D1521643

RESEARCH GUIDE
TO AMERICAN LITERATURE

Realism and Regionalism
1865–1914

RESEARCH GUIDE
TO AMERICAN LITERATURE

RESEARCH GUIDE
TO AMERICAN LITERATURE

Realism and Regionalism
1865–1914

Gary Scharnhorst
University of New Mexico
and
Tom Quirk
University of Missouri–Columbia

A BRUCCOLI CLARK LAYMAN BOOK

Facts On File
An imprint of Infobase Publishing

Research Guide to American Literature: Realism and Regionalism, 1865–1914

Copyright © 2010 by Gary Scharnhorst and Thomas Quirk

Facts On File, Inc.
An imprint of Infobase Publishing
132 West 31st Street
New York NY 10001

Library of Congress Cataloging-in-Publication Data
Research guide to American literature. — New ed.
    p. cm.
"A Bruccoli Clark Layman book."
Includes bibliographical references and index.
ISBN 978-0-8160-7861-5 (v. 1 : acid-free paper)—ISBN 978-0-8160-7862-2 (v. 2 : acid-free paper)—ISBN 978-0-8160-7863-9 (v. 3 : acid-free paper)—ISBN 978-0-8160-7864-6 (v. 4 : acid-free paper)—ISBN 978-0-8160-7865-3 (v. 5 : acid-free paper)—ISBN 978-0-8160-7866-0 (v. 6 : acid-free paper)—ISBN 978-0-8160-7867-7 (v. 7 : acid-free paper) 1. American literature—Research—Methodology—Handbooks, manuals, etc. 2. American literature—History and criticism. 3. Canon (Literature) I. Franklin, Benjamin, 1939– II. Vietto, Angela III. Habich, Robert D., 1951– IV. Quirk, Tom, 1946– V. Scharnhorst, Gary. VI. Anderson, George Parker, 1957– VII. Cusatis, John. VIII. Moser, Linda Trinh, 1964– IX. West, Kathryn, 1962– X. Facts on File, Inc.
PS51.R47 2010
810.7'2—dc22

                         2009047815

Text design by Erika K. Arroyo
Composition by Bruccoli Clark Layman
Cover printed by Art Print, Taylor, PA
Book printed and bound by Maple Press, York, PA
Date printed: March 2010
Printed in the United States of America
10 9 8 7 6 5 4 3 2 1
This book is printed on acid-free paper.

In memory of George Arms

Contents

Contributors

Series Introduction

Research Guide to American Literature is a series of handbooks for students and teachers that recommends strategies for studying literary topics and frequently taught literary works and authors. The rationale for the series is that successful study is predicated on asking the right questions and then devising a logical strategy for addressing them. The process of responsible literary investigation begins with facts and usually ends with opinions. The value of those opinions depends on the ability of the reader to gather useful information, to consider it in context, to interpret it logically, and finally to decide what the interpretation means outside the confines of the literary work. Often the answers to questions a sophisticated reader asks about a literary topic are subjective, involving a reader's perception of an author's or a character's motive; always the search for the answer to a meaningful question involves a process of self-education and, in the best of circumstances, self-awareness.

RGAL is intended as a resource to assist readers in identifying questions to ask about literature. The seven volumes in this series are organized chronologically, corresponding to generally accepted literary periods. Each volume follows this general pattern:

Part I provides the social and historical context for a literary period, explaining its historical boundaries, describing the nature of the literary output of the time, placing the literature in its social and historical contexts, identifying literary influences, and tracing the evolution of critical approaches.

Part II comprises ten study guides on general themes or topics related to the period, organized alphabetically. Each guide first provides necessary background information, then suggests questions or research topics that might be fruitfully considered, along with specific primary and secondary works that students will find useful. Each guide also includes an annotated checklist of recommended secondary works and capsule identifications of people mentioned.

Part III comprises some thirty study guides for particular literary works or authors, organized alphabetically by the author's name. Each guide begins with a brief overview of the author's career to provide context, and then suggests some half a dozen topics for discussion and research, with advice about how to begin investigating the topic. These topics are meant to facilitate classroom discussion as well as to suggest interesting ideas for research papers. Each guide includes an annotated checklist of recommended secondary works.

Part IV is an annotated general bibliography recommending the most useful general works of literary history, literary criticism, and literary reference pertinent to the period.

Part V is a glossary of terms used in the volume.

A keyword index is included in each volume.

The purpose of *RGAL* is not to tell students what literature means but to help them determine the meaning for themselves by asking significant questions and seeking answers diligently and thoughtfully. That is how learning that matters takes place. The method is as old as Socrates.

—Richard Layman

Part I
Overview

Boundaries of the Period

With the publication of Charles Darwin's *On the Origin of Species* in 1859, the start of the American Civil War in 1861, and the deaths of Henry David Thoreau in 1862 and Nathaniel Hawthorne in 1864, the literary landscape was ripe for a new generation of American writers who emphasized verisimilitude (similarity to truth) or Realism in the arts. These writers—among them, Mark Twain, Henry James, William Dean Howells, Sarah Orne Jewett, Mary Wilkins Freeman, and John William De Forest—chose not to allegorize or sentimentalize or sensationalize experience in their fiction, preferring instead to represent the world as objectively as possible. "Let fiction cease to lie about life," Howells declared in *Criticism and Fiction* (1891); "let it portray men and women as they are, actuated by the motives and the passions in the measure we all know; . . . let it not put on fine literary airs; let it speak the dialect, the language, that most Americans know—the language of unaffected people everywhere." Ambrose Bierce facetiously defined Realism in his *Devil's Dictionary* (1911) as "The art of depicting nature as it is seen by toads."

Many Realists (for example, Twain, Howells, Bierce, Bret Harte, Hamlin Garland, and Stephen Crane) began their careers as journalists, and they addressed the questions of "who, what, when, where, why, and how" in their fiction no less than in their newspaper reporting. Howells even advanced a scientific model of literary development, with Realism having evolved from literary romance much as birds evolved from lizards. Though Howells admired Hawthorne's fiction, he nevertheless believed it occupied a lower rung on the evolutionary scale of literature than "the truthful treatment of material" *(Criticism and Fiction)*. Purporting to offer a transcript of life, the Realists often depicted middle-class experience. They shared with such pragmatists as William James a philosophical attitude that affirmed freedom of the will, deliberate and purposeful behavior, and individual responsibility.

In addition to Howells, many other novelists of the period defended the aesthetics of Realism. James compared realistic fiction to painting in his essay "The Art of Fiction" (1884). According to James, the only reason a novel should exist "is that it does attempt to represent life. When it relinquishes this attempt, the same attempt that we see on the canvas of a painter, it will have arrived at a very strange pass" (*Partial Portraits*, 1888). James's brand of Realism was a form of literary portraiture, as may be inferred from several of his titles (for example, *Portraits of Places, The Portrait of a Lady, Partial Portraits*). In his humorous essay "Fenimore Cooper's Literary Offenses" (1895) Twain listed "nineteen rules governing literary art." Among them are "when the personages of a tale deal in conversation, the talk shall sound like human talk" and "the personages of a tale shall confine themselves to possibilities and let miracles alone." Crane similarly asserted that he had "developed all alone a little creed of art which I thought was a good one. Later I discovered that my creed was identical with the one of Howells and Garland. . . . we are the most successful in art when we approach the nearest to nature and truth" (*The Correspondence of Stephen Crane,* edited by Stanley Wertheim and Paul Sorrentino, 1988).

Dominant Genres and Literary Forms

The literary landscape in the late nineteenth century featured no monolithic school of Realists. There were, in effect, many realities or varieties of Realism, including local color or Regionalism (for example, the tales of Twain, Jewett, Freeman, Kate Chopin), psychological Realism (James, Charlotte Perkins Gilman), critical Realism (Howells), and Naturalism (Crane, Upton Sinclair, Jack London). The various Realists did not necessarily appreciate all contributions to the form: Twain wrote Howells in 1885 that he "would rather be damned to John Bunyan's heaven" than be forced to read a novel by James (*Selected Letters of Mark Twain*, edited by Charles Neider, 1982). With their interest in local customs, mores, and dialects, local colorists were, in a sense, local historians. Their tales often took the form of the anecdote or character sketch (for example, Freeman's "A New England Nun," 1887). James's psychological Realism was a more aestheticized form of fiction written in a prolix and periphrastic style (thus prompting the joke that James "chewed more than he bit off"). By experimenting with refined narrators or "centers of consciousness," James presumed to re-create the play of their imaginations. The reader of James's "Daisy Miller" (1879), for example, knows nothing more than the thoughts of the prim and stiff-necked expatriate Winterbourne. In the novella, James subverted the sentimental plot of love triumphant by contrasting the social codes of the parvenue Daisy and the Euro-Americans, and the tale ends not with the reconciliation of the young lovers but with the unexpected death of the heroine.

The forte of the Realists, especially of the critical Realists, was topical fiction. Even James's international stories such as "Daisy Miller" exploited the growth in international travel during the last third of the nineteenth century. (With the development of the steamship, passenger departures from the United States for Europe increased from around 20,000 in 1860 to around 110,000 in 1900.) In "Roman Fever" (1934), Edith Wharton played an intriguing variation on the international theme, virtually parodying James's "Daisy Miller." More to the point, Realists often protested conditions, pilloried hypocrisy, or proposed social reforms. Few subjects escaped their notice. Among the topics that concerned them were immigration (for example, Sui Sin Far's *Mrs. Spring Fragrance,* 1912), small-town parochialism or "the revolt from the village" (Twain's *Adventures of Tom Sawyer,* 1876; Wharton's *Ethan Frome,* 1911; Edwin Arlington Robinson's *Tilbury Town*), military adventurism (Howells's "Editha," 1905), urban squalor, prostitution, and the "fallen woman" (Crane's *Maggie: A Girl of the Streets,* 1893; Sinclair's *Jungle,* 1906), and economic injustice (Garland's "Under the Lion's Paw," 1889). Other narratives were devoted to the institution of marriage and the rights of women, including Chopin's *Awakening* (1899), and Gilman's "Yellow Wallpaper" (1892). Realistic fiction was often influenced by race, too. The decade of the 1890s was punctuated by the *Plessy v. Ferguson* decision of the Supreme Court (1896) sanctioning "separate but equal" public facilities for blacks and whites and represented the nadir of race relations in the United States. The African American writers Charles Chesnutt, Paul Laurence Dunbar, and Alice Dunbar-Nelson published dozens of stories of the color line and dialect poems around the turn of the twentieth century that ridiculed the evil of racial discrimination, and Chopin's "Desirée's Baby" (1893) exposed the hypocrisy that rationalized the prohibition of racial intermarriage.

Despite the early successes of Harte and Twain, Western American writers were slow to warm to Realism. Western American literature consisted for most of this period of blood-and-thunder dime novels celebrating westward expansion and conquest. As late as 1902 the novelist Frank Norris complained that rather than a school of Western Realists there were "the wretched 'Deadwood Dicks' and Buffalo Bills of the yellowbacks" and writers such as James Fenimore Cooper, "who lied and tricked and strutted in Pathfinder and Leather-Stocking series" (*The Literary Criticism of Frank Norris,* edited by Donald Pizer, 1964). Among the harbingers of Western Realism during the first decades of the twentieth century was London, especially in such tales as "To Build a Fire" (1908). This story also illustrates the strategy of literary Naturalism, perhaps best defined in three words as "Realism plus Darwin."

All Realists adopted a quasi-scientific method of detailed observation, but in the case of the Naturalists the science was rooted in Darwin's theory of natural selection. As Malcolm Cowley explained, "The Naturalistic writers were all determinists in that they believed in the omnipotence of abstract forces. They were pessimists so far as they believed that men and women were absolutely incapable of shaping their own destinies." Most literary Naturalists were also social Darwinists who applied Darwin's biological theories of natural selection to models of social organization, arguing by analogy that just as the fittest of each species in nature struggles for existence by adapting to its environment, the fittest human competitors best adapt to social conditions and thrive. Theoretically, the Naturalistic tale might be a success story, but in practice it was almost always a failure story, with the unfit protagonist doomed to death, as in "To Build a Fire." Cowley concluded that the net effect of Naturalism was "to subtract from literature the whole notion of human responsibility." Crime in the Naturalistic novel—for example, prostitution in Crane's *Maggie*—was the result of uncontrollable and impersonal forces, not personal choice. As Crane inscribed on the flyleaf of presentation copies of *Maggie,* "It is inevitable that you will be greatly shocked by this book, but continue, please, with all courage to the end. For it tries to show that environment is a tremendous thing in the world and frequently shapes lives regardless. If one proves that theory, one makes room in Heaven for all sorts of souls, notably an occasional street girl, who are not confidently expected to be there by many excellent people" *(Correspondence of Stephen Crane).*

Yet, Crane's comment also illustrates a dilemma faced by the Naturalist. To the extent that he objectively portrayed the plight of the underclass and described the forces that shape character, he was faithful to the tenets of Naturalism. To the extent he prepared a brief for the defense of the underclass, however, he violated the principle of scientific objectivity and instead advocated for reform. Though several of the Naturalists were socialists (for example, London and Sinclair), their literary theory warred with their politics. These proletarian writers attempted to graft their leftist politics onto Naturalism, a project that met with decidedly mixed results. Sinclair's *Jungle* is often credited with catalyzing support for the Pure Food and Drug Act, but it is crudely constructed and basically breaks in half when the hero is thrown in jail. As Sinclair later conceded, he "aimed at the public's heart and by accident I hit it in the stomach" (*The Autobiography of Upton Sinclair*, 1962). Given the deterministic bias of Naturalism, the proletarian writers were simply unable to explain the conversion of a character to a political point of view.

A corollary to the doctrine of determinism professed by the Naturalists was the indifference if not malevolence of nature. As Crane declared in one of his idiosyncratic poems:

> A man said to the universe
> "Sir, I exist!"
> "However," replied the universe,
> "The fact has not created in me
> A sense of obligation." (*War is Kind*, 1899)

As the correspondent in Crane's "Open Boat" (1897) considers his chances of survival, he realizes "the serenity of nature amid the struggles of the individual." Nature "did not seem cruel to him then, nor beneficent, nor treacherous, nor wise. But she was indifferent, flatly indifferent." In "To Build a Fire," London similarly described how the "cold of space smote the unprotected tip of the planet" in the Klondike and the doomed miner, "being on that unprotected tip, received the full force of the blow." As a literary school, the Naturalists exhibited an epistemological skepticism, a disbelief in a purposeful, end-directed, or teleological universe.

However crude and disturbing the Naturalistic style, it exhibited certain recurring characteristics. Virtually all Naturalistic tales were written from a third-person omniscient point of view. The Naturalist was, after all, a type of scientist; the story, a type of lab report. Whereas the Realist aimed to draw "rounded" or credible individual characters, the Naturalist portrayed representative and recurring types such as the brute or the spectator. Unfortunately, the trend among Naturalists to portray types also prompted them to reinforce some racial and ethnic stereotypes and to assert the superiority of Anglo-Saxons according to the standard science of the day. Moreover, the Naturalists frequently employed animal metaphors to describe characters. Obviously such metaphors had been used for millennia, but after the publication of Darwin's *On the Origin of Species* they had a new resonance. For example, Crane compared Maggie's brother and her ex-lover in the midst of a bar fight with wild animals, roosters, bulldogs, and cats. The men in "The Open Boat" are compared to ants in their plight, the workers in *The Jungle* to rats in a trap. Naturalists also often invoked sports or gaming metaphors, as when Crane compares a soldier to a football player in *The Red Badge of Courage* (1895). Naturalistic novels were often bloated with detailed descriptions of insulated settings (for example, Rum Alley in *Maggie*, based on Hell's Kitchen on the Lower West Side of New York, and Packingtown in *The Jungle*). If a writer was an environmental determinist, after all, he labored under the obligation to depict the environment in minute detail.

Above all, the Naturalists tended to be critical of the so-called teacup tragedies of Howellsian Realism. "Realism is minute; it is the drama of a broken teacup, the tragedy of a walk down the block, the excitement of an afternoon call, the adventure of an invitation to dinner," Norris complained. In contrast, "terrible things"—particularly death—"must happen to the characters in a Naturalistic novel" *(The Literary Criticism of Frank Norris)*. Broadly speaking, too, there were generational differences between Realists and Naturalists: James and Howells matured as writers in the 1870s and 1880s, whereas Crane and Norris matured in the 1890s. In her short novel *Ethan Frome* (1911) Wharton revised the local-color Realism of Freeman and Jewett; she averred later in her autobiography that she tried in the novel to "draw life as it really was" in rural New England, in contrast to the depiction of it through the "rose-coloured spectacles" of her predecessors (*A Backward Glance*, 1934).

Some of Crane's writings, including *The Red Badge of Courage* and "The Open Boat," represented an advance on the Naturalistic tradition and presage the advent of literary modernism. Crane once asserted that he was attempting to imitate in words what the French impressionistic painters were doing with light and color: "I bring this to you merely as an effect—an effect of mental light and shade, if you like: . . . something meaningless and at the same time overwhelming, crushing, monstrous" ("War Memories," 1899). Put another way, Crane tried to develop Naturalistic themes in an impressionistic style. Events in *The Red Badge of Courage* are mediated entirely through Henry Fleming's imagination like strokes of color from a painter's brush. Reality in the novel exists only insofar as Fleming apprehends it. These tales anticipate Ernest Hemingway's terse style, with frequent shifts in point of view.

Few American poets of the period are remembered today, justifiably so. Most of the forgotten ones were heirs of the sentimental tradition of British Romanticism, their verses buried in the morgues of newspapers and magazines. Howells, Harte, and other Realists wrote poetry, to be sure, but most of it was utterly conventional. Twain parodied sentimental verse in *The Adventures of Huckleberry Finn* (1884), but his own poetry was equally forgettable. Still, the major American poets of the late nineteenth century, Walt Whitman and Emily Dickinson, rebelled against the didacticism and formal conventions of the midcentury Fireside Poets (for example, Henry Wadsworth Longfellow, John Greenleaf Whittier, Oliver Wendell Holmes Sr., James Russell Lowell, and William Cullen Bryant). At the turn of the twentieth century, both Crane and Edwin Arlington Robinson wrote a brand of Naturalistic poetry that deserves to be resurrected from the footnote. Crane's verse was enigmatic and bitterly ironic, influenced stylistically by Dickinson's lyrics, and Robinson wrote such dour dramatic monologues as "Richard Cory" (1897) and "Miniver Cheevy" (1907). While Robert Frost was committed to traditional poetic forms—he famously declared that writing free verse was like playing tennis without a net—his best verses were profoundly disturbing. A transitional poet, he was hardly a glib versifier of the New England woodlands in such verses as "Mending Wall" (1914) and "The Death of the Hired Man" (1914). T. S. Eliot's "The Love Song of J. Alfred Prufrock," published in 1915, inaugurated a modernist tradition in American poetry distinct from both the innovative verse forms of Dickinson and Whitman and the terrifying tropes of Frost. That is, this poem, more than any other literary work in the early twentieth century, marked the close of one era in American literature and the start of another.

—Gary Scharnhorst

Historical and Social Context

This volume is concerned with the years 1865–1914. In other words, the age of Regionalism, Realism, and Naturalism begins with the end of the Civil War and concludes with the beginning of World War I. The era has been described in many ways—as an "era of good feelings"; an age in "ferment"; an age of "progress," of "reform," of "energy." The extravagant displays of wealth and abuses of power from 1865 until 1890 are aptly captured by the title of an 1873 novel by Mark Twain and Charles Dudley Warner—"The Gilded Age." The efforts to curb these abuses after the economic depression of 1893 until 1920 characterize what is known as the "Progressive Era." The 1890s are sometimes regarded as a time of decadence, the "mauve decade"; the opening decade of the twentieth century, on the other hand, has been called an "end of American innocence." There is some truth in all of these labels, but together they underscore the social and cultural confusion of the times. Realist and naturalist writing sought to depict the age and often to offer in imaginative terms answers and remedies to current dilemmas. In so brief a space, one can only be suggestive of the historical period, and, broadly speaking, the most vital aspects of that history have to do with the aftermath of the Civil War, the political and social unrest of the day, patterns of migration and immigration (and with them the growth of the cities), the dramatic increase in wealth and poverty that created an ever-widening gulf between rich and poor, and the increasing authority of science and technology in everyday life.

By any reckoning, the death toll of the Civil War is appalling—well over 600,000 men died in combat or from disease. The figure is difficult to grasp, but Mathew Brady's troop of daguerreotypists made the carnage vivid for the nation. Widows and fatherless children, empty sleeves, run-down homes and farms would serve as bitter reminders of the conflict for decades to come. Insofar as the Civil War affected literary production in the country, there were several important consequences that prepared the ground for Regionalist and Realist writing. First, the war broadened the perspective of men and women alike. Men who might have otherwise lived out their lives without traveling more than twenty miles from their birthplace had been mustered out and had become acquainted with people who had different customs, different speech patterns, different habits. Those who stayed behind anxiously searched the newspapers for word of where their loved ones were or whether they were still alive and as a result acquired a better understanding of the geography of the nation and the significance of national, as opposed to local, politics. At the same time that Americans broadened their perspectives, they acquired a greater appreciation for place, and Regionalist writing became popular. Moreover, the newspapers increased significantly both in number and readership, and the number of magazines published in the country jumped from a few hundred before 1865 to more than three thousand by 1885. Clearly, local-color writing had a ready outlet in both these venues.

It was difficult to glorify or sentimentalize the war after the sad knowledge of so many lives lost, but there were many who did so nonetheless. Pastors, politicians, and others saw the triumph of the North in the Civil War as a great moral victory and cultivated the notion that the nation's ills could merely be reformed out of existence. Such reformist impulses included the populist and temperance movements. Others took away different lessons from the experience of the war. It was quickly perceived that the expenditure of large amounts of capital and the mobilization of great numbers of individuals, whose energies were directed at a single object, could yield surprisingly effective results. These lessons could be applied to manufacturing, and thus the industrialization of the country became a transformative event. Hank Morgan, in Twain's *Connecticut Yankee in King Arthur's Court* (1889), learned the blacksmith trade from his father but soon became a superintendent of an arms factory in charge of some two thousand workers. More and more, American men, women, and children were getting a living in factories. By 1900, 20 percent of all manufacturing workers were women, and 13 percent were children under the age of sixteen. Working conditions were often deplorable, and dangerous; industrial accidents accounted for some twenty-five thousand deaths a year. Rebecca Harding Davis presciently described the devastating effects of factory life upon the soul in "Life in the Iron Mills" in 1861; Upton Sinclair dramatized similar conditions in the meatpacking industry in his popular novel *The Jungle*. Sinclair's socialist ambitions and his sympathies for American laborers were largely ignored; instead, sickened by the descriptions of meat preparation, Americans demanded changes and the Pure Food and Drug Act was enacted the same year. At all events, writers counted themselves among those who might help to reform a nation that appeared badly in need of repair.

On the surface, it would seem that there should have been political stability during this period; with the exception of the elections of Grover Cleveland and Woodrow Wilson, Republicans occupied the White House for five successive decades. Nonetheless, during the same period, the country was fraught with continuing political dissatisfaction and social unrest, and in fact three of those Republican presidents were assassinated. Financial panics contributed to the discontent. The economic depression of 1873 lasted six years and put three million out of work; the panic of 1893 was of briefer duration, but its consequences were even more severe. Economic uncertainty and rapid industrialization gave birth to labor organizations, most important, the National Labor Union, the Knights of Labor, and the American Federation of Labor. The Populist Party was organized in 1892 to defend the rights of western farmers against falling prices and farm foreclosures. Edwin Markham's extremely popular poem "The Man with a Hoe" (1899) and Hamlin Garland's stories about farm life on the middle border dramatized the backbreaking and often futile struggles to get a decent life from the land. In urban areas, strikes, work stoppages, and other forms of protest publicized the workers' plight, but, by and large, unions were ineffective in their opposition to their treatment by management and industry, as were the populists in trying to reform monetary policy unfriendly to their interests. The relation between management and organized labor was a source of violent conflict, most notably with the Haymarket riot in 1886 and the Pullman strike in 1894.

The efforts of Reconstruction to heal the divisions between North and South were an utter failure. With the end of Reconstruction in 1877, the institution of Jim Crow laws throughout the South contributed to bitter tensions and sometimes to race riots. Charles Chesnutt dramatized the Wilmington, North

Carolina race riot of 1898 in his novel *The Marrow of Tradition* (1901). Theodore Dreiser and Paul Laurence Dunbar wrote short stories about lynch mobs, and James Weldon Johnson described the burning alive of a black man in the South in *The Autobiography of an Ex-Colored Man* (1912). Twain wrote a satirical essay titled "The United States of Lyncherdom." Race riots and lynchings were not exclusively directed toward African Americans (there were anti-Chinese, anti-Greek, and anti-Italian riots as well), nor were they an exclusively Southern phenomenon. The problems of migration and immigration added volatile elements to the brew. Great numbers of African Americans, motivated by fear, repression, or simple poverty, moved north, mostly into the swelling cities. Until World War I, the United States had a more or less unrestricted immigration policy, except with regard to Orientals. Successive waves of immigration also increased the urban population, but immigration complicated problems of labor and industry, as well, and cultivated certain racial and ethnic fears in those Americans who had definite ideas about what an American was. They sometimes described themselves as "hundred per-centers," and the feeling that those of Anglo-Saxon descent were a superior race destined to dominate civilization here and abroad was a general one. Prior to 1870, most of the immigrants to the United States were, with the exception of the Irish, Anglo-Saxon Protestants. After that date, immigrants from Russia and southern and eastern Europe introduced a Jewish or Catholic element into American society that made the so-called real Americans nervous and suspicious. The anti-Catholic American Protective Association was established in 1887 and the Immigration Restriction League in 1896. Those who had immigrated to the United States to find religious tolerance and economic opportunity were discovering that these commodities were hard to come by.

Racial and ethnic tensions were particularly acute in the cities. Between 1880 and 1900, American cities grew by fifteen million people. At a time when "urban planning" was nonexistent, the consequences were dire. Pollution, open sewers, and overcrowding in poorly ventilated tenement buildings contributed to an alarming increase in death by disease. In *How the Other Half Lives* (1890) Jacob Riis sensationally documented with photographs the squalor of New York tenements. The population did not divide neatly into halves, of course. Ward McAllister coined the phrase "the four hundred" to designate the only people who really matter in New York City; in answer, O. Henry published a volume of short stories about ordinary people in the city and called it *The Four Million* (1906). Before the introduction of electric streetcars, workers had to live within walking distance of the workplace. Eventually, however, commuting became a real possibility, and as a result many people began to live in "suburbs." In turn, as a rapidly increasing middle class emerged, the social strata started to segment in territorial ways. Some parts of the city were particularly dangerous or unwholesome. Stephen Crane depicted life along the Bowery in *Maggie: A Girl of the Streets,* and the African American writer Paul Laurence Dunbar rendered both the harsh life in the rural South and the debilitating conditions in New York's Tenderloin district in his novel *The Sport of the Gods* (1902).

Despite the undeniable facts of hard living, whether on the farms or in the cities, the prevailing belief in the rags-to-riches myth persisted. Virtue, talent, and hard work were the tools for success, this myth maintained. Twain satirized this belief with antic glee; William Dean Howells, Henry James, and Edith Wharton treated the subject more seriously but with equal disdain. Still, there were well-known examples of those who rose from obscure and difficult circumstances to become rich and powerful. Andrew Carnegie began working at the age of thirteen and rose through the strata of American society to become one of the richest men in the nation. But he is only one example. Before the Civil War, there were perhaps one hundred millionaires in this country; by the 1890s, there were over four thousand. Much of that wealth was gotten or sustained by graft, bribes, monopolies, and other sorts of abuses. The Crédit Mobilier scandal, which involved fraudulent manipulation of more than $20 million worth of construction contracts for building the Union Pacific Railroad, was exposed in 1872, during the Ulysses S. Grant administration. The president was not implicated in the influence peddling, but the vice president was, and thereafter this sort of political corruption was known as "Grantism." Backroom dealing was perversely combined with exuberant displays of opulence and excess; the phrase "conspicuous consumption" was coined during this era, and the so-called robber barons were guilty of it. The well-to-do sat down to ten-course dinners at the famous New York restaurants of the day, Waldorf or Delmonico's; in one instance, a dog dinner was staged in Newport, Rhode Island, and one dog collapsed from overeating. Gambling was another indulgence—John W. "Bet-You-a-Million" Gates, who had made his money in barbed wire, is said to have lost $250,000 in a single poker game. Immense wealth combined with simple bad taste gave rise to an examination of the conflict between "old money," founded on tradition and a genteel sensibility, and "new money," accompanied by a certain extravagance and coarseness that were deemed vulgar. This was a theme Howells, James, and Wharton treated with accomplished literary results.

With the depression of 1893, these lavish displays appeared all the more unseemly, and, by the turn of the century, "muckraking" journalists began to publish articles on a variety of scandals and abuses involving industrialists and politicians. Before that, political progressives had argued for more government intervention in the affairs of business and commerce. Among those reforms were, notably, the Interstate Commerce Act (1887) and the Sherman Antitrust Act (1890). These measures were not strictly enforced, however, until the presidencies of Theodore Roosevelt and Woodrow Wilson in the early years of the twentieth century. Not so coincidentally, perhaps, during this same period there was a surge of philanthropy by rich benefactors. Andrew Carnegie published a famous essay, "The Gospel of Wealth," in the *North American Review* in 1899 arguing that the wealthy were stewards and had social obligations to contribute to the public good. From 1893 to 1903 over $600 million in the form of gifts and bequests were donated to one institution or another. Large sums were contributed to public libraries, concert halls, museums, universities, or to foundations dedicated to helping the poor. Despite the coarse behavior of some of the well-to-do, these same people enriched the cultural life of the nation in various and important ways.

Finally, one has to note the tremendous impact of science and technology during this era. Running alongside all the tumult and confusions of the social life, and strangely somehow apart from it, was the advance of science. If social progress was made at all, it was made by fits and starts. Not so with scientific innovation. It seemed to purr right along, unhindered or undisturbed by the chaos. A partial list of innovations or inventions is suggestive: dynamite (1867), the telephone (1876), the phonograph (1879), the internal combustion engine (1885), electric streetcars (1887), the electric motor (1888), the box camera (1888), radio telegraphy (1895), the X-ray (1895), the first flight (1903), and Albert Einstein's special theory of relativity (1905). But the list does not indicate more-efficient methods of industrial production and distribution, improved methods of railroad and bridge construction, faster and generally safer modes of transportation, and many other changes. Some proposed that science, particularly Darwinian evolution, had declared war on religion. However, orators such as John Fiske and Reverend Henry Ward Beecher reassured the public that the two realms were entirely compatible. Whatever else Darwinism meant to the popular mind, it surely meant progress, that the best days lay ahead. It was also clear that the advances in science and technology touched the lives of everyone in one way or another.

To the extent that the United States participated and contributed to the revolutionary developments in scientific discovery and technological innovation, progress also seemed to fortify notions of American exceptionalism. It was a great question, at any rate, whether the U.S. military adventures in Cuba and the Philippines were wars of liberation or examples of imperialism. As it entered the early twentieth century, the United States was a very different country from the one that emerged after the Civil War. It was larger, wealthier, and more powerful. Its populace was more diverse, and the lives of its people were more complicated, even if its citizens were not necessarily more sophisticated. Gertrude Stein once remarked that America was actually older than other nations because it had entered the twentieth century in the 1880s. For good or ill, the United States had joined the community of nations on a more-or-less equal footing. With World War I looming on the horizon in 1914, it would have its chance, and its obligation, to prove its membership.

—*Tom Quirk*

Literary Influences

Late-nineteenth- and early-twentieth-century American literature was shaped by a variety of influences, many of them imported from Europe. Certainly American literature of this period was not written in an intellectual vacuum. Much as the European Romantics Thomas Carlyle, Samuel Taylor Coleridge, and Immanuel Kant inspired the Transcendentalism of Emerson, the literary Realism of Europeans was rebranded a generation later by American writers. The influence of George Eliot, Henrik Ibsen, August Strindberg, Gustave Flaubert, Émile Zola, Alphonse Daudet, Guy de Maupassant, Leo Tolstoy, Ivan Turgenev, Fyodor Dostoevsky, and other European Realists on Henry James, William Dean Howells, Kate Chopin, Frank Norris, Stephen Crane, and other American Realists literally cannot be overstated. In particular, Howells championed the English, French, and Russian Realists. As Lars Åhnebrink has explained, "In his vindication of modern European literature Howells stood out perhaps more than any other American writer or critic. His knowledge of contemporary European literature was extensive." While editor of the *Atlantic Monthly*, Howells "published articles on Stendhal, Dostoevsky, the brothers Goncourt, Flaubert, Zola, Mérimée, Alfred de Musset, Baudelaire, Gautier, Björnson, Renan, and many others." Howells was profoundly influenced in the late 1880s by Tolstoy's ideas about nonviolence and economic equality. Similarly, Winfried Fluck asserts that "The American writer who was most fully at home in a transatlantic culture of letters and most observant of European movements was Henry James" ("Morality, Modernity, and 'Malarial Restlessness': American Realism in its Anglo-European Contexts," in *A Companion to American Fiction, 1865–1914*, 2005). As James wrote Howells in 1884, "there is nothing more interesting to me now than the effort & experiment of this little group [Flaubert, Turgenev, Zola, Daudet, Maupassant] with its truly infernal intelligence of art, form, manner—its intense artistic life. They do the only kind of work, to-day, that I respect; & in spite of their ferocious pessimism & their handling of unclean things, they are at least serious and honest" (*Letters, Fictions, Lives: Henry James and William Dean Howells*, edited by Michael Anesko, 1997).

Unfortunately, Howells and James paid a heavy price for championing the European Realists. As in the political debate over the protective tariff, natives and nativists in the literary debate taxed the foreign import. During the so-called war against Realism beginning in 1887, the Hoosier poet Maurice Thompson, president of the Association of Western Writers, repeatedly complained that Howells had foisted the "raw, nauseous Realism of the Russians and the Zola school of France" upon an American reading public hungry for pleasant and patriotic books (Scharnhorst). As Thompson protested in his essay "Foreign Influence on American Fiction," "Just now we are trying to be French; yesterday we were cultivating the Russians; last week the English had us under their thumbs" (*North American Review*, July 1889). Thompson and others of his ilk responded with a flood of trite historical romances about wholesome rural maidens, medieval chivalry, and so forth, including *Alice of Old Vincennes* (Thompson, 1900), *Ben-Hur* (Lew

Wallace, 1880), *Prince Saroni's Wife* (Julian Hawthorne, 1882), and *When Knighthood Was in Flower* (Charles Major, 1898).

In the long run, of course, Howells, James, Mark Twain, and the other Realists won the war. Though controversial on its first publication, James's "Daisy Miller" (1879) was modeled on Victor Cherbuliez's *Paule Méré* (1865), and James's novel *The Portrait of a Lady* (1881) betrayed the influence of Eliot's *Daniel Deronda* (1876) and Flaubert's *Madame Bovary* (1857). Howells's novel *Annie Kilburn* (1889) glossed Tolstoy's *Anna Karenina* (1875–1877), as the initials of their eponymous heroines suggest. Twain was indebted to both Thomas Malory's *Morte d'Arthur* (1485) and Thomas Carlyle's *French Revolution: A History* (1837) in *A Connecticut Yankee in King Arthur's Court* (1889). Bret Harte's best stories, including "The Luck of Roaring Camp" (1868) and "The Outcasts of Poker Flat" (1869), were written in the "Dickensian mode," and Upton Sinclair claimed that he tried to put "the content of Shelley into the form of Zola" in his novel *The Jungle* ("What Lives Means to Me," *Cosmopolitan,* October 1906). Chopin read Maupassant's stories in 1888 "and marveled at them. Here was life, not fiction; for where were the plots, the old fashioned mechanism and stage trapping that in a vague, unthinking way I had fancied were essential to the art of story telling" (Per Seyersted, *Kate Chopin: A Critical Biography,* 1969). She echoed Maupassant's tales "Solitude" and "Suicide" in parts of *The Awakening* (1899). Not that the American Realists merely wished to copy the Europeans. They preferred to "draw on Realism's cultural capital as a 'modern' movement in order to define modern life in American terms" (Fluck, "Morality, Modernity, and 'Malarial Restlessness'").

The European intellectual influence on American literary Naturalism was even more pronounced. In his pamphlet *Le Roman expérimental* (translated as "The Experimental Novel," 1893), Zola developed an elaborate analogy between empirical fiction and medical science. According to Zola, the experimental (that is, the Naturalistic) novelist simply adopts "the scientific method, which has been in use for a long time." He "institutes the experiment, that is, sets the characters of a particular story in motion, in order to show that the series of events therein will be those demanded by the determinism of the phenomena under study" (Becker). The Naturalistic novel was something of a lab report, usually narrated from an omniscient narrator. "By substituting for the word 'doctor' the word 'novelist,'" Åhnebrink adds, Zola "could make his meaning clear and give to the work of art the rigidity of a scientific truth." Norris sometimes signed his letters "the boy Zola" and modeled entire chapters of his novel *McTeague* (1899) on Zola's *L'Assommoir* (1877). Crane's *Maggie,* according to Åhnebrink, also "owes a considerable debt to *L'Assommoir,*" and *The Red Badge of Courage,* according to Vernon Parrington, was inspired partly by Zola's *Le Débâcle* (1892) and Tolstoy's *War and Peace* (1865–1869; *Main Currents in American Thought,* 1930).

As Bert Bender and others have shown, moreover, Charles Darwin's theories of natural selection and sexual selection also inform Naturalistic texts. Crane allegorized the notion of natural selection—in a nutshell, the idea that species must adapt to their environments to survive and reproduce—in one of his poems:

The trees in the garden rained flowers.
Children ran there joyously.
They gathered the flowers
Each to himself.
Now there were some
Who gathered great heaps—
Having opportunity and skill—
Until, behold, only chance blossoms
Remained for the feeble.
Then a little spindling tutor
Ran importantly to the father, crying:
"Pray, come hither!
See this unjust thing in your garden!"
But when the father had surveyed,
He admonished the tutor:
"Not so, small sage!
This thing is just.
For, look you,
Are not they who possess the flowers
Stronger, bolder, shrewder
Than they who have none?
Why should the strong—
The beautiful strong—
Why should they not have the flowers?"
Upon reflection, the tutor bowed to the ground,
"My lord," he said,
"The stars are displaced
By this towering wisdom." (*War is Kind*, 1899)

The concept of sexual selection, too, was hotly contested in the fiction of the period. When in chapter 4 of *McTeague* Marcus Schouler yields to the dentist his claim to his cousin Trina—"Mac, I'll give her up to you"— Norris affirms that men select their mates and that women have little or no say in the matter. He illustrates the conventional understanding of sexual selection that Darwin proposed in *The Descent of Man* (1871). But when Edna Pontellier in chapter 36 of *The Awakening* spurns the overtures of Robert Lebrun, Chopin challenges Darwin, no less: "I give myself where I choose. If he were to say, 'Here, Robert, take her and be happy; she is yours,' I should laugh at you both." Like the peahen or the female pigeon, Edna selects her mate in the world of Chopin's imagination.

Even more than Darwin's writings, Herbert Spencer's philosophy appealed to American readers. As Richard Hofstadter has explained, Spencer became "the metaphysician of the homemade intellectual and the prophet of the cracker-barrel agnostic." Whereas Darwin had applied the notion of cutthroat competition or survival of the fittest to organisms, Spencer applied it to society and social institutions. (The complex of ideas that paraded under the banner of "social Darwinism" was, in fact, more indebted to Spencer than to Darwin. It was Spencer, not Darwin, who coined the phrase "survival of the fittest.") While on the surface Spencer's social ethics seemed progressive and optimistic—evolution would inevitably lead to the perfection of humankind—the devil was in the details. Spencer opposed all forms of state aid to the poor, believing they were inherently "unfit" and that permitting them to survive and propagate would prolong the course of social evolution. The only justification for altruism, he allowed, was that it ennobled the giver. He even opposed publicly supported, universal education. The purpose of sociology and other social sciences was to demonstrate the impracticality of reform or of intervening in the operation of natural laws. Among Spencer's champions, predictably enough, were the "captains of industry" John D. Rockefeller and Andrew Carnegie. But the literary Naturalists, even leftists such as Theodore Dreiser, Hamlin Garland, and Jack London were apostles, too. In chapter 13 of his semiautobiographical novel *Martin Eden* (1909), London described his own enthusiasm for Spencer's *First Principles* (1860–1862): "here was the man Spencer, organizing all knowledge for him, reducing everything to unity, elaborating ultimate realities, and presenting to his startled gaze a universe so concrete of realization that it was like the model of a ship such as sailors make and put into glass bottles. There was no caprice, no chance. All was law." He incorporated these deterministic ideas into such stories as *The Call of the Wild* (1903) and "To Build a Fire" (1908). In all, the Naturalists gleaned from Zola a scientific model for diagnosing social ills; from Darwin the metaphor of the jungle; from Spencer the notions of "struggle for existence" and "survival of the fittest"; from Karl Marx a sense of economic determinism; from Hippolyte Taine the idea of literature as the product of race or national character, moment, and social milieu; and from Sigmund Freud the discovery of the irresistible force of the unconscious (C. Hugh Holman, *Handbook to Literature*, 1986).

American Realist/Naturalist texts often fit hand in glove with many of the social essays of the period, including Henry Demarest Lloyd's *Wealth against Commonwealth* (1894), a muckraking exposé of the Standard Oil Company; Thorstein Veblen's *The Theory of the Leisure Class* (1899), a satire of the "conspicuous consumption" and "pecuniary canons of taste" of the wealthy and privileged; Jacob Riis's *How the Other Half Lives,* a photoessay documenting the plight of the urban poor; and Henry George's *Progress and Poverty* (1879), which proposed a "single tax" on the "unearned increment" in property values, a measure designed to discourage land speculation. The predatory policies of Standard Oil loom in the background of Howells's novel *A Hazard of New Fortunes* (1889), for example, and Crane's *Maggie* has often been compared to *How the Other Half Lives.* Hamlin Garland wrote "Under the Lion's Paw" (1889) specifically as a campaign document on behalf of the single tax and even read it aloud at political rallies. The story resonated with midwestern farmers who lost land and money during the drought and economic depression of the 1890s.

Only one American writer of fiction from the previous era seems to have exerted much influence on post–Civil War U.S. authors: Nathaniel Hawthorne. He epitomized for James, Howells, Mary Wilkins Freeman, Sarah Orne Jewett, and other postwar writers the critically and commercially successful American man of letters. Little wonder so many of Hawthorne's stories became paradigm texts for the Realists. Richard H. Brodhead asserts that Hawthorne "is the only American author always to have been part of our significant past," the "only major American author never to have been underestimated," and Brodhead tracks his influence on the works of the Realists, particularly James, who knew him personally and wrote a book about him (*The School of Hawthorne,* 1986). Both Howells's *Undiscovered Country* (1880) and James's *Bostonians* (1886), for example, may be best understood as Realist rewritings of Hawthorne's *Blithedale Romance* (1852). Freeman's short story "The Slip of the Leash" (1904) and the Joanna Todd episode in Jewett's *Country of the Pointed Firs* (1896), in which characters resign their places on the "electric chain of humanity," should be read in light of Hawthorne's similar sketch "Wakefield" (1837).

The writings of the Realists were featured throughout the late nineteenth century in the pages of the leading middle-class parlor magazines, the *Atlantic, Harper's, Century,* and *Cosmopolitan,* all of them published in Boston or New York. Howells, in fact, was editor of three of these four monthlies at different times between 1871 and 1892, and he served as a literary patron over the years to Twain, James, Freeman, Jewett, Crane, and Dreiser. Partly as a result of the invention of the linotype machine, the number of magazines published in the United States increased from about 200 in 1860 to 1,800 in 1900 with a corresponding increase in the opportunities for literary careers. Most commercially successful novels and magazines were pitched to middle-class women readers. Howells estimated that some 75 percent of all books sold in the United States during this period were bought by women, and John W. De Forest similarly asserted that women composed four-fifths of the reading public. Once asked why he "always had a boy and girl in love" in his books, De Forest explained that "it was the only kind of plot a writer could get the public interested in" (Edwin Oviatt, "J. W. De Forest in New Haven," *New York Times Saturday Review,* 17 December 1898). According to H. H. Boyesen, the American writer during this period was condemned to mollify "the young American girl. She is the Iron Madonna who strangles in her fond embrace the American novelist; the Moloch upon whose altar he sacrifices, willingly or unwillingly, his chances of greatness" (Borus). The novel, even the realistic novel, usually contained a love interest to spur sales. *The Adventures of Huckleberry Finn* and *The Red Badge of Courage* were rare and notable exceptions to the rule, and in the case of other realistic tales, for example, "Editha," *The Awakening,* "Daisy Miller," and *Ethan Frome,* it was a love interest often disappointed.

—*Gary Scharnhorst*

Evolution of Critical Opinion

American literary Realism is often described as a movement shaped in part by its reaction against earlier and mostly sentimental fiction; American literary history generally may be seen as a series of cultural rebellions. These assumptions are valid enough, so far as they go. There was a good deal of give-and-take in the contest, however, and the student of this period will find abundant research opportunities in exploring certain features of an ongoing and changing literary debate.

In 1837 Ralph Waldo Emerson delivered his "The American Scholar" address at Harvard, in which he observed, "The literature of the poor, the feelings of the child, the philosophy of the street, the meaning of household life are the topics of the time." These were the materials of an American literature, and Emerson was only one of many calling for an authentic and native literature that reflected the qualities of a then relatively young democratic nation. Part of that call was for American artists and readers to free themselves from a worship of European conventions and models. Bold as his pronouncements were, Emerson's celebration of the common and familiar did not so much threaten prevailing literary taste, which for the most part was genteel, as refocus it, for he also insisted that what is near at hand symbolizes a spiritual and ultimately transcendental meaning. The origins of local-color writing date from around the same time as Emerson's speech, but those authors' purposes were more casual and not so lofty. Particularly among the frontier humorists there were no overt literary aims other than to faithfully record the speech and flavor of a specific region at a particular time, and they tended to think of their productions as "sketches" or anecdotes rather than as short stories. Though many of these sketches were later collected and published as books, such as Augustus B. Longstreet's *Georgia Scenes* (1843) and J. J. Hooper's *Some Adventures of Captain Simon Suggs* (1845), they were often first published in newspapers.

Since these early efforts at local-color writing were generally considered a low form of journalism, the first critical judgment passed upon the movement was simply neglect—skepticism, depreciation, even disdain would come later. Actually, the eventual consequences of this critical neglect were rather salutary. For one thing, writers such as Longstreet and Hooper tended to think of themselves as merely transcribing what they saw and heard; they were attentive to accuracy of detail but were not so much "objective" observers of life as they were indifferent to the opinion of the literary establishment, and this gave them a freedom from constraints they might otherwise have felt. Another consequence was that this sort of writing had a certain underground popularity among male readers, generally, who enjoyed the coarse and racy stories coming out of the South but frequently published in the New York sporting weekly, *The Spirit of the Times*. Local-color writers and, later, Realists tended to make their appeal directly to the everyday reader, whose literary judgment was based upon common experience instead of the instructed vision taught in schools or handed down from on high. Still a third consequence of critical neglect was that these early local colorists were all unknowingly contributing to what William Dean Howells eventually called the "literary decentralization" of our culture (*Criticism and Fiction*, 1891)—a democratic emphasis upon diversity and variety instead of upon a unified and homogenous literary taste created by an educated elite. Even though Howells himself was editor of the prestigious Boston-based *Atlantic Monthly*, he no doubt would have approved of the editorial remark published in *Scribner's Monthly* (September 1881): "New England is no longer king. . . . The South and West are hereafter to be reckoned with." Boston and, later, New York remained the literary centers of the nation, nonetheless.

To the extent that local color prefigured the purposes of American Realism, it offered later writers the example of a set of practices and themes that, if they were not openly hostile, were at least antagonistic to dominant critical opinion. The resistance to literary Realism was, according to Warner Berthoff, grounded in fear—fear that the moral fiber of the country was breaking down before one's eyes and that the new writers were contributing to that dissolution. Broadly speaking, there were two schools of literary thought that stood in opposition to the Realist movement. The first we may call idealistic or sentimental criticism. It was devoted to the idea that literature ought to be elevating and ennobling; literature should express what ought to be, not what is. In the prose and poetry of this stripe, virtue should be rewarded and vice punished; likewise, literature ought to recommend heroic self-sacrifice, unswerving loyalty, high religious and moral feelings, expansive sympathy and the like. As T. S. Perry once remarked, genuine literature must be true "to those higher laws and passions that alone are real, that exist above all the petty, accidental caprice of time and place" ("American Novels," *North American Review,* October 1872).

The second school ultimately opposed the logic of Realism for different but related reasons. One might call it the nationalist school, and it tended to revolve around questions of genre. Realists preferred the novel over popular sentimental romance and believed that form might accurately describe the whole of American life and gain a wide readership. Additionally, there was the question of whether there is or even ought to be something that might be called the "Great American Novel." John William De Forest introduced the topic in 1868 in an essay by that name. Something of a Realist himself, De Forest promoted the notion that, ideally, such a work would dramatize a truly national (as opposed to a sectional) character and help foster ideas of unity and consolidated American themes and interests. The great American novel would help to heal the rift between North and South and establish an artistic version of the political "union" that Lincoln had sought to preserve.

Any effort to write such a work assumed that there is a distinctive "American" character that somehow represents the whole of the country, and behind that assumption lay others—including, for many, the premise that the American character was fundamentally Anglo-Saxon in its bearing and outlook. Here, ironically, was the very sort of sentimental stereotype of a figure that never really existed that Realists sought to dispute. Nevertheless, important and sophisticated Realists were tempted to try their hand at that sort of depiction—Henry James did in *The American* (1877), and, in different fashion, so did Mark Twain, Howells, and Edith Wharton.

By the 1890s, a proliferation of Regionalist stories gave evidence that many writers and critics believed the future of a truly national literature lay in a heterogeneous compound of individuated tales and novels rooted in place. In 1892 Edward Eggleston, in his preface to *The Hoosier Schoolmaster*, declared, "The 'great American novel,' for which prophetic critics yearned so fondly twenty years ago, is appearing in sections." And Howells himself, in 1891, insisted on the "universal rule against universalizing" and that a full representation of American literature would, quiltlike, consist of a hundred "patches" of American life. So it becomes clear that, even within the ranks of the Realists, there was a considerable difference of opinion. Nevertheless, much of American literary history can be framed by these two oppositions—the contest between highbrow and lowbrow literary expression and the problem of the one and the many. The problem was further complicated by the lack of a clear definition of what Realism was. As Hamlin Garland observed, "The meaning of the word 'Realism' varies with the outlook of every person who uses it" ("Productive Conditions of American Literature," *Forum*, August 1894). Perhaps due to its very vagueness, Realism was capacious enough for a great many gifted writers to identify themselves as Realists, and as a literary movement it appeared hospitable not only to women writers, but immigrants from both Europe and Asia, as well as African American and Native American writers.

Nevertheless, when Howells pleaded, "let literature cease to lie about life," he was challenging the art and usefulness of genteel and largely sentimental fiction *(Criticism and Fiction)*. When Howells also, echoing Edmund Burke, announced that the "true standard of the arts" lay within every man's and woman's power, he meant to appeal to and empower the ordinary reader whose own experience with the way day-to-day life actually works was the sufficient criterion for aesthetic judgment; at the same time he meant to encourage a genuinely democratic literature. And when he declared the appeals of sentimental literature morally "poisonous" to the individual and the social fabric, he was advocating a largely pragmatic, or at least utilitarian, ethical view as its replacement. This was a genuine revolutionary creed for the day, and the aesthetic satisfaction Realist fiction afforded was a "recognition," in the readers, that, yes, this was a very picture of life as they knew it to be. As Garland, himself a Realist though he preferred the term "veritism," sadly knew, however, the ordinary man and woman, whose hands were callused and whose backs were aching, were more often apt to turn to fiction as a means of escape or entertainment.

By virtue of being editor of the *Atlantic Monthly* and later supplying a monthly "Editor's Study" column for *Harper's Monthly,* Howells became the chief spokesman for the Realist movement. For a man who was by temperament so open and cordial a critic, it is a bit surprising how controversial a figure he came to be. He was attacked from both sides. Aristocratic critics objected to the advocate of a literature that invited us to become acquainted with the sorts of common characters one would, in real life, take some pains to avoid, and William Roscoe Thayer called him the "champion of crude causes" ("The New Story-Tellers and the Doom of Fiction," *Forum,* December 1894). From the other side, the Naturalist Frank Norris thought Howells as too fastidious, "proper as a deacon."

The French novelist Émile Zola had set forth the essential tenets of Naturalism in his pamphlet *Le Roman expérimental* (1880; translated as "The Experimental

Novel," 1893), arguing the new novelist should follow the example of the scientist and show in man and society "the mechanism of the phenomena which science has mastered." American Naturalist writers such as Norris came to believe that Realism dealt too exclusively with the surfaces of life and did not probe the disturbing complexities that motivate men and women—sexual urges, instinctive violence, economic desperation, a Darwinian struggle for existence. In *The Responsibilities of the Novelist* (1903) and elsewhere Norris called for a reinvigorated Romanticism, full of melodrama and extreme situations, for the responsible novel must tell the truth, even though it might be unwelcome. Naturalists defied the critics and shocked their readers. They depicted individuals under extreme circumstances (freezing to death on the Alaskan tundra or dying of dehydration in Death Valley); they chronicled suicides, perversities, gross social injustice, greed that drifted into madness. They were pessimistic and deterministic in their outlook, and yet they, too, took the high moral ground. If society were ever to advance, it must awaken from its complacency and confront honestly the meanness of life and the vanity of human striving.

Because Naturalist writers often sought to dramatize human life as governed by forces quite beyond the control or understanding of their created characters, they implicitly challenged the general assumption of traditional Realists that if one looked on life directly, one might also make sound, individual moral choices that accrued to the benefit of society. In other words, human beings might make the necessary mental corrections of perceived realities and thereby achieve some sort of informed perspective of experience. For Garland, literary Realism is the "truthful statement of an individual impression corrected by reference to the fact" *(The Literary Criticism of Frank Norris)*. Clearly, Naturalism occupied different ground. As Theodore Dreiser put it in *Sister Carrie* (1900), man's instincts are "dulled by too near an approach to free-will, his free-will not sufficiently developed to replace his instincts"; thus, he is a mere "wisp in the wind."

Naturalism was perhaps the most vigorous challenge to the Realist agenda, though many Naturalists thought of themselves as continuing that project by appropriating a certain kind of subject matter that disclosed the stresses and fractures of life sadly in need of social, as opposed to moral, reform. Norris at least thought Naturalism split the difference between Romanticism (primarily concerned with truth) and Realism (devoted to accuracy). But there were other extensions of or departures from Realism. Three literary movements (each with their critical adherents or detractors) are worth mentioning here: literary Impressionism, aestheticism, and Imagism.

Aestheticism is associated with the fin de siècle literary movement and may be loosely considered to include such offshoots as bohemianism, vagabondia, and decadence. The central premise of aestheticism is that art is its own excuse for being, that it is essentially free from all social and moral obligations. Despite the fact that many critics thought this largely imported literary movement was un-American in its alternate gestures of escape and revolt, a large segment of the population was fascinated by such figures as Oscar Wilde and Aubrey Beardsley. Certainly a portion of Ambrose Bierce's and Stephen Crane's canons may be described as bohemian, but out-and-out American aesthetes (Edgar Saltus or Lafcadio Hearne, for example) are no longer of much interest. Nevertheless, aestheticism challenged the positions of both the genteel tradition and literary Realism; on the one hand it was more highbrow than the Boston Brahmins, and on the other it was countercultural in its manner and its selection of subject matter.

Imagism and Impressionism share an interest in representing the immediacy of experience. That is to say, unlike Realism, which allows for the mental correction of perceptions and therefore of making informed moral judgments, these movements emphasized the primacy of sensation. And unlike Naturalism, which tended to diagnose social and political realities with an eye to reform, they were chiefly concerned with rendering the unpremeditated and immediate sensation. In this country, Imagism was a short-lived poetic movement that importantly influenced modern American poetry. Among its practitioners were the early Ezra Pound, H.D. (Hilda Doolittle), and Amy Lowell. Pound defined the image as "that which presents an intellectual and emotional complex in an instant in time" and thereby gives a "sense of freedom from time limits and space limits."

Impressionism may be thought of as a literary manner which, in the words of Richard Chase ("Introduction" to *The Red Badge of Courage,* 1960), attempts to deliver the "shimmering flow of experience." However, to some degree literary Impressionism opposed traditional Realism because it meant to show the distinction between a perceived actuality and an objective one. Garland wrote several painterly sketches in this manner, and there are many passages in James's fiction that are deliberately impressionistic. Crane is probably the most thoroughgoing American literary impressionist of the era. In some of his better fiction (*The Red Badge of Courage* or "The Blue Hotel," for example) he manages to dramatize a picture of life, full of color and urgency and irony, that makes Impressionism more than a literary technique; instead, it describes an existential condition under a given set of circumstances and at the same time delivers astute and sometimes whimsical social analysis and incisive psychological portraits of those in the grip of confusion or fear or other immediate emotional conditions.

Literary movements do not end quickly or decisively. This is true of Realism and Naturalism, as well. Even among American Realists themselves there was a temptation to go beyond the doctrinal prescriptions of William Dean Howells. The psychological Realism of Henry James, as it was manifested in *The Wings of the Dove* (1902), *The Ambassadors* (1903), and *The Golden Bowl* (1904), caused James's sympathetic brother William to complain that he had gone too far; and the late work of Mark Twain, such as "The Great Dark" or *No. 44, The Mysterious Stranger,* was fantastic to a degree that seems to have cut any ties to conventional Realism. Naturalists were particularly critical of Howells, claiming he was too timid and too limiting in his fiction and his criticism, avoiding aspects of the ordinary life, particularly sex, that were fundamental. Norris and Dreiser made such criticisms, and in his Nobel Prize acceptance speech in 1930, Sinclair Lewis appeared to have delivered the postmortem: Howells "had the code of a pious old maid whose greatest delight was to have tea at the vicarage. He abhorred not only profanity and obscenity but all of what H. G. Wells has called 'the jolly coarseness of life.'" The examples of modern writers such as Theodore Dreiser, Sherwood Anderson, and Ernest Hemingway served to cement the point. High modernists such as Ezra Pound, T. S. Eliot, and James Joyce certainly did not take it as an article of faith that the true standard of the arts lay within every man or woman's power; to the contrary, their work displayed a disregard for the so-called common reader. As for literary Naturalism, tied as it was to nineteenth-century scientific and economic theories, it too began to seem dated, even irrelevant. The scientific discoveries of Marie Curie, the relativism of Albert Einstein, and the theory of "creative evolution" advanced by Henri Bergson all called the determinism of a nineteenth-century scientific materialism into deep question. Freudian psychoanalysis also posed a challenge to the Naturalist position, though Bert Bender has argued in *Evolution and "The Sex Problem"* (2004) that Freud actually extended and enlarged evolutionary contexts for understanding Naturalist writing. At any rate, Naturalism survived into the twentieth century in such writers as Richard Wright and Tillie Olsen, just as Realist fiction survived in Eudora Welty, Tom Wolfe, and John Updike.

Beginning in the 1970s, critical theorists and academic critics posed a different sort of challenge to Realism and Naturalism. Jacques Derrida's dictum will serve in a shorthand way to express the problem: "There is nothing outside the text." Formulated in a variety of ways, poststructuralists held that reality itself is a verbal construct, and therefore attempts to represent the outside world, to render life as it is lived is vain, even absurd. Considered in this way, writing is more about writing than anything else. The novelist William H. Gass declared the task of the writer to be to hold his readers "kindly imprisoned in language," for there is nothing beyond this language. This sort of fiction is subjective in the extreme, even solipsistic. Novelist Tom Wolfe took a different view: "With very few exceptions, the towering achievements [in the novel] have taken the form of a detailed Realism. . . . And why? Because a perfectly sound and natural instinct told them that it is impossible to portray characters vividly, powerfully, convincingly, except as part of the society in which they find themselves." The student should inspect the annotated bibliography to see the variety of ways that theory has affected academic criticism of nineteenth-century literary Realism and Naturalism. Amy Kaplan, for example, in her *The Social Construction of American Realism* (1988) argues that the work of Howells, Wharton, and Dreiser actually reflects a sense of "unreality," which they counter with social constructions of reality. Walter Benn Michaels in *The Gold Standard and the Logic of Naturalism* (1987) gives a new historicist reading of Norris, Wharton, and Dreiser, contending that economic circumstances enter into virtually every aspect of life in these texts, though they may seem far removed from economic themes or issues. There remain articulate advocates of the ambitions of early Naturalists and Realists, however. The historian David E. Shi observes that, "By rendering the ordinary significant and the hidden visible, by refusing to offer easy consolations or to rest content with cheap ironies, they demonstrated the power of representation to sustain, assure, and enlarge us." More recently, the critic James Wood has spoken elegantly on behalf of Realism in *How Fiction Works* (2008), insisting that readers still want to connect to a world out there and to read of a life that is familiar and therefore comprehensible. It seems clear that, no matter how transformed or ingeniously analyzed, a genuine interest in Realism and Naturalism will continue for some time to come.

—Tom Quirk

Part II
Study Guides
on General Topics

Biography and Autobiography

Biographical narratives typically have been constructed according to a standard format, a chronicle from cradle to grave. In contrast, autobiographical narratives have been less formulaic or more experimental, taking multiple forms. The earliest biographies were intended to glorify the lives of so-called great men and to chronicle the ebb and flow of history in the manner of Plutarch's *Lives*. "All history resolves itself very easily into the biography of a few stout and earnest persons," Ralph Waldo Emerson declared in "Self-Reliance" (1841), and he illustrated the point by sketching the lives of six movers and shakers in his book *Representative Men* (1850), among them Plato, Shakespeare, Goethe, and Napoleon.

Biographies published in the late nineteenth and early twentieth centuries, however, were more often designed to instruct readers on how to live or to encourage them to pattern their behavior after exemplary lives. As a result, biographies of the Founding Fathers became popular. Benjamin Franklin's autobiography, though completed in 1788 and published in French translation in 1791, was not published in the United States until 1867. At least fifteen book-length Franklin biographies appeared between 1876 and 1910, however, and his life acquired an unprecedented cachet during the period. Thomas Mellon, the founder of the Mellon family fortune, reminisced in his 1885 autobiography that he regarded "the reading of Franklin's Autobiography as the turning point of my life," and T. L. Haines in his success manual *Worth and Wealth* (1883) repeatedly cited Franklin and quoted from his autobiography. William Dean Howells proclaimed Franklin's memoirs "one of the greatest autobiographies in literature," one that "towers over other autobiographies as Franklin towered over other men," in 1905. Charles W. Eliot, the president of Harvard University from 1869 to 1909, published Franklin's memoirs in the first volume of his multivolume Harvard Classics, the so-called "Harvard Five-foot Shelf," in 1909. That is, Franklin's autobiography became an American culture text that resonated with readers whatever their social class. Brothers Paul Leicester Ford and Worthington Chauncey Ford, the grandsons of Noah Webster, published biographies of George Washington in 1896 and 1900, respectively. Owen Wister wrote a biography of Ulysses S. Grant in 1900 before his best-selling Western, *The Virginian* (1902), and afterward he wrote the biography *The Seven Ages of Washington* (1907). Abraham Lincoln's life was also memorialized in numerous biographies after his assassination in 1865. A prime example of this trend is the monumental ten-volume *Abraham Lincoln: A History* (1890) by the sixteenth president's secretaries John Nicolay and John Hay. During this time, campaign biography was also an important branch of the genre. Campaign biographies were written during a political campaign, often by a hired author, to extol a political candidate and increase his popularity among the voters. Among the most important examples of the period were *Sketch of the Life and Character of Rutherford B. Hayes* (1876), by Howells, and *Life of Gen. Ben Harrison* (1888), by Lew Wallace. Juvenile biographies of some of the great politicians of the age were in vogue, epitomized perhaps by three works by Horatio Alger Jr.: *From Canal Boy to President, or, The Boyhood and Manhood of James A. Garfield* (1881), *From Farm Boy to Senator; Being the Boyhood and Manhood of*

Daniel Webster (1882), and *Abraham Lincoln, the Backwoods Boy; or, How a Young Rail-Splitter Became President* (1883).

In contrast, autobiography as a genre is a more experimental form. While autobiography is most clearly defined by its content—the representation of an individual life—it is also distinct as a genre intended for public consumption. Also, unlike journals and diaries that describe current life events over a period of time, autobiographies generally reflect on the author's life from a single point in time. Autobiographical authors often use a combination of memory, historical knowledge, and literary devices to construct themselves as meaningful, unified individuals. What is often most interesting about autobiography is not the truth or falsity of the representation but the way an author chooses to construct his or her persona. In American literature especially, autobiography has often been viewed as a democratic genre in which each individual can shape identity as he or she chooses.

The examples of experimental autobiography are myriad. *The Education of Henry Adams* (1907) recounts the life of the author in standard prose, but it is narrated in third-person and in an ironic tone. In it, Henry Brooks Adams laments his poor education despite his upbringing in a distinguished American family. Several authors glided smoothly among the genres of fiction, biography, and autobiography. The novelist Henry James, for example, wrote the life of an American expatriate sculptor in *William Wetmore Story and His Friends* (1903) and contributed a biography of Nathaniel Hawthorne (1879), whom James viewed as his predecessor, to the English Men of Letters series published by Macmillan. Later, he wrote a series of autobiographies titled *A Small Boy and Others* (1913), *Notes of a Son and Brother* (1914), and the unfinished *The Middle Years* (1917). Similarly, the novelist and editor Howells pioneered a new form of literary auto/biography in *Literary Friends and Acquaintance: A Personal Retrospect of American Authorship* (1900) and *My Mark Twain* (1910). Like James and Howells, Mark Twain also moved flawlessly among genres, with such fictionalized autobiographical travel books as *The Innocents Abroad* (1869), *Roughing It* (1872), *A Tramp Abroad* (1880), *Life on the Mississippi* (1883), and *Following the Equator* (1897) interspersed with novels such as *The Adventures of Tom Sawyer* (1876), *The Adventures of Huckleberry Finn* (1884), and *Pudd'nhead Wilson* (1894). Twain dictated his autobiography late in life in nonchronological order, publishing some of this material serially in the *North American Review* as "Chapters from My Autobiography" (1906–1907). These multiple types of autobiography reflect not only the author's self-construction but also various editors' ideas about narrative form.

The most commercially successful autobiography of the period was arguably *Personal* memoirs *of U. S. Grant* (1885–1886), completed as the Civil War commander and former president was dying. Twain's publishing house Webster & Co. paid his widow several hundred thousand dollars in royalties. The success of Grant's memoirs led to the publication of similar projects, such as the *Memoirs of Gen. W. T. Sherman* (1891) and *Theodore Roosevelt: An Autobiography* (1913). For the record, the biographies of politicians and war heroes easily outsold biographies of religious heroes. During the Gilded Age, few "spiritual autobiographies" akin to Jonathan Edwards's "Personal Narrative" (c. 1740) or Henry David

Thoreau's *Walden* (1854) appeared, and none of any significance. Twain believed that a biography of the reigning pope would rival the popularity of Grant's autobiography, given its potential worldwide audience but Bernard O'Reilly's *Life of Leo XIII, from an Authentic Memoir Furnished by His Order* (1887), also published by Webster & Co., was a commercial failure.

Biography and autobiography also became important modes of expression for minority voices in America in the late nineteenth and early twentieth centuries. Charles W. Chesnutt and W. E. B. Du Bois wrote biographies of Frederick Douglass (1899) and John Brown (1909). Sarah Winnemucca's *Life among the Piutes* (1883) detailed her experiences in a Native American tribe that repeatedly aided the U.S. military but was then deemed hostile and removed to a reservation in the northwest United States. Douglass, whose most famous work was *Narrative of the Life of Frederick Douglass, an American Slave* (1845), continued to revise and add to it until he published the final version as *The Life and Times of Frederick Douglass* (1892). Among other significant autobiographies by minority writers were Booker T. Washington's *Up from Slavery* (1901), Sui Sin Far's "Leaves from the Mental Portfolio of an Eurasian" (1909), and Zitkala-Ša's "Impressions of an Indian Childhood" (1900), "The School Days of an Indian Girl" (1900), "An Indian Teacher among Indians" (1900), and "Why I am a Pagan" (1902). In addition, at least two immigrant autobiographies merit mention here: the Danish journalist Jacob Riis's *The Making of an American* (1901), which describes the horrific living and working conditions of poor New York immigrants; and Mary Antin's *The Promised Land* (1912), the account of a Polish Jew's assimilation.

During this period biographies were increasingly written by scholars and literary authors. One of the most famous biographers of this time was George Edward Woodberry, professor at Columbia University, scholar, and poet, who wrote numerous biographies of both British and American authors, including Edgar Allan Poe (1885), Hawthorne (1902), A. C. Swinburne (1905), and Emerson (1907).

TOPICS FOR DISCUSSION AND RESEARCH

1. In examining autobiography, what persona is the author presenting of him or herself, and why has the author chosen this representation? What themes has the author found in her/his life, and how does the author use these themes to make sense of her/his identity?
2. Ask if a biography you are examining is scholarly or popular. If it is a popular biography, what about the subject makes him or her an appropriate figure of popular interest, and how does the author play on this popular interest to draw readers? What might be classified as "sensational" in the popular biography, and how does that represent the social mores of the period?
3. How might the form of biography or autobiography be influenced by either slave narrative or captivity narrative? What kind of transformation does the subject of a slave or captivity narrative undergo, and how is that transformation presented by the author?

4. Closely examine the form of the biography or autobiography. Is it written in first person? How does the chronology of the narrative compare to the historical chronology of the subject's life? Does the narrative emphasize factual historical information, or does it utilize literary and artistic devices to emphasize metaphorical meaning and aesthetic coherence? How does this narrative form affect the content of the biography or autobiography, and how does it affect your response to the text?

RESOURCES

Criticism

G. Thomas Couser, *American Autobiography: The Prophetic Mode* (Amherst: University of Massachusetts Press, 1979).

Closely examines more than twenty American autobiographies, from colonial to contemporary, in order to explore the genre thoroughly. Couser sees autobiography as a response to communal crisis, which transforms into an obsessive desire to understand what it means to be an American.

James Olney, ed., *Autobiography: Essays Critical and Theoretical* (Princeton: Princeton University Press, 1980).

A collection of sixteen essays that explores autobiography and its construction of self-identity from a variety of perspectives. It covers autobiographies from diverse national origins and time periods in order to question the form and purpose of autobiography.

Albert E. Stone, *Autobiographical Occasions and Original Acts: Versions of American Identity from Henry Adams to Nate Shaw* (Philadelphia: University of Pennsylvania Press, 1982).

A central text for students of American autobiography that focuses on modern (late-nineteenth- to mid-twentieth-century) autobiographies. Especially helpful for exploring and understanding autobiographies of marginalized individuals, such as Black Elk.

Stanley Weintraub, ed., *Biography and Truth* (Indianapolis, Ind.: Bobbs-Merrill, 1967).

A collection of essays in which biographers discuss their predicaments in interpreting the truth for their biographies and then crafting that truth into a compelling narrative. Each author's reflections on writing are accompanied by a sample of his or her biographical work.

PEOPLE OF INTEREST

Henry Brooks Adams (1838–1918)

Grandson and great-grandson of presidents and a journalist, editor, novelist, and academic.

Horatio Alger Jr. (1832–1899)

Graduate of Harvard College and the Divinity School, the author of more than a hundred juvenile novels between 1864 and his death.

Frederick Douglass (1818–1895)

Former slave and civil-rights activist best known for his *Narrative of the Life of Frederick Douglass* (1845). As one of the most famous slave narratives, Douglass's autobiography is a foundational text for scholars of autobiography and African American literature.

Jacob Riis (1849–1914)

Muckraking journalist best known for his photo-essay *How the Other Half Lives* (1890).

Lew Wallace (1827–1905)

Best known as the author of the historical romance *Ben-Hur* (1880), he was governor of the New Mexico Territory (1878–1881).

Booker T. Washington (1856?–1915)

Founder of the Tuskegee Institute in Alabama and the leader of middle-class African Americans across the country during the last quarter-century of his life.

—Erin Murrah-Mandril

Crime and Detective Fiction

Since the inception of the related genres of crime and detective fiction in the early nineteenth century, readers of all ages find thrill, fascination, and ultimately intellectual and social comfort in the adventures of criminals and the detectives who hunt them down. Crime narratives, the larger generic category into which detective fiction is a subset, detail the commission of a crime, which may range from physical assault to theft to psychological exploitation, its investigation, and then an eventual outcome or judgment. Such a crime upsets or has the potential to upset the social order. Detective fiction is related in that it, too, narrates the investigation and solution of a crime, but with one important difference. According to John G. Cawelti's study of the genre, "the classical detective story required four main roles: the victim, the criminal, the detective, and those threatened by the crime but incapable of solving it."

Suspense, mystery, crime, and the constant interplay between right and wrong, good and evil, are popular and resilient plots. Yet, these plots are still riveting for the very puzzles they present and the ways they allow their readers to participate both as amateur criminals—committing blackmail or espionage in a fictional world—and as armchair detectives—matching wits with the best fictional minds to bring order back into a chaotic world. Readers and writers can, by engaging in the criminal imagination, safely walk on the moral wild side, knowing full well that, as Julian Symons avers, "those who tried to disturb the established social order" will be "discovered and punished," social order will be restored, and the armchair detective will take comfort in a criminal discovered and a mystery solved.

The ability of crime fiction's readers to relate to its narratives is, perhaps, what contributed to its popularity—a literate American public daily read accounts in newspapers and mass-market magazines that covered, and in many cases, sensationalized, criminal events. Edgar Allan Poe's "The Mystery of Marie Rogêt" (1842), in fact, is purportedly based on the actual murder of Mary Cecilia Rogers, whose body was found floating in the Hudson River a few days after her disappearance on 25 July 1841.

Creating mystery and detective fiction from real-life scenarios continued in the United States with the publication of the Pinkerton detective series, based on the cases of the Pinkerton National Detective Agency, and containing elements commonly seen in crime and detective fiction: multiple suspects, surveillance, and advanced technology, such as photography or lie detectors, to whittle down the list of possible criminals. *Recollections of a Detective Police-Officer* (1856) by Englishman William Russell, who called himself "Waters," appeared in the United States as a "yellowback," a cheaply produced book with a yellow cover; it detailed purportedly real-life exploits and cases.

In addition to Pinkerton's and "Waters's" stories, readers of crime and detective fiction, particularly adolescents, turned in the late nineteenth century to "dime novels" or "penny dreadfuls," inexpensive publications aimed at quick sales, which recounted sensationalized crime stories that some Americans believed contributed to an increase in crime among their juvenile readers. Nick Carter was the most famous and widely read of all characters to appear in dime novels and is considered to be the second most published character in all of American literature. He first appeared in "The Old Detective's Pupil; or, The Mysterious Crime of Madison Square" in the 18 September 1886, issue of the *New York Weekly*, then continued through 1990 in various detective magazines, radio shows, comic books, and more than 250 novels.

The second half of the nineteenth and the first decades of the twentieth centuries witnessed an explosion of the crime and detective genre, introducing some of the most resistant detectives, memorable criminals, and social worlds that resembled very much the everyday realities of many readers. With this increased popularity of the genre, however, came a shift in its focus. No longer content to lavish their creative acumen on the criminal, authors began to provide more lively detail about both the detective, making the person who solved the crime the heroic, if quirky, protagonist and in some cases, the social conditions that surrounded or even contributed to the crime.

Talented crime and detective fiction writers are adept at capturing society's fears, and the popularity of their hero-detectives may be telling markers of what and who American society values. The middle of the nineteenth century brought the rise of industry, and the concomitant increase in the belief in the power of science and technology to enhance daily life, a theme Ronald R. Thomas explores in his study of detective fiction and the nineteenth-century rise of forensic science. Craig Kennedy, the so-called American Sherlock Holmes, created by Arthur B. Reeve, predicted many advances in criminology.

Authors such as Metta Fuller Victor, perhaps best known for her two detective novels *The Dead Letter* (1866), believed to be the first American detective novel, and *The Figure Eight* (1869), and Mary Roberts Rinehart, Anna Katharine Green, Mary E. Wilkins Freeman, and Pauline Hopkins created memorable female sleuths and criminals who had direct lineage from the women's and African Americans' rights movements and ideologies, while the male author Edward Lytton Wheeler (1854/5–1885) created the "Deadwood Dick" series, which ran from 1877 to 1897 and included the sleuth "Lady Kate, the Dashing Female Detective." Rinehart subscribed to the American school of "scientific" detection, a focus that mixed adventure stories with mysteries in need of a solution, a combination developed even further in the hard-boiled school later in the twentieth century. Greene was an enormously successful author and in fact wrote the first American best-selling detective novel, selling more than 250,000 copies. Although Greene opposed giving women the right to vote, her fiction often focuses on problems facing women, including the nightmarish control men exert over women's lives.

Women's-rights advocacy was not the only civil-rights commentary delivered along with the mysteries. African American Hopkins, writing a short detective story, "Talma Gordon" (1900), addresses the nervous concerns about racial intermarriage or "amalgamation," the "crime" in the story. Stephen F. Soitos, in his study of African American detective fiction, explores what he terms the "blues detective" during this same era. Mark Twain's *Pudd'nhead Wilson* (1894) introduces David Wilson, who not only employs fingerprint analysis to solve the mystery; since he discovers that a white and a light-skinned black boy have been switched at birth, this novel offers an important polemic on the morality of judging people according to their skin color, and the dangerous path of racial discrimination.

As the United States moved into the twentieth century, crime and detective stories lost some of their melodrama and detectives, and criminals functioned in a more realistic world of human frailty, error, miscalculation, and social networks. Detectives and readers were asked to consider both crime and its consequences. When organized crime threatened American social integrity, for example, mobsters became prominent in the genre and required equally tough detectives to bring them to justice, characters and tropes Dashiell Hammett mastered in the 1920s and 1930s. Detectives, criminals, and the fiction they populated entered a morally relative world and tried their best to eradicate the troublesome elements in order to enact justice.

At its heart, though, crime and detective fiction addresses what seem to be some of humans' most foundational concerns and needs. Howard Haycraft suggests that a detective story "embodies a democratic respect for law," while John G. Cawelti has argued that "our fascination with mystery represents unresolved feelings about the primal scene." Cawelti also suggests that detective fiction was not only a "pleasing artistic form" for nineteenth- and early-twentieth-century readers, but it also provided a "temporary release from doubt and guilt," generated from the overwhelming changes in culture. In his "Defence of Detective Stories" (1902) G. K. Chesterton intoned that "we live in an armed camp, making war with a chaotic world, and that criminals, the children of chaos, are nothing but traitors within our gates." Until the world no longer needs them to work through the ethics of human nature that lead some to murder or steal, the detectives, and the crimes they solve and the criminals they bring to justice, are here to stay on our fictional pages.

TOPICS FOR DISCUSSION AND RESEARCH

1. How does the detective fiction by such authors as Mary Roberts Rinehart, Anna Katharine Greene, and Mary E. Wilkins Freeman reflect the social environment and historical era in which it was produced?
2. How has the character of the detective changed since Poe's introduction of C. Auguste Dupin? How has the character of the detective remained consistent over time? What do you think accounts for these differences and similarities?
3. How have technological advancements appeared in detective and crime fiction, and what do those advancements suggest about the culture? Consider, particularly, the Pinkerton Detective Agency and series, as well as the fictional character "Craig Kennedy's" use of investigative techniques.
4. How do you see crime fiction at work in other areas of culture? How do crime dramas on television or in movies compare to fiction? What do you think accounts for the popularity of crime drama?

RESOURCES

Criticism

John G. Cawelti, *Adventure, Mystery, and Romance: Formula Stories as Art and Popular Culture* (Chicago: University of Chicago Press, 1976).
A pioneering study of formula fiction.

Howard Haycraft, ed., *The Art of the Mystery Story: A Collection of Critical Essays* (New York: Simon & Schuster, 1946).
Compiles the most authoritative writings on the genre in the first half of the twentieth century.

Stephen Knight, *Form and Ideology in Crime Fiction* (Bloomington: Indiana University Press, 1980).
Argues that the commercial success of a text should not deter critics from studying it; instead, the criticism should look toward the societal interests in which it was produced.

Stephen F. Soitos, *The Blues Detective: A Study of African American Detective Fiction* (Amherst: University of Massachusetts Press, 1996).
Beginning with Pauline Hopkins in 1901, traces the lineage of African American detective fiction written by black Americans about black detectives and incorporating themes of race and racial tension.

Ronald R. Thomas, *Detective Fiction and the Rise of Forensic Science* (New York: Cambridge University Press, 1999).
Links the nineteenth century's increasing reliance on technological expertise—such as fingerprinting, photography, and lie detectors—with the burgeoning genre of detective fiction in both Britain and the United States. Thomas's focus on forensic science is especially concerned with the authority of the literary detective and the way in which those devices relate to broader questions of cultural and individual authority.

PEOPLE OF INTEREST

Anna Katharine Green (1846–1935)
American poet and novelist, one of the first writers of detective fiction in America, distinguished by adherence to legal accuracy. When her poetry failed to gain recognition, she produced her first and best-known novel, *The Leavenworth Case* (1878). She became a best-selling author, eventually publishing about forty books.

Pauline Hopkins (1859–1930)
African American poet, journalist, playwright, and fiction writer best known for her serialized novel *Of One Blood* (1902–1903).

Edgar Allan Poe (1809–1849)

American writer, poet, editor, and literary critic, considered part of the American Romantic Movement. Best known for his tales of mystery and the macabre, Poe was one of the earliest American practitioners of the short story and is considered the inventor of the detective-fiction genre with his trio of stories "The Murders in the Rue Morgue," "The Purloined Letter," and "The Mystery of Marie Rogêt." Arthur Conan Doyle, inventor of Sherlock Holmes, said, "Each [of Poe's detective stories] is a root from which a whole literature has developed. . . . Where was the detective story until Poe breathed the breath of life into it?"

Mary Roberts Rinehart (1876–1958)

The so-called American Agatha Christie, best known for her mystery novel *The Circular Staircase* (1908) and her frequent contributions to *The Saturday Evening Post* early in the twentieth century.

—Laura Behling

Ethnic Writing

A simplified definition might describe "ethnic" literature in the United States as a literature written by, about, or for people whose national, racial, religious, or linguistic background differs from what is perceived as the dominant national standard which is seen as synonymous with the culture of "White Anglo-Saxon Protestants."

The true complexity involved in defining the term "ethnic literature" arises from the word "ethnic" which, according to the *American Heritage Dictionary*, is used with reference to "a group of people sharing a common and distinctive racial, national, religious, linguistic, or cultural heritage." Although recent scholarship on the subject has emphasized the artificial character of ethnic labels and has undermined a static conception of ethnicity, a more traditional view and common usage frequently imply a distinction between the particular elements of ethnic cultures and the features of the dominant national mainstream. In this sense, the word retains a component of its earlier meaning as "pagan," "heathen," or, by extension, "non-standard"— terms which highlight a deviation from a particular doctrine. In the United States, this standard has long been seen as synonymous with the culture of White Anglo-Saxon Protestants. People identified as "ethnics" were therefore defined by their difference from a real or imagined standard; they were regarded as figures on the margin, outsiders, "others."

With such categories in place, it was easy to label immigrants from foreign countries as representatives of ethnic cultures. But recent arrival on American shores was not the only criterion applied. The cultural ways of Native Americans, African Americans, and Mexican Americans, communities that had long lived within the boundaries of the United States, were also deemed outside of the American mainstream and thus qualified as examples of ethnic identities.

Although it is important to realize the specific histories and contexts, as well as the differences within each ethnic culture, it is possible to identify a few recurrent themes in ethnic writing. Located on the margins of American society and culture, ethnic groups had to contend with negative stereotypes and various forms of discrimination and oppression. Therefore, ethnic writers often confronted and opposed a literary record that demeaned their culture and their people. This fact notwithstanding, the writing of ethnic groups goes far beyond tales of suffering and victimization. Caught in a clash between their traditional world and a new environment and faced with the strains of marginality and the pressures of assimilation, ethnic literature reflects the relationship between subordinate and dominant cultures and is centrally concerned with the question of identity formation. But ethnic writing has interest and value beyond the realm of non-mainstream groups insofar as it sheds a revealing light on the established writers in the American literary canon. Seen from this perspective, it becomes clear that the idea of "difference" is ultimately less interesting than the dynamic interaction between cultural groups, the crossing and recrossing of cultural borders, emphasizing the hybrid, or bicultural, situation in which ethnic American writers find themselves.

Owing to their social status and the educational and economic conditions that lay at its base, members of ethnic groups were slow to emerge as active voices in the growing body of American literature, and it took until the second half of the twentieth century for an ethnic label to become an asset rather than a liability. Despite this fact, it would be wrong to assume that ethnic writing was nonexistent before the twentieth century. The birth of an African American literary tradition can be said to have started with black poet Phillis Wheatley in the late eighteenth century. Slave narratives began to be published as early as the late eighteenth century and recorded the experiences of human bondage in the Southern states from the perspective of the oppressed. Important representatives were Harriet Jacobs's *Incidents in the Life of a Slave Girl* (1861) and Frederick Douglass's *Life of Frederick Douglass, an American Slave* (1845). In the second half of the nineteenth century, African American autobiographical memoirs and narratives gradually gave way to fiction as a means of expression, and writers such as Charles W. Chesnutt, Paul Laurence Dunbar, and Alice Dunbar-Nelson turned their talents to writing poetry, short fiction, and novels. Both Chesnutt and Dunbar attracted the attention of William Dean Howells, earning his praise and support as skillful and talented imaginative writers. With the publication of Booker T. Washington's *Up from Slavery* (1901), W. E. B. Du Bois's *The Souls of Black Folk* (1903), and James Weldon Johnson's *The Autobiography of an Ex-Colored Man* (1912) African American writing set milestones in the early twentieth century.

Native American traditions go back to the time before white Europeans arrived on the North American continent, but since they were mostly preserved in an oral tradition, they did not come to the general public's attention until they were published in print. By the nineteenth century, American Indians were beginning to tell their own stories. As is typical for the early phase of an ethnic literature, the initial publications were nonfiction prose, especially autobiographies, historical accounts, and protest literature in response to the curtailment of Native Americans' rights. When Indians lost their traditional homelands and were forcefully removed to reservations, they began to collect and publish the myths, history, and customs preserved in their respective tribe's oral heritage. Prominent examples are Sarah Winnemucca Hopkins's *Life among the Piutes* (1883), and Zitkala-Ša's *Old Indian Legends* (1901).

As the nineteenth century neared its end, more and more writers for whom immigration was a recent experience began to publish material in which they either recorded their personal stories in biographical formats or used them as a basis for writing fiction. Notable representatives are Jewish writers of Eastern European background such as Abraham Cahan (*The Imported Bridegroom and Other Stories of the New York Ghetto,* 1898, and *The Rise of David Levinsky,* 1917), Mary Antin (*The Promised Land,* 1912), and Anzia Yezierska (*Hungry Hearts,* 1920, and *The Bread Givers,* 1925).

Also toward the end of the nineteenth century Asian American writers began to depict the life of their cultural groups, using both fact-oriented and fictional forms of representation. A major and influential voice was Sui Sin Far (Edith Maude Eaton), whose short fiction dealing with the struggles and joys of Chinese families living on America's Pacific Coast was published in popular periodicals and later collected in her book *Mrs. Spring Fragrance* (1912).

Apart from ethnic literature written in English, immigrants and members of other minorities also created a large body of texts in their native languages. Older literary histories, such as *The Cambridge History of American Literature* (1917–1921) and Robert Spiller's *Literary History of the United States* (1948), draw attention to the fact that writing by Americans who used languages other than English was a substantial part of America's literary production. A chapter in Spiller's book surveys the literature and literary cultures of German, French, Spanish, Italian, Norwegian, Swedish, Danish, and Jewish ethnic groups in the United States. To this day, many of America's major archives and libraries are well stocked with multilingual materials still untapped by scholars.

The term "ethnic writing" can also be expanded to include texts by authors of a non-ethnic background who appropriated ethnic voices and styles. In vaudeville theaters and other venues of the popular stage, performers masqueraded as African Americans, Irishmen, Germans, and other minorities and attracted large audiences who subsequently bought cheaply made pamphlet anthologies filled with humorous dialogs and sketches. Writers such as Thomas Nelson Page (*Pastime Stories*, 1894) and Joel Chandler Harris (*Uncle Remus: His Songs and Sayings*, 1880) wrote narrative fiction drawing on their outsider's perception of African American culture. Categorized as "blackface minstrelsy" or specimens of the "plantation tradition," these texts have come under severe critical scrutiny.

Viewed in its entirety, ethnic American writing covers a spectrum which has far more to offer than exotic people and scenes or instances of ethnic self-description and self-discovery. With its thematic variety, its stylistic range, and its cultural contexts, ethnic writing is a vital category in American literature and offers a broad field for exploration and study.

TOPICS FOR DISCUSSION AND RESEARCH

1. What are the criteria for distinguishing "ethnic" literature from other types of literature? Would you expect ethnic writers to write about topics and in a style that differs from so-called mainstream writers?
2. History books often refer to the United States as a nation made up of immigrants from all parts of the world. At the same time, contemporary debates about ethnic writing tend to be limited to Native American, African American, Latino, and Asian American writers. Why do you think other groups virtually play no role in the discussion of ethnic literature?
3. Can you imagine why the term "ethnic literature" might carry a negative connotation?
4. Can you explain why people would object to the idea that an author might adopt the voice of an ethnic group to which he or she does not belong?

RESOURCES
Criticism

David R. Peck, *American Ethnic Literatures: Native American, African American, Chicano/Latino, and Asian American Writers and Their Backgrounds. An Annotated Bibliography* (Pasadena, Cal.: Salem, 1992).

In its coverage of the four major American ethnic literatures, lists bibliographies on individual ethnic groups and on ethnic history and immigration. It also provides background information for teachers, selected reading lists of primary works, and an annotated bibliography of relevant literary criticism.

Emmanuel S. Nelson, *The Greenwood Encyclopedia of Multiethnic American Literature,* 5 volumes (Westport, Conn.: Greenwood Press, 2005).

A comprehensive resource that covers the topic of American ethnic writing by offering its readers more than 1,100 entries not only on individual writers, their major works, and the traditions to which they belong but also on literary and linguistic issues, historical and social contexts. With its cross-references, bibliographic information, and illustrations, it is an invaluable reference tool.

Werner Sollors, *Beyond Ethnicity: Consent and Descent in American Culture* (New York: Oxford University Press, 1986).

Covers a broad range of texts, combining ethnicity theory with an examination of literary and rhetorical patterns to arrive at an understanding of how people from various ethnic backgrounds came to see themselves as Americans.

Sollors, "Literature and Ethnicity," *Harvard Encyclopedia of American Ethnic Groups,* edited by Stephen Thernstrom (Cambridge, Mass.: Belknap Press of Harvard University, 1980), pp. 647–665.

Traces the word "ethnicity" through its etymological development and through a broad cross-section of American writings and observes that ethnicity is a pervasive theme in all American literature. In the course of time ethnicity has been transformed from a liability to an asset.

Sollors, ed., *Multilingual America: Transnationalism, Ethnicity, and the Languages of American Literature* (New York: New York University Press, 1998).

A collection of scholarly essays on Yiddish, Chinese American, Italian American, and other forms of ethnic writing that presents stimulating views of America's multilingual heritage. It invites readers to expand their notion of what constitutes American literature.

Berndt Ostendorf, "Literary Acculturation: What Makes Ethnic Literature 'Ethnic'?" *Callaloo,* 25 (Autumn 1985): 577–586.

Specifies the elements that characterize ethnic writing. It distinguishes between literature about immigrants, for immigrants, and literature growing out of the ethnic-groups experience and discusses the various pressures (linguistic, literary, commercial) that result from the traditionalist demands and progressive desires.

Henry Pochmann, "The Mingling of Tongues," *Literary History of the United States,* volume 2, edited by Robert E. Spiller et al. (New York: Macmillan, 1948), pp. 676–693.

Together with the "The Indian Heritage" (pp. 694–702), serves as a reminder that literature in the United States was not only written by Americans and not only in English. It lists and comments on German, French, Yiddish, Spanish, Italian, and Scandinavian writings.

William Peterfield Trent et al., eds., "Non-English Writings I" and "Non-English Writings II," in *Cambridge History of American Literature,* volume 3 (New York: Putnam, 1917), pp. 572–634.

Devotes more than sixty pages to works written in other languages than English, drawing attention to texts produced by European immigrants in German, French, and Yiddish. They also highlight the literature of Native American, "the richest field of unexploited aboriginal literature . . . anywhere in the world" (610).

Brom Weber, "Our Multi-Ethnic Origins and American Literary Studies," *MELUS,* 2 (March 1975): 5–19.

Argues in favor of a position that acknowledges the "historical significance and qualitative value of American ethnic literatures" and claims that "all American literature has been written or recounted by members of ethnic groups."

PEOPLE OF INTEREST

Mary Antin (1881–1949)
Lecturer, progressive politician, immigrant-rights activist, and autobiographer.

Abraham Cahan (1860–1951)
Lecturer, translator, novelist, and editor of the *Jewish Daily Forward* from 1903 to 1946.

W. E. B. Du Bois (1868–1963)
Civil-rights activist, founding member of the NAACP, and longtime editor of its magazine, *The Crisis.*

Joel Chandler Harris (1848–1908)
Georgia humorist, lecturer, journalist, and folklorist.

Sarah Winnemucca Hopkins (c. 1841–1891)
Piute author, lecturer, and educator.

James Weldon Johnson (1871–1938)
African American journalist, civil-rights activist, poet, and teacher.

Thomas Nelson Page (1853–1922)
Major proponent of the "plantation tradition" in Southern American literature.

Booker T. Washington (1856–1915)
Founding principal of the Tuskegee Institute, an industrial and normal school in Alabama for African American men and women.

Anzia Yezierska (c. 1881–1970)
Author of semiautobiographical tales of the assimilation of immigrants.

Zitkala-Ša (aka Gertrude Bonnin, 1876–1938)
Lakota author and educator.

—Holger Kersten

Humor Writing

Humor writing between 1865 and 1914 flourished under the general rubric of "The Literary Comedians." The "Phunny Phellows" made vulgar dialect, misspelling, and local urban scenes their defining characteristics. Humor may thus have contributed to the drive for urban, realistic language and staging. At the same time, newspapers and national magazines published pieces from various regions, combining humor and local color in the manner of the American cracker-barrel philosophers such as Joel Chandler Harris's Uncle Remus and Mark Twain, the American humorist who gained prominence as the most important humorist-Realist of the period.

A variety of regional humors, including the Southwestern, Northeastern, Yankee, Knickerbocker, and Western, led up to the era under discussion. From the Southwest came the raucous vulgarity of the fistfight, the bear hunt, and hard drinking. From the Northeast, urban dialect and settings combined with national and class perspectives; from the Yankees came pragmatism and practicality and a notable suspicion of claims to higher motives; from the Knickerbockers, a thorough sense of upper-class pretensions; and from the West, skepticism. As early as 1862, Charles G. Leland in *Sunshine in Thought* proclaimed that labor and industry were in a transition stage in art, and "Through their dusty, steam-engine whirling Realism, society will yet attain a Naturalism, or a living and working in nature, more direct, fresher and braver, than history has ever recorded." William Dean Howells, a minor humorist himself at times, followed Leland's direction. Humor and Realism in America interconnected on many levels.

Literary comedy of the period was represented across a wide spectrum of authors. Major literary comedians included Artemus Ward (aka Charles Farrar Browne), who died at thirty-three in 1867, and Twain (Samuel L. Clemens). Twain borrowed Ward's casual deadpan manner as a humorous lecturer. Twain's social-historical irony, ear for language, and eagle eye for detail, the most prominent features of his comedy, also benefited from the influence of the "old showman" persona exhibited in Ward's letters and sketches. Max Adeler (aka Charles Heber Clark), author of *Out of the Hurley-Burley* (1874); Josh Billings (aka Henry W. Shaw), famous for his aphorisms and almanacs; James M. Bailey, widely known as "the *Danbury News* Man"; Robert J. Burdette, "the Burlington *Hawkeye* Man"; and Eli Perkins (aka Melville D. Landon) were oriented toward domestic comedy and thin jokes; longer fiction was outside their scope, and comic trivia sometimes replaced a feeling of narrative objectivity. Bill Nye of the Laramie, Wyoming, *Boomerang* and Finley Peter Dunne, writing as "Mr. Dooley," a whimsically cynical Chicago bartender, put themselves forth as speakers on the topics of the day, and escaped didacticism by manifesting themselves as "real" commentators in commonplace style, thought, and speech, who remarked on American and international politics and a wide variety of social topics. Harriet Beecher Stowe's Sam Lawson, a Yankee cynic, offered a realistic perspective in stories of small-town experience, and "Josiah Allen's Wife" (aka Marietta Holley), a spinster who lived almost reclusively in a small town in upstate New York, produced volume after volume of travel narratives providing tart commentary on the status of women, all in the ironic voice of a determined farm wife. The narrators themselves and their characters were not elevated or refined, and their moralizing was in persona and part of the objective scene. Poets writing with similar comic style included James Whitcomb Riley, William Carleton, and Sam Walter Foss, all of whom combined local color, sentiment, and humor. All used the narrative style localized by voice, dialect, and subject matter, even when addressing larger issues. A host of lesser and long-forgotten local reporters filled columns in papers across the nation with local descriptions of slapstick comic events, local and newspaper slang, and commonplace vernacular speech. Ambrose Bierce, the most bitter and cynical of the humorists of his age, stands in a category by himself for his acrid aphorisms concerning politics, society, and American life.

TOPICS FOR DISCUSSION AND RESEARCH

1. Can Realism as a genre coexist with humor, or are they mutually exclusive? Students might wish to compare passages of humorists and Realist authors to discover and discuss how viewpoints are expressed and whether or not the "voice" of the humorist creates a feeling that could be characterized as a realistic portrait of themselves in persona.

2. An allied topic is whether or not poetry can be realistic enough to fall within the genre of Realism. William Carleton's *Farm Ballads* (1873) and *City Ballads* (1885) provide an array of poems to discuss in terms of style, sentimentality—as in Carleton's famous "Over the Hill to the Poorhouse"—and imagery and other poetic devices.

3. Major comedians of the period, although paralleling the careers of Realist and Naturalist writers, are virtually unknown, though their writings were extremely popular and Ward and Leland were considered by English critics to be unique specimens of American pragmatic attitudes and irreverence. Would they have been remembered if they had written longer works? Is literary humor too localized on historical events to offer broader visions of humanity with the seeming objectivity of great Realist novels and short stories?

4. Henry James in the opening of *The American* (1877) describes the hero Christopher Newman as he seeks a trophy wife and shows him as grotesquely naive in his first visit to the home of the Bellegardes, his adversaries in his quest. Bellegarde, for example, only flinches as Newman innocently but vulgarly appraises the quality of the main hall, but suppresses all emotion as the unsophisticated Newman rattles on. Is this unrecognized realistic humor in a novel that is usually taken as serious? Is James's depiction realistic?

5. Literary comedians of the Realist period usually write in persona as "real" persons, use popular language and style, and depend on local settings. Doesn't it follow that their works would appear objective and reportorial, thus qualifying easily as Realism? Commentary in Jesse Bier's *The Rise and Fall of American Humor* (1968) and Walter Blair and Hamlin Hill's *America's Humor: From Poor Richard to Doonesbury* (1978) may be helpful in addressing this question.

RESOURCES

Primary Works

Walter Blair, *Native American Humor* (1937; reprinted, San Francisco: Chandler, 1960).

Hennig Cohen and William B. Dillingham, *The Humor of the Old Southwest* (Boston: Houghton Mifflin, 1964; reprinted, Athens: University of Georgia Press, 1994).

Mark Twain's Library of Humor, edited by Mark Twain and William Dean Howells (New York: Webster, 1888).

Reference

Stanley Tractenberg, ed., *Dictionary of Literary Biography*, volume 11: *American Humorists, 1800–1950*, 2 volumes (Detroit: Bruccoli Clark Layman/Gale, 1982).

Criticism

Kenneth S. Lynn, *Mark Twain and Southwestern Humor* (Boston: Little, Brown, 1960).

David E. E. Sloane, *The Literary Humor of the Urban Northeast, 1830–1890* (Baton Rouge: Louisiana State University Press, 1983).

PEOPLE OF INTEREST

Charles Farrar Browne (1834–1867)
Native of Maine, adopted the persona of Artemus Ward, a vulgar showman from Baldwinsville, Indiana, modeled on P. T. Barnum. His comic sketches of American life contributed to Mark Twain's comic Realism and narrative voice. He died in London of consumption at the height of his popularity.

Finley Peter Dunne (1867–1936)
Used his persona as "Mr. Dooley," a Chicago bartender, to express direct responses in Irish dialect to American experience.

Marietta Holley (1836–1926)
As "Josiah Allen's Wife" took up major social issues in sketches, local humor narratives, and travel volumes directed at a popular readership. Her vernacular voice and persona carried feminist messages and social irony on race, children's rights, feminism, and travel, as in *My Opinions and Betsy Bobbet's* (1873) and other works.

Charles G. Leland (1824–1903)
Author of *Hans Breitmann's Party, With Other Ballads* (1868) was recognized in England as a fresh American voice. Other volumes and collections followed, and his later studies of gypsies and the Algonquin legends of New England make him of importance as a sociologist and linguist. He also wrote extensively on arts and crafts. A Philadelphia native, most of his later life was spent abroad.

—David E. E. Sloane

Naturalism

"Naturalism" refers to a literary movement that began in about 1880 and ended in about 1940, with its major practitioners in the United States being Stephen Crane, Frank Norris, Jack London, Edith Wharton, Ellen Glasgow, Theodore Dreiser, Hamlin Garland, and Willa Cather. These writers imbued their writing with a scientific view of reality based on social Darwinism. Partly as a consequence, they often described their works as objective case studies, but the purpose, as with the earlier Realists, was often an implicit plea for social reform.

Whereas earlier European and American fiction generally assumed a moral universe in which good was ultimately rewarded and evil punished, the Naturalists generally imply an amoral, mechanistic universe. Further, human beings within Naturalism are seen as fundamentally animals, rather than divine creatures, whose lives are entirely, or almost entirely, shaped by natural forces such as heredity, instincts, and the environment.

Social Darwinism was based on a misunderstanding of Charles Darwin's theory of evolution. Two misconceptions espoused by influential social Darwinists Herbert Spencer and Auguste Comte are particularly significant. They extrapolated from Darwin's point that the creatures best adapted to any given environment were more likely to survive, that social progress is achieved through the survival of the fittest, and that successful societies are inherently superior to less successful ones. These ideas captured the imaginations of the Naturalists and became dominant themes in such works as Jack London's *The Call of the Wild* (1903), *The Sea-Wolf* (1904), and *White Fang* (1906); Stephen Crane's *Maggie: A Girl of the Streets* (1893), *The Red Badge of Courage* (1895), "The Open Boat" (1897), and "The Blue Hotel" (1898); and Theodore Dreiser's *Sister Carrie* (1900) and *An American Tragedy* (1925), to name but a few classic examples.

Like the earlier Realists, the Naturalists focus on factual details and avoid sentimentality. Partly because they attempt to describe life from a scientific point of view, however, their writing often creates a greater sense of distance between the readers and the characters. Journalistic objectivity is a common, though not consistent, characteristic. Frank Norris, a fan of Edgar Allan Poe, in particular, often resorts to romantic flourishes, and most works of Naturalism seem romantic insofar as they focus on the unusual rather than the commonplace. Another result of the Naturalists' focus on case studies is that their writing often seems less artistic than earlier fiction; this is particularly true of the writing of Norris and Dreiser.

In addition to focusing on the lower classes, the Naturalists write more frankly about previously taboo subjects—such as human sexuality, alcoholism, disease, and depravity—often describing aberrant, irrational, or cruel behavior. In Crane's *Maggie: A Girl of the Streets,* for example, the reader discovers how social forces can lead a good girl to become a prostitute and how, as a consequence, the community, and her own family, ultimately abandon her to inevitable destruction. In Norris's *McTeague,* the lesson is how greed can lead to other irrational behavior, including murder. Theodore Dreiser's *An American Tragedy*—based on a true story—shows how social ambition based on the American dream can lead a young man, almost inevitably, to murder.

By highlighting natural forces, the Naturalists question the possibility of human free will. Their characters, rather, often appear to be defined by their environments and genes, that is, powers beyond their control. Consequently, the Naturalists seem ironically akin in their worldview to the earlier Puritans, who also attributed human actions to powerful forces beyond their control and questioned the possibility of free will, so that Naturalism has been described as secular Calvinism.

Ironically, too, the Naturalists, who were usually educated Anglo-Saxons, focus primarily on the plight of poor people of marginalized ethnic backgrounds, and they often identify characters by their ethnicity, such as the "Frenchman" or the "Swede." These ethnic labels need to be understood within the context of social Darwinism, which suggests people's ethnicities shape them, thus legitimizing ethnic stereotypes. The Jewish character Zerkow in Norris's *McTeague,* for example, is stereotypically defined by greed, as the more complex main characters only slowly become so. Similarly, often in these works being of Anglo-Saxon descent implies a hereditary advantage. While these ideas are discredited today, it is important to recognize that the Naturalists are not so much endorsing social Darwinism—or racism—as they are questioning its significance and portraying its potential ramifications. Further, significant exceptions exist, such as Paul Laurence Dunbar, an economically disadvantaged African American whose groundbreaking 1902 Naturalist novel, *The Sport of the Gods,* deals in ethnic stereotypes while challenging white superiority.

Also, one should keep in mind that distinctions between literary genres are far from exact. An author's collected writings often display varying degrees of allegiance to the tenets of any particular literary school or philosophy. Works traditionally identified as Realism often exhibit characteristics associated with Naturalism, just as many works associated with Naturalism fit into other categories as well, such as modernism. Consequently, it may be more accurate to say that these writers' works are Naturalistic rather than label them works of Naturalism, if that suggests they embody all the values of social Darwinism.

Further, while American Naturalism often seems pessimistic, it is important to remember that the goal is almost always social reform, including more sympathy for ethnic minorities and the economic underclass. As Charles C. Walcutt explains, "The more helpless the character, the stronger the proof of determinism; and once such a thesis is established the scientist hopes and believes men will set about trying to control the forces which now control men."

TOPICS FOR DISCUSSION AND RESEARCH

1. Given the social Darwinian context of works of Naturalism, the characters' free will and, therefore, personal responsibility are always questioned. Consider, for example, Maggie's responsibility for becoming a prostitute in Crane's *Maggie: A Girl of the Streets*, or Clyde Griffiths's responsibility for becoming a killer in Dreiser's *An American Tragedy*. What responsibility do environmental and social forces have for their actions?

2. Frank Norris suggests that there is a more primitive, instinct-driven animal lurking just beneath the surface of our civilized veneer. What are the results of these animalistic impulses in *McTeague*? Is the greed described the result of this "beast" or of modern capitalistic values? Similarly, in *Vandover and the Brute* Norris suggests that Vandover's faults are the result of the brute—primarily his sexual desire—within him. On the other hand, Vandover often seems too passive, too civilized. Which is it?

3. Do London's novels—particularly *The Call of the Wild, White Fang,* and *The Sea Wolf*—support or challenge the idea of the "survival of the fittest"? What does London suggest are the characteristics that make one "fit" to survive either in nature or in modern society? How important are intelligence and the ability to cooperate?

4. Consider the role economic forces play in determining the value of the major characters—Carrie, Drouet, and Hurstwood—in Dreiser's *Sister Carrie*. Are human relationships seen as a type of commodity exchange? Are there examples of true love in the story?

5. Willa Cather is often associated with modernism rather than Naturalism. Consider one of her major works, such as *O Pioneers!* (1913) or *My Ántonia* (1918), and write a paper either challenging or defending calling her a Naturalist.

RESOURCES

For more serious study of a specific author, begin with one of the many excellent biographies. To better understand Naturalism, consider examining one of these critical works:

Criticism

Lars Åhnebrink, *The Beginnings of Naturalism in American Fiction: A Study of the Works of Hamlin Garland, Stephen Crane, and Frank Norris, with Special Reference to Some European Influences, 1891–1903* (New York: Russell & Russell, 1961).
Notes several European influences on American Naturalism and argues for including Hamlin Garland as an early American Naturalist. Åhnebrink defines Naturalism as "a manner and method of composition by which the author portrays life as it is in accordance with the philosophic theory of determinism (exemplified by Zola's *L'Assommoir*). In contrast to a Realist, a Naturalist believes that man is fundamentally an animal without free will."

June Howard, *Form and History in American Literary Naturalism* (Chapel Hill: University of North Carolina Press, 1985).
Sees Naturalism as a method for society to confront new threats to the social order brought about by capitalism, as well as the stress to the old order brought about by the influx of working-class immigrants into the United States.

Walter Benn Michaels, *The Gold Standard and the Logic of Naturalism* (Berkeley: University of California Press, 1987).
Like Howard, all but ignores the influence of Darwin and looks instead at the social and economic forces that produced Naturalism. Michaels suggests that

earlier critics have mistakenly described the Naturalists as outside society objectively looking in. Instead, the Naturalists were integrally tied to their society and necessarily reflected its values. Naturalism, then, reflects tensions that the society's worldview inevitably creates, tensions between materialism and idealism, self as inherently valuable and self as object. According to Michaels, there is no real distinction between the novels and the culture. Both are social constructs: the fiction merely supports the larger ideology, another fiction.

Donald Pizer, *Realism and Naturalism in Nineteenth-Century American Literature* (Carbondale: Southern Illinois University Press, 1966).
Defines Naturalism as "essentially Realism infused with a pessimistic determinism" and asserts that "Naturalism reflects an affirmative ethical conception of life, for it asserts the value of all life by endowing the lowest character with emotion and defeat and with moral ambiguity, no matter how poor and ignoble he may seem."

Pizer, ed., *The Cambridge Companion to American Realism and Naturalism* (Cambridge, England & New York: Cambridge University Press, 1995).
Interprets Naturalism as reflecting social and economic forces: "the burden of most of the essays in this volume . . . is to reaffirm—through a variety of approaches and emphasis—the belief that Realism and Naturalism arose in large part as responses to what Louis Budd calls the 'disjunction' between rhetoric and actuality in American life—between the language of hope in America's civil religion and the actuality of the world encountered."

Eric J. Sundquist, ed., *American Realism: New Essays* (Baltimore: Johns Hopkins University Press, 1982).
Offers several newer approaches to Naturalism, including feminist, New Historicist, and Marxist readings.

Charles C. Walcutt, *American Literary Naturalism: A Divided Stream* (Minneapolis: University of Minnesota Press, 1956).
Traces Naturalism to American Transcendentalism, particularly because the Transcendentalists relied on physical observation to discover truth. Walcutt asserts that the only consistent characteristic of Naturalism is a philosophic stance based on social Darwinism.

PEOPLE OF INTEREST

Willa Cather (1873–1947)
Chronicled early pioneering life on the Great Plains, which she obviously loved, and the people it formed, whom she obviously admired. At the same time, works such as "The Sculptor's Funeral" (1905) and *A Lost Lady* (1923) illustrate that she also was aware of the loneliness, small-mindedness, and other potential problems with life in the early West. Her works highlight how environment shapes character.

Stephen Crane (1871–1900)
Died at twenty-eight; wrote several brilliant short stories as well as several significant novels, most notably *Maggie: A Girl of the Streets* (1893) and *The Red Badge of*

Courage (1895). His writing is known for its artistry, impressionistic descriptions, and unsentimental objectivity.

Theodore Dreiser (1871–1945)
Was particularly interested in portraying a non-Romantic view of human sexuality and the negative influence of capitalism. His *Sister Carrie* (1900) and *An American Tragedy* (1925) are particularly important works.

Jack London (1876–1916)
An ardent socialist who valued individualism and freedom. He believed in social Darwinism and the racism it suggested, but fought for social equality, women's suffrage, and prohibition. His novels can be didactic, but his best works reveal his own struggles to reconcile these opposing impulses.

Frank Norris (1870–1902)
A disciple of Auguste Comte's philosophy and Émile Zola's literary Naturalism. *McTeague* (1899) and the posthumously published *The Pit: A Story of Chicago* (1903) and *Vandover and the Brute* (1914) are particularly important works.

—Richard Randolph

Reform Literature

Reform literature of the period 1865–1914 shows the precedence of antebellum social reform writing about abolition, women's rights, temperance, and other causes. This writing relied heavily on the literary mode of sentimentalism, which sought to touch readers' hearts and move them to acknowledge their common humanity with oppressed groups. Although "the belief in the transcendental, usually religious moral order" of sentimentalism had lost its cultural dominance by the Realist period, William A. Morgan argues that sentimentalism influenced both the "questions about society that Realist literary texts ask" as well as "the resolutions they consider."

Besides the legacy of antebellum reform literature, late-nineteenth-century reform writing was significantly fueled by the representational form, purpose, and possibilities of literary Realism. In its serious literary representation of concrete social problems and its commitment to depicting ordinary, common life as the writer saw it—even in all its ugliness—literary Realism became a powerful reformist tool for illuminating social problems and arousing the social conscience of readers.

The pervasive economic and social transformations of the second industrial era were a third major influence on reform literature, which took for its main, but not exclusive, target, the consolidation of wealth and power and the conflicts between labor and capital engendered by industrialization and the rise of consumer capitalism. The de-skilling and disempowering of workers through the increased mechanization of mass production, the unregulated boom and bust cycles of capitalism, and labor's response—organizing unions, boycotting, and striking—sharpened the battle lines between labor and employers. In the 1890s, when corporate employers increasingly used force and governmental power to break strikes and punish strikers, this enhanced alliance between big business and the government further widened the gulf between classes. This economic and social strife and the need for socioeconomic changes it signaled became the focus of much reform literature.

Reform literature grappled with the major philosophical, sociological, and ethical controversies of the late nineteenth century: disputes over individualism, heredity/natural hierarchy of social classes, and conditions of the environment; disagreements about the historical inevitability of industrialization and the growth of the market; and questions about the possibility of social cohesion and ethical commitment to others in an increasingly fragmented, uncontrollable social world lacking agreed-upon ethical/spiritual principles. Much reform literature challenges the controversial cultural discourse of individualism espoused by Andrew Carnegie and other captains of industry; the philosophy of social Darwinism; and the laissez-faire economic and political ideology—all of which supported the belief that the "fit" thrive through their individual effort and innate superiority and deserve the success of their wealth. Many texts expose the role of economic and political power structures, greed, and corruption, and raise questions about responsibility, agency, and the need for systemic change.

Some reform literature targets exploitive factory work—low wages, long work hours, child labor—the impoverished conditions of workers' lives, and the unjust distribution of wealth. Exhibiting traces of sentimentalism amidst their harsh, realistic descriptions, these novels seek to change their readers' assumptions about the working class. Elizabeth Stuart Phelps used the Reports of the Massachusetts Bureau of Statistics of Labor to provide a factual base for her novel *The Silent Partner* (1871). Fusing women's rights and temperance issues with the exploitive treatment of workers in textile mills, Phelps uses the awakening social conscience of her main character, the privileged Perley Kelso, to stir readers to reckon with their own "wide-spread ignorance . . . regarding the abuses of our factory system." Another novel about a New England manufacturing town, William Dean Howells's *Annie Kilburn* (1888), also explores class relations and the lives of factory workers through the character of the affluent Annie, who helps to create the Peck Social Union. Like Phelps, Howells sensitively wrestles with questions of social responsibility for the economic injustice of factory conditions and the gulf between classes.

Other novels show their reform impulse by complexly addressing the way corporate capitalism has contaminated business and challenged ethics and even the possibility of moral, humanitarian action. Howells's *A Hazard of New Fortunes* (1890) realistically portrays characters deeply entangled with the forces of modernization: advertising and commercialism. Through his main character, Basil March, the middle-class editor of a New York magazine, Howells bravely confronts the diminishing possibility of social cohesion in late-nineteenth-century America and the complicity of even compassionate citizens in the social evils they wish they could change. In the character of Silas Lapham, a paint manufacturer who turns his small family business into a big venture in the novel *The Rise of Silas Lapham* (1885), Howells examines the way that capitalism, with its competition and speculation, warps personal ethics. Working with these same broad themes, Frank Norris's *The Octopus* (1901) is based on his research into the Mussel Slough gunfight between San Joaquin wheat ranchers and the Southern Pacific Railroad. Controversially interweaving strands of Realism, Naturalism, and mystic Romanticism, Norris portrays the wheat farmers as profit seekers exploiting the fertility of their land and engaging in bribery in their desperate fight against the corruption and power of railroad monopolies to fix transportation rates and the price of land. The optimistic determinism of the novel suggests the need for reform of an economically, socially, and environmentally oppressive system.

Some reform literature actually envisioned alternative societies: the roughly one hundred works of progressive, pastoral, and feminist utopian fiction, which Jean Pfaelzer calls a remarkable "literary expression of social anxiety and political hope, a cultural event closely corresponding to the militant struggles for industrial, agrarian and feminist reform." Building on the tradition of Thomas More's *Utopia* (1516) about an imagined society that was a good place (the Greek word "eutopia") and "nowhere," the utopian fiction of the Progressive period sought to explain the problems of industrial capitalism—movement of people off the farms and into crowded cities, labor strife, and the disparity between the very rich and everyone else—and suggest a reform agenda.

Edward Bellamy's *Looking Backward, 2000–1887* (1888), the most popular novel of the post–Civil War years, is considered the period's most significant work of utopian literature. It inspired a political movement, a magazine called *The*

Nationalist, and Nationalist clubs throughout the country, in which many writers and social reformers participated. In this story, wealthy Bostonian Julian West falls asleep in 1887 and wakes up in 2000 to discover that the country has evolved into a socialist paradise: the means of production are owned communally; wealth is equally distributed; technology has made life comfortable—all the socioeconomic problems of late-nineteenth-century America have been solved by egalitarian solidarity.

Another novel, Howells's pastoral utopia *A Traveler from Altruria* (1894), presents a visitor from the imaginary Altruria, who comes to America, the great land of democracy and equality, and instead teaches his middle-class host that Altruria is a much more socially enlightened and egalitarian culture. The novel satirically attacks the discrepancy between America's purported values and its social realities, and the greed and corruption of the Gilded Age.

Other examples of this genre focusing on women's rights are the feminist utopian novels of the Progressive period such as Elizabeth Burgoyne Corbett's *New Amazonia: A Foretaste of the Future* (1889) and Charlotte Perkins Gilman's *Herland* (serialized, 1915). Some novels played out the problems of the day to their frightful conclusions, creating dystopian warnings: for example, Jack London's *The Iron Heel* (1908), a vision of capitalism's potential to become fascist oppression, and Ignatius Donnelly's *Caesar's Column* (1890), depicting economic conflict that ends in an apocalyptic battle.

During the Progressive period a major vein of reform writing became documentary, pragmatic investigative writing, known as "muckraking" (a derisive term used by Theodore Roosevelt in 1906 to refer to one of the allegorical characters in John Bunyan's *The Pilgrim's Progress,* 1678). The muckrakers, journalists and authors, sought to bring social problems to the attention of ordinary citizens and the government with the goal of instituting tangible legislative, commercial, and social reforms. They targeted a wide range of problems: corruption in government; corporate monopolies; stock swindles; the persecution and disenfranchising of African Americans and Native Americans; the inequality of women; the conditions of the poor; the treatment of children; the sick and the mentally ill; medical quackery; life in the coal mines and factories; and the pursuit of profit at the expense of the health and well-being of the working class. Integrating interviews and firsthand experience with documentary research, they often brought a quality of eyewitness testimony to their arguments and made a significant contribution to the modern idea of investigative journalism.

Two key vehicles for the dissemination of muckraking writing were *Collier's* and *McClure's*. Often serialized articles in these magazines became major book-length works. *Collier's Once a Week* was launched in 1888 by Irish immigrant P. F. Collier, ran until 1957, and published such significant muckrakers as Ida Tarbell, C. P. Connolly, and Ralph Stannard Baker. Upton Sinclair's *The Jungle* was commissioned by the socialist journal *The Appeal to Reason* in 1905, researched on the scene, and published as a volume in 1906. Although Sinclair wrote *The Jungle* with the primary purpose of revealing the suffering of immigrant laborers who were working in the horrifically unsanitary conditions of Chicago's meatpacking industry and were exploited by employers, real estate speculators, and the legal system, the public latched on to food safety issues, and the novel led to the Meat

Inspection Act and the Pure Food and Drug Act in 1906. *McClure's* (1893–1929), along with *Everybody's* and *American Magazine,* also published the work of muckrakers such as Tarbell, Baker, and Lincoln Steffens.

One of the most famous muckraking works was Jacob Riis's *How the Other Half Lives* (1890), which was inspired by his exposure to tenement living, crime, and poverty in New York City. In this landmark photojournalistic exposé of life in city tenements, Riis appealed to the public conscience by recounting the history of these tenements, the speculation and greed behind the business of owning them—including owners' willful neglect of repairs and sanitation—and the disproportionately high rents paid by poor immigrants. Although Riis generalized about ethnic groups and created a touristic portrait of poverty that affirmed middle-class values, he also underscored the way living conditions contributed to disease, moral decay, and crime; nurtured the Social Gospel ("the gospel of justice" and care for the poor); and prodded the public to call for sanitation, better design, and just management of tenements.

Other popular and influential muckraking include the pamphlet *Southern Horrors: Lynch Law in All Its Phases* (1892) by Ida B. Wells-Barnett, an African American suffragist, journalist, and newspaper editor, who exposed the atrocities against blacks; Tarbell's *The History of the Standard Oil Company* (1904), revealing the corrupt workings of the powerful oil monopoly; and John Spargo's *The Bitter Cry of the Children* (1906), protesting the grueling work of child laborers who were coal breakers in the mining industry.

TOPICS FOR DISCUSSION AND RESEARCH

1. What relationship does the writer of the reform text establish with his/her reader, and through what literary devices or rhetorical strategies is this relationship constructed? For instance, is the narrator an interpreter of the problem for the middle-class readers? Does the writer convey a positive and persuasive ethos through the use of extensive documented research? Does the writer employ the popular reformist strategy of the investigative visit (used effectively by Riis's explorations of tenement housing in New York City)?

2. In terms of literary elements and modes—characterization, plot, irony, sentimentalism's appeal to readers' sympathy, or Realism's fidelity to experience through graphic detail (scenes outside middle-class comfort and familiarity)—how does a particular work of reformist fiction confront readers with the need for reform? If a text has a strong socially activist thrust, how polemical and propagandist is it? How do Realism and social purpose, or fictional world and social purpose, work together in this text? For example, in utopian fiction, how much do plot action and character development contribute to the impact of the novel?

3. From research about a specific reform text, determine what was controversial about the issue examined and about the text itself in its historical moment. How class-based and class-bound, how objectifying, how sensational, and how instrumental in its effects was this reform text? In literary and historical scholarship, what is controversial about a late-nineteenth-century reform text?

RESOURCES

Criticism

Ann Bausum, *Muckrakers: How Ida Tarbell, Upton Sinclair, and Lincoln Steffens Helped Expose Scandal, Inspire Reform, and Invent Investigative Journalism* (Washington, D.C.: National Geographic, 2007).
Provides a lively introduction to muckraking with visuals (political cartoons, photographs, book covers).

Paul Boyer, *Urban Masses and Moral Order in America, 1820–1920* (Cambridge, Mass.: Harvard University Press, 1978).
Examines reform as a means of social control and explores charity movements, settlement houses, and other efforts to manage the urban masses.

Sharon M. Harris, *Rebecca Harding Davis and American Realism* (Philadelphia: University of Pennsylvania Press, 1991).
Offers a major early feminist study of Davis's writing and place in literary history, exploring her complex attitude toward reform.

William M. Morgan, *Questionable Charity: Gender, Humanitarianism, and Complicity in U.S. Literary Realism* (Hanover: University of New Hampshire Press, 2004).
Offers an accessible, scholarly study, linking Realism to both antebellum literature and modernism and deepening the moral and aesthetic complexity of various Realist writers, especially Howells.

Jean Pfaelzer, *The Utopian Novel in America 1886–1896: The Politics of Form* (Pittsburgh: University of Pittsburgh Press, 1984).
Offers a detailed, scholarly but readable analysis of utopian fiction of the period, looking at the aesthetic principles of the genre in relation to its political and social subject matter.

Mark Pittenger, "A World of Difference: Constructing the 'Underclass' in Progressive America," *American Quarterly*, 49 (March 1997): 26–65.
Analyzes the complex mixed messages sent by middle-class writers who went "down and out" to investigate the lives of the poor and often ended up reinforcing hereditarian assumptions about the culture of poverty.

Alan Trachtenberg, *The Incorporation of America: Culture and Society in the Gilded Age* (New York: Hill & Wang, 1982).
Offers a social history of this period that enriches and challenges the meaning of reform efforts.

Arthur Weinberg and Lila Weinberg, *The Muckrakers* (Chicago: University of Illinois Press, 1961).
Offers a good sampling of muckrakers' investigative journalism from the Progressive period, including writings by Steffens, Baker, Tarbell, David Graham Phillips, and William Hard, reprinted from *McClure's, Collier's, Cosmopolitan,* and other prominent Progressive magazines.

PEOPLE OF INTEREST

Edward Bellamy (1850–1898)

Came from a New England family of ministers. His early education and career include schooling in Germany, where he learned about socialism; training as a lawyer; and work as a journalist for reform newspapers. During this time, he also published twenty-three short stories in magazines, such as *Atlantic Monthly*, *Harper's*, and *Scribner's*, and wrote four novels, among them *Six to One* (1878) and *Dr. Heidenhoff's Process* (1880). His hugely popular utopian novel *Looking Backward, 2000–1887* (1888) remains his most notable work. Its sequel, *Equity* (1897), was less successful. Bellamy edited his weekly newspaper, the *New Nation*, and lectured widely on his nationalist vision.

Frank Norris (1870–1902)

Reported on the Boer War in South Africa, wrote for *McClure's* from Cuba during the Spanish-American War of 1898, and wrote feature articles for the new California periodical *The Wave*. Influenced by the French school of Naturalism, late-nineteenth-century scientific and psychological theories, and the political movement Populism, Norris's novels nevertheless defy clear categories. In 1892 his exposé of agricultural corruption, "A Deal of Wheat," appeared in *Everybody's Magazine*.

Elizabeth Stuart Phelps (1844–1911)

Wrote fiction for children and adults that reflects her roots in New England intellectualism and Christian culture; is known for her best-selling novel, *The Gates Ajar* (1868), which actually had more affinities with spiritualism than orthodox Christianity. Her social activism and use of interviews and research inform her novels *Up Hill; or, Life in a Factory* (1865) and *The Silent Partner* (1871) and her story "The Tenth of January" (1868). Women's conflicts with gender roles and their need for independence are prominent in her fiction, notably in her novel *The Story of Avis* (1877), about a woman artist.

Jacob Riis (1849–1914)

Muckraking journalist, pioneer of photojournalism, and social reformer. As an immigrant from Denmark in 1870, he experienced the life of the poor in New York City and then became a newspaper reporter covering police news for the *New York Tribune*. With the use of primitive flash techniques, he photographed his visits to the poorest parts of New York City and recounted his findings in his startling book *How the Other Half Lives* (1890). He continued to produce photojournalistic exposes: *The Children of the Poor* (1892), *Out of Mulberry Street* (1898), *The Battle with the Slum* (1902), and *Children of the Tenements* (1903), among other works, and for years gave visual presentations on the urban living conditions of the poor.

—June Johnson Bube

Regionalism and Realism

The student of this period in American literary history will learn soon enough that there are a great many "ism" words used in connection with it—Regionalism, Naturalism, Realism, veritism, provincialism, Impressionism, and the like. One should not conclude, however, that the writing produced under these labels came from a stable and agreed-upon theory or doctrine. To the contrary, these forms of writing evolved from a loosely organized set of conventions, practices, and assumptions. Nevertheless, it is useful to have some sort of working definitions for the terms in order to recognize the purposes of the author and significance of the movement as a whole.

REGIONALISM

At one point, "Regionalism" and "local color" were used more or less interchangeably; Hamlin Garland used the word "provincialism" to describe the same literary manner. However, more recently the phrase "local color" has been avoided by some because it seemed to imply an inferior literary mode, or because critics have made distinctions between the terms. Some have argued that Regionalist writing depicts characters with greater psychological depth and with greater sympathy than does local-color writing, which is often comic, racy, even to the point of burlesque. More broadly, one may say, as a test more than a definition, that if a given text could not have happened in any other locale, or least not in the same way, then that is a specimen of Regionalist or local-color writing. In other words, there is something distinctive about it—the manners, dialects, legends, inborn attitudes of mind, and so forth are firmly rooted in place. The New England mind-set is qualitatively different from that of the South, and both are different from the slangy communities of miners in the West, who were apt to be from all over the country. As noted in the "Historical and Social Contexts" essay in this volume, there developed a great curiosity about other regions of the country after the Civil War, and thereby a market for this kind of fiction developed. It is true that there were antebellum antecedents for local-color writing, particularly in the humorous writing of the Old Southwest (Georgia, Mississippi, Alabama, Louisiana, Kentucky, and Tennessee), but the full flowering of the movement came later, especially in the 1890s. Women writers were particularly accomplished in this literary school.

As is to be expected, setting figures prominently in Regionalist writings, at times functioning as a character, or at least a dominant force in the tale. Regionalist settings are often pastoral, though not always idyllic. In Bret Harte's "The Luck of Roaring Camp" the baby seems to commune with nature, and a flood, not human choices, determines final events; in George Washington Cable's "Belles Desmoiselles Plantation," it is a breached levee that transforms the action; and in Sarah Orne Jewett's "A White Heron," the child Sylvy seems to get encouragement from the natural surroundings as she ascends a tall pine tree in search of the heron. One can see from these few examples that Regionalists were not reluctant to mingle vivid realistic details with romantic elements. This is true as well in such stories as Alice Dunbar-Nelson's "The Goodness of St. Rocque," where Creole magic plays a role, or Charles Chesnutt's "Po' Sandy" and Tennessee writer Mary Noailles Murfree's "The 'Harnt' that Walks Chilhowee," where supposed ghosts have a part.

Regionalism often renders characters as types representative of the locale rather than highly individualized people, though there are important exceptions to this generalization, as with Mary Wilkins Freeman's fiercely independent women who tend to defy established tradition. Some Regionalist stories are written as first-person narratives. In these instances, the student has to remember that the vernacular narrator is usually part of the region itself. Third-person narratives tend to establish a distance between the author and the characters or the place, and the student will need to discern whether that distance is ironic or sympathetic. Thematically, Regionalist stories are often regarded as nostalgic, their authors mindful of the great social changes occurring and a bit wistful about the passing of rural and communal values. However, more recently literary historians have tended to see Regionalist authors as participating in the unification of a so-called national identity after the rupture brought about by the Civil War.

REALISM

Regionalism is no longer regarded as the poor cousin of Realism. Nevertheless, there are differences between the two genres worth pointing out. American Realism may be understood as both a reaction against the idealizations and sentimentality of the Romantic era and as a positive literary program, with its own set of premises and its own social ambitions. Broadly speaking there are at least four ways to understand what Realist writing is. First, Realism assumes that sentimentalism and idealism are based on a philosophical idea that "reality" transcends human experience as it is ordinarily lived, and the Realist rejects this notion, maintaining instead that the real is a social, not a spiritual, phenomenon and that it is available to human beings through shared experience. Second, Realists generally believe that individuals are capable of making free moral choices, and that if their minds are not clouded by stereotypical or idealized biases (what Huckleberry Finn would call "tears and flapdoodle"), they are apt to make proper choices that benefit themselves and the world at large. Third, one may perhaps discern and define Realist works by the subject matter—common characters living lives and encountering difficulties that average readers recognize and can identify with. In other words, Realism is democratic in its focus and addresses readers as fully capable of judging and understanding literary works without the aid of lofty critical postulates. And, fourth, Realism may be understood as a literary manner, as distinct from subject matter. In other words, Realists try to represent life in recognizable ways: the characters speak a colloquial discourse and act according to comprehensible motives, the author tries to be nonintrusive in order to permit the reader to evaluate the plausibility and effectiveness of representation, and the author has a greater concern for character than action and attempts to project the commonly understood life of the times. These are generalizations, of course, and there is a great deal of slippage involved when the student grapples with individual texts.

The Realist writer tends not to confine subject matter to the local but to bring characters of varying backgrounds (in terms of race, gender, class, education, or geography) into close contact. This is true of Henry James, who often has an American character confront the burden of the past by visiting Europe and being tested by an older and more conservative environment. It is also true of Edith Wharton, who moved her heroine in *The House of Mirth* (1905) through the social economic strata of New York City, as does Stephen Crane in a very different way when he inspects the life of the poor in the flophouses or the Bowery, or Harold Frederic in *The Damnation of Theron Ware* (1896) when he has a Methodist minister's faith tested by what he regards as an exotic Catholic woman on the one hand and a godless scientist on the other. One could give many more examples, but the point to be made is that Realist writers often regarded their texts as a pragmatic testing of character with this sort of question in mind: What would such and such a character, with a certain temperament and background, do under given circumstances?

TOPICS FOR DISCUSSION AND RESEARCH

1. Since Realism and Regionalism are related movements, the distinctions between them tend to blur. Mark Twain's *Adventures of Huckleberry Finn* or Kate Chopin's *The Awakening* may be read either as Realist or Regionalist works, depending on what aspects of the novel are foregrounded. How might a certain work be read and understood in different ways? Is this a problem of analysis or an enhancement and enlargement of the meaning of the work?
2. Regionalist writing of the late nineteenth century was largely dominated by women writers. Why should this be the case?
3. Realism is generally considered a "democratic" movement. William Dean Howells said the "true standard of the arts" is within every man and woman's power. How is reading and understanding literary texts different when one disregards the authority of critics and reviewers? Are the requirements placed upon the reader more difficult in some ways?
4. Regionalist and Realist writing often uses regional dialects, many of which have changed or passed away by this time. How can the contemporary reader learn to appreciate dialect in literature?
5. One of the aims of Regionalist and Realist writers was to overturn stereotypes, whether they be stereotypes concerning race, gender, class, or region. Does this aspect of the literary works constitute a form of social satire?

RESOURCES

Students should not overlook a generally available and accessible resource—the anthology. The introductions and headnotes to individual works are pertinent and often insightful. Among those anthologies worth examining are:

Primary Works

Judith Fetterley and Marjorie Pryse, eds., *American Women Regionalists, 1850–1910* (New York: Norton, 1992).

James Nagel and Tom Quirk, eds., *The Portable American Realism Reader* (New York: Penguin, 1997).

Donald Pizer, ed., *Documents of American Realism and Naturalism* (Carbondale: Southern Illinois University Press, 1998).
Composed of three sections—The Critical Debate, 1874–1950; The Early Modern Period, 1915–1950; and Modern Academic Criticism, 1951–1995. It contains a healthy selection of critical statements by the practitioners of Realism, including Howells and Hamlin Garland, as well as more-recent essays or excerpts of critical commentary.

Claude M. Simpson, ed., *The Local Colorists: American Short Stories 1857–1900* (New York: Harper, 1960).

Willard Thorp, ed., *Great Short Works of American Realism* (New York: Harper & Row, 1968).

Criticism

Edwin H. Cady, *The Light of Common Day: Realism in American Fiction* (Bloomington: Indiana University Press, 1971).
Cady argues that Realism cultivates a certain "common vision" in readers and that successful Realist works dramatize the relation between ordinary experience and art.

Josephine Donovan, *New England Local Color Literature: A Woman's Tradition* (New York: Ungar, 1983).
Posits a distinctly female literary tradition among New England Regionalists, one that existed apart from and opposed to the male-dominated world and that represented strong and independent women characters.

Harold H. Kolb Jr., *The Illusion of Life: American Realism as a Literary Form* (Charlottesville: University of Virginia Press, 1969).
Begins with chapters defining American Realism in lucid and convincing ways, followed by chapters on individual writers. Kolb's book emphasizes Realism as a literary manner, and his treatment of the rejection of omniscient narration in favor of a restricted narrative consciousness in Henry James, Mark Twain, and William Dean Howells is instructive.

Literary Movements <http://www.wsu.edu/~campbelld/amlit/litfram.html> [accessed 20 August 2009].
A particularly valuable website created and maintained by Donna Campbell. In addition to time lines, profiles of individual authors, and literary movements, this site provides useful links to other reliable sites, including the Society for the Study of American Women Writers.

David E. Shi, *Facing Facts: Realism in American Thought and Culture, 1850–1920* (New York: Oxford University Press, 1995).
A solid and highly readable cultural and social history of the period. Of particular value is his placement of Realist art, architecture, and literature together in a cultural context.

Kenneth Warren, *Black and White Strangers: Race and American Literary Realism* (Chicago: University of Chicago Press, 1993).
Demonstrates the centrality of race in late-nineteenth-century American Realism and puts writers not usually associated with one another in critical conversation.

PEOPLE OF INTEREST

George Washington Cable (1844–1925)
Born in New Orleans. Cable's parents freed their slaves long before the Civil War, and though he served in the Confederate army, he wrote passionately for racial equality, particularly in *The Negro Question* (1890). His first collection, *Old Creole Days* (1879), established him as a Southern Regionalist writer; his Realist novel *The Grandissmes* (1880) is considered his masterwork. He was known for local-color Realism combined with keen psychological insight and a willingness to confront social issues of the day.

Harold Frederic (1856–1898)
Born in upstate New York. Frederic was an editor for a pair of upstate New York newspapers before becoming the London correspondent for *The New York Times* in 1884. He wrote his fiction mostly in England; his work ranges from historical romances to satirical portraits of English society to Realist novels and stories. After a visit to Russia, Frederic wrote *The New Exodus* (1892) condemning anti-Semitism. *Marsena and Other Stories* (1894) comprises fiction about the Civil War. His best-known work is the novel *The Damnation of Theron Ware* (1896).

Mary Noailles Murfree (1850–1922)
Born in Murfreesboro, Tennessee. After a childhood illness left her lame, Murfree turned to writing. The family's summers were spent in the Cumberland Mountains, where she became fascinated with the Tennessee mountain people she wrote about in local-color stories. She published more than ten volumes of stories, including *Down the Ravine* (1885) and *The Mystery of the Witch-Face Mountain* (1895), and several novels. She blended lyrical and somewhat romantic description with realistic Appalachian dialect and an eye for detail.

—*Tom Quirk*

War Writing

Three conflicts inspire the war writing that one finds between 1865 and 1914: the American Civil War (1861–1865), the Spanish-American War (1898), and the War of the Philippines (1899–1902). Of these three, the Civil War dominated the American literary imagination. More than any previous conflict, it generated untold numbers of works of all genres, from histories and memoirs to poems, novels, and short stories. When the war was over, publishers took advantage of advances in print technology and a new infrastructure of roads and rail lines to distribute their wares across the reunited country. The careful documentation of the conflict, the large number of people who experienced events firsthand, and the changing literary tastes of the postwar period all seemed to lead naturally to a proliferation of realistic literary accounts. While some important literary works were published in the years immediately following the Civil War, however, the genre of war writing only began to rise to prominence in the 1880s.

Two of the most important early works of war writing following the end of the conflict were works of poetry. Walt Whitman, who nursed wounded soldiers in the hospitals in Washington, D.C., during the war, began publishing his collection of poetry *Drum-Taps* in 1865—only to pause the printing to add more poems, including his famous tributes to the slain President Abraham Lincoln "When Lilacs Last in the Dooryard Bloom'd" and "O Captain! My Captain!" *Sequel to Drum-Taps*, also published in 1865, includes poems that describe the poet's own evolving feelings about the war, as seen in the contrast between such early poems such as "Beat! Beat! Drums!" (1861), meant to inspire volunteers, and later poems such as "The Wound-Dresser" (1865), which describes the suffering in the hospitals.

Less well known is Herman Melville's *Battle-Pieces and Aspects of the War* (1866). While the author did not serve in the military, he did travel to the front in 1864, took part in a cavalry expedition, and spoke with Union general Ulysses S. Grant. He followed events of the war closely, and many of his poems were inspired by newspaper accounts. His subject matter ranges from particular battles, as in "Battle of Stone River" (1863), to historical figures, as in "A Dirge for McPherson, Killed in Front of Atlanta" (1864). Fewer than five hundred copies of the work were sold at the time of its publication, but in recent years literary scholars have shown an increasing interest in *Battle-Pieces* and its vision both of the war and of the imperial nation that would emerge from it.

One of the most important war novels of the period was also published soon after the conflict. John W. De Forest's *Miss Ravenel's Conversion from Secession to Loyalty* (1867) was hailed at the time of its publication for its realistic characters and portrayal of combat. De Forest, already a published author when he enlisted with the Union army, wrote first-person accounts of his experiences for *Harper's Monthly* before drawing on his experience to write what is largely considered the first serious war novel in American literature. The title character, Lillie Ravenel, is a secessionist who moves north from New Orleans to the fictional town of New Boston with her father, a Union loyalist. There she meets two contenders for her affection, the virtuous Edward Colburne and the dashing Lieutenant-Colonel

Carter, a Union officer from Virginia. The romantic subplot plays out against the backdrop of the war, with Lillie eventually abandoning both her Confederate leanings and her home in favor of Colburne and the North.

A Southern counterpart to De Forest is Sidney Lanier. Lanier began work on his war novel, *Tiger-Lilies* (1867), while serving in the Confederate army. The novel is composed of three books: the first introduces the Sterling family of Tennessee, who, in addition to a German named Paul Rubetsahl, are the protagonists of the work. The scene shifts suddenly in book 2 to the Civil War, where the novel follows the adventures of Philip Sterling and his friends, as well as the treacherous plotting of Cranston and a Confederate deserter named Gorm Smallin. Here Lanier draws considerably on his personal experiences of the war. Sterling, like Lanier, spends time in a Union prison, and the description of prison life is noteworthy. The novel ends abruptly in the brief book 3 with the fall of Richmond and the reunion of the surviving characters.

While war fiction was largely replaced by writing that told stories of Reconstruction and the aftermath of the conflict during the 1870s, nonfictional accounts of the Civil War began to become more prominent during this decade. Walt Whitman published a prose account of his time in the hospitals in *Memoranda during the War* (1875–1876), which draws on notes he kept. William Tecumseh Sherman, the Union general famous for his "march to the sea" through Georgia, published the first edition of his memoirs in 1875. Works such as these helped to set the stage for the proliferation of war memoirs in the 1880s. *The Century* magazine published the immensely popular "*The Century* War Series" from 1884 through 1887, which invited participants from both sides of the conflict to share their stories and perspectives. At around the same time, Ulysses S. Grant, who published two articles in the *Century,* turned to writing his own memoirs. The two-volume *Personal Memoirs of U. S. Grant* (1885) was completed in a heroic effort as the general lay dying of cancer. Mark Twain encouraged Grant to publish with his company, and the work was a huge success. The autobiography begins with the general's ancestry and his birth and ends with the conclusion of the Civil War. There is no mention of his presidency, his failed business dealings, or his famous world travels. Despite these omissions, it is generally considered one of the best war autobiographies.

As war writing became increasingly popular during the 1880s, the San Francisco journalist Ambrose Bierce, a Union army veteran, began writing about his experiences during the war. Bierce, who took part in many of the war's most significant combat operations, scorned what he saw as the increasingly romantic and self-aggrandizing accounts; his stories often show the cruelty and waste of war. One of his most famous stories, "An Occurrence at Owl Creek Bridge" (1890), tells the story of Peyton Farquhar, a Confederate sympathizer who is executed for espionage. In his final moments, he fantasizes about a daring and miraculous escape, only to have the fantasy abruptly ended by his death. Bierce's writing is often marked both by irony and graphic detail. He collected his Civil War fiction in *Tales of Soldiers and Civilians* (1891).

Another work that eschews romantic portrayals of the war is Stephen Crane's *The Red Badge of Courage* (1895). Although Crane was born six years after the

Civil War ended, his novel is considered one of the best pieces of war writing of the period and, indeed, in American literature. It tells the tale of Henry Fleming, a young volunteer who goes off to war fired with romantic ideals of combat, only to confront the realities of war and his own uncertainty about his courage under fire. Crane also produced the well-received collection *The Little Regiment and Other Episodes of the American Civil War* (1896) and a collection of Spanish-American War stories, *Wounds in the Rain* (1900).

Ellen Glasgow's *The Battle-Ground* (1902) offers an interesting combination of what is generally referred to as the romance of the "Lost Cause," highly sentimentalized and idealistic portrayals of the Confederacy, with the Realism of writers such as De Forest and Bierce. It tells the story of Dan Montjoy, a Confederate who goes to war accompanied by his loyal slave Big Abel. Although Montjoy and many of the other Southern characters speak in favor of both the Union and abolition, they fight for their states, paying high personal costs. The novel is noteworthy for some graphic battle scenes and for its portrayal of the efforts of Southern society to survive in a war zone. It also depicts the class differences between soldiers fighting for the Confederate side.

Neither the Spanish-American War nor the War of the Philippines inspired the volume of war writing that the Civil War did. William Dean Howells's "Editha" (1905) is one of his most anthologized short stories, and it tells the story of a young woman who encourages her fiancé, who is largely a pacifist, to enlist to fight in the Spanish-American War. When he dies during his first engagement, Editha is confronted by her culpability in the form of the man's grieving mother, only to dismiss her guilt with a return to an idealistic view of herself. The story is Howells's critique both of sentimentalism and the jingoistic fervor that swept the nation in wartime. Similarly, Mark Twain's posthumously published "The War Prayer" (1923), written in response to the war in the Philippines, criticizes patriotic prayers for victory by pointing out that such prayers are also prayers for the death and loss of family members on the opposing side.

TOPICS FOR DISCUSSION AND RESEARCH

1. How does one define and evaluate "war writing"? Must it feature graphic scenes of combat? Howells's short story "Editha" is set during the outbreak of what appears to be the Spanish-American War; the point of view, however, is fixed firmly on the home front. Is this war writing?

2. What role does gender play in war writing? How are women portrayed in these texts? One might consider Lillie Ravenel in *Miss Ravenel's Conversion* or Henry Fleming's mother in *The Red Badge of Courage,* for example. Ellen Glasgow's novel *The Battle-Ground* has recently gained more attention and could inform exploration of war writing by women.

3. Southern war writing is sometimes dismissed as overly sentimental or unrealistic in its portrayal of "The Lost Cause." Are such critiques valid? Compare *The Battle-Ground* with book 2 of Lanier's novel *Tiger-Lilies.*

4. What does war writing suggest about the writers' attitudes toward particular conflicts or war itself? Some critics have seen *The Red Badge of Courage* as a

profoundly antiwar novel, despite its hero's assertion that he emerges from battle a "man." Often war writing of the early twentieth century is described as "anti-imperial" in its relation to American military activity in Cuba and the Philippines. All war writing contains a political element worthy of close attention.

RESOURCES

Criticism

Daniel Aaron, *The Unwritten War: American Writers and the Civil War* (New York: Knopf, 1973).
A thorough cataloguing of authors who wrote on the war from its beginning and into the twentieth century.

Alice Fahs, *The Imagined Civil War: Popular Literature of the North and South, 1861–1865* (Chapel Hill: University of North Carolina Press, 2001).
Offers a greatly broadened canon to consider by concentrating on popular literature rather than simply those works that have gained critical acclaim. Fahs examines works from the period following the war, and her epilogue will be of particular interest to those desiring another perspective on Civil War writing.

Edmund Wilson, *Patriotic Gore: Studies in the Literature of the American Civil War* (New York: Oxford University Press, 1962).
The essential starting place for those approaching the writing of this period. Wilson examines works from a variety of genres by numerous prominent figures of the period, ranging from Harriet Beecher Stowe to Ambrose Bierce.

PEOPLE OF INTEREST

John W. De Forest (1826–1906)
Union veteran credited with providing the first "realistic" portrayal of the Civil War in fiction in *Miss Ravenel's Conversion from Secession to Loyalty* (1867). De Forest published several other novels, including a "reunion romance" set during Reconstruction titled *The Bloody Chasm* (1881), but he died in relative obscurity.

Ellen Glasgow (1873–1945)
Born and raised in Virginia and went on to become a leading literary figure, winning the Pulitzer Prize for fiction in 1942. *The Battle-Ground* (1902) is Glasgow's only Civil War novel, and although both Wilson and Aaron are generally dismissive of it (Wilson pays it no mention), other critics have argued that it provides a realistic account of the Civil War South.

Sidney Lanier (1842–1881)
Began work on his Civil War novel *Tiger-Lilies* (1867) while serving in the Confederate army; his tour of duty ended in a federal prison when he was captured in 1864. Lanier gained fame as a poet and later became a professor at Johns Hopkins University before dying of tuberculosis.

Herman Melville (1819–1891)
Wrote several novels and short stories but is best known today for *Moby-Dick* (1851). In addition to *Battle-Pieces* (1866), Melville published an extended poem titled *Clarel* in 1876. The Melville Society hosts a website with further information on the author at <http://people.hofstra.edu/john_L_bryant/Melville/index.html> [accessed 21 August 2009].

—*Martin T. Buinicki*

Westerns

Few literary forms conform as rigidly to formulaic definition as does the Western, and yet the genre has undergone an almost continuous process of revision and reinvention since its appearance in the early nineteenth century. For most readers, the term describes a work of popular fiction set in the period after the Civil War and before the supposed "closing of the frontier" famously described by historian Frederick Jackson Turner in 1893. Indeed, the genre has been irrevocably linked to Turner's "frontier thesis," the claim that the experience of western expansion and settlement serves as the defining feature in the establishment of a uniquely American national character. As popular and critical attitudes toward Turner's ideas and an underlying ideology of American exceptionalism have evolved, so too has the Western adapted to a shifting cultural context. Likewise, the cultural turn in the study of literature has encouraged critical scholarly exploration of popular culture, including the Western, and this scholarly scrutiny has led to increased recognition of the genre's aesthetic and ideological significance in the literary history of the United States.

Among the distinctive generic characteristics of the Western is the presence of a solitary male protagonist, whose sense of honor and dignity invoke the chivalric hero of romance, yet whose temperament and personal history render him unfit for full participation in an increasingly bureaucratic and industrialized society. The origins of this figure, as well as the basic contours of the Western narrative, can be found in James Fenimore Cooper's Leatherstocking novels, a series of five books published between 1823 and 1841 and modeled on Sir Walter Scott's immensely popular historical romances. Cooper's novels chronicle the life of Natty Bumppo, or "Leatherstocking," a white man raised among Indians, whose prodigious skills as a frontiersman help to ensure ongoing westward settlement during the years before and after the American Revolution.

Following the model established by Cooper's self-described "national epic," similar historical romances began to appear within an increasingly lucrative American publishing marketplace. Indeed, the same market forces that oversaw western expansion helped to create a middle-class audience that eagerly read such stories in ever-larger numbers. In 1860 the firm of Beadle and Adams began marketing sensational adventure tales, usually shorter than thirty thousand words, for ten cents each, and these "dime novels" sold millions of copies within a decade of their first appearance. Among the best-selling titles were Edward Ellis's *Seth Jones; or, The Captives of the Frontier* (1860) and Edward L. Wheeler's Deadwood Dick series, which included over thirty novels, beginning with *Deadwood Dick, the Prince of the Road* (1877). Wheeler's inclusion of contemporary events and real-life figures in the novel, set in the Black Hills following George Armstrong Custer's historic 1876 defeat at Little Bighorn, exemplifies the blurring of distinctions between historical fact and fiction that characterized the Western for generations. The presence of Sitting Bull and Calamity Jane in Wheeler's fictional tale lends an air of authenticity to the narrative, written in Philadelphia by a writer who never traveled west, and also presents an imagined history of western expansion to a curious public, even as the events themselves are unfolding in real time.

Dime novels served as a crucial conduit for the mythological Western narrative that gripped American society in the late nineteenth century. The partnership between William Cody, a sometime hunter and army scout, and the prolific Ned Buntline (aka Edward Z. C. Judson) helped generate the mass-culture phenomenon known as Buffalo Bill Cody, hero of dozens of dime novels, legendary Indian fighter, and entrepreneur behind the "Wild West," a theatrical spectacle that toured worldwide well into the twentieth century. In fact, Turner delivered his address "The Significance of the Frontier in American History" to the American Historical Association at the World's Columbian Exposition in Chicago literally across the street from the site where the "Wild West" was staged in 1893. The ritual reenactment of western expansion as "manifest destiny," exemplified by scores of virtually interchangeable dime novels and Buffalo Bill's long-running extravaganza, rendered the line between fact and fiction virtually indistinguishable in the popular imagination.

At the turn of the century, as dime novels began to disappear in favor of even cheaper magazines marketed toward younger readers, the publication of Owen Wister's *The Virginian* in 1902 breathed new life into the genre and heralded the arrival of the highbrow "literary" Western. Like so many writers of Westerns, Wister was an Easterner caught in the thrall of the mythology of the West, and his characterization of the protagonist of *The Virginian* solidified several elements of the modern Western hero: a displaced Southerner, he is a natural aristocrat who rejects convention and pretense, a reluctant yet deadly warrior, and an articulate advocate who is reticent by choice. Most significantly, the hero is a cowboy. Whereas dime-novel heroes might serve in any number of roles, including soldier, scout, mountain man, it is the prototypical cowboy, leading cattle across unfenced plains, that occupies iconic pride of place within the Western story. By 1900 long-distance cattle drives were a thing of the past; modern industrial ranching had radically circumscribed the cowboy's role. Wister's evocative vision of a Wyoming landscape not yet conquered by the forces of civilization, therefore, resonated in an industrial America nostalgic for its myth-laden agrarian origins. Like Leatherstocking, the Virginian and his cultural descendants reflect the ambivalent combination of mourning and optimism that characterizes twentieth-century attitudes toward modernity itself.

Among the thematic concerns raised by Wister's seminal novel, are shifting gender roles, racial conflict, and the changing demography of the United States, all of which loom large in subsequent retellings of the Western narrative. To a great extent, *The Virginian* reinforces the dictates of the "strenuous life" defended and exemplified in Theodore Roosevelt's writings and political career. Moreover, in response to the increasing influence exerted by urbanization, industrialization, and corporate capitalism on the lives of American citizens, the Western has consistently reflected the appeal of a restored tradition, albeit one largely invented within fiction itself. Although Westerns generally acknowledge the presence of women, Native Americans, and other groups in the historical development of the American West, their roles within the genre are, for the most part, greatly circumscribed by the ideological imperatives of the "westering" narrative. Although several literary works, such as Helen Hunt

Jackson's *Ramona* (1884), Sui Sin Far's *Mrs. Spring Fragrance* (1912), and Willa Cather's *O Pioneers!* (1913) are deeply concerned with the history, stories, and people of the western United States, their focus on the perspectives of Native Americans, Asian immigrants, or women places them outside the boundaries of the Western genre. In other words, these works, along with such canonical texts as Mark Twain's *Roughing It* (1872), Stephen Crane's "The Bride Comes to Yellow Sky" (1898), and Frank Norris's *The Octopus* (1901), are widely acknowledged as "Western literature" but not as "Westerns."

Although Wister's novel gained currency within the sphere of high culture, one of the most prominent inheritors of Wister's legacy was Zane Grey, among the most popular and successful writers of the twentieth century. Amazingly prolific, Grey published fifty-seven novels, the most famous of which, *Riders of the Purple Sage* (1912), further codified the heroic elements of Wister's Virginian. Grey's protagonist, Lassiter, embodies the dark, brooding mystery, highly personal moral code, and capacity for sudden violence that characterizes the modern Western protagonist. His arrival in the narrative is both an affront to the society he shuns and a necessary step to ensure its survival. When Jane Withersteen, a Mormon woman running a cattle ranch under the manipulative and cruel eyes of the local church elders, watches the arrival of "a horseman, silhouetted against the western sky, coming riding out of the sage," she intuitively understands what he represents. The combination of strength and vulnerability and of skepticism and idealism marked the prototypical hero of countless Western stories and reinforced the Wesern's role as a stabilizer of cultural anxieties regarding social change. Like Wister's schoolteacher Molly in *The Virginian,* Jane represents a "New Woman," strong, independent, and confident. Although these qualities make her fascinating to both the protagonist and audience, she nonetheless represents a potential threat to the prevailing social order that must be subsumed and contained through her involvement with the protagonist.

TOPICS FOR DISCUSSION AND RESEARCH

1. In his famous address "The Significance of the Frontier in American History" (1893), Turner defined the frontier as "the meeting point between savagery and civilization." In what ways does the Western as a literary form reflect the coexistence of these two ideas, and how do the protagonists of these stories negotiate between them?

2. How has the success of the Western been facilitated by changes in the publishing and entertainment industry? How does the form and impact of the Western reflect such phenomena as the spread of magazine publishing and the manufacture and marketing of cheap paperbacks?

3. How do the dynamics of gender operate in Westerns? Are male and female roles always stable or clearly established, or do these stories sometimes reflect cultural instability or uncertainty with regard to gender?

4. Westerns have always laid claim to a level of truth and authenticity. How do the mythical elements of the Western complicate assertions of historical accuracy and the veneer of Realism typical of the genre?

5. The Western has proven adaptable to other storytelling conventions, from mysteries to science fiction. What are some identifiable characteristics of the Western that have been translated into other genres and other cultures? What are some examples of the lasting prominence of the Western?

RESOURCES

Primary Works

Bill Brown, ed., *Reading the West: An Anthology of Dime Westerns* (Boston: Bedford, 1997).

Includes four quite different examples of the nineteenth-century dime novel: Ann Stephens's *Malaeska; or, the Indian Wife of the White Hunter;* Edward Ellis's *Seth Jones; or, the Captives of the Frontier;* Edward Wheeler's *Deadwood Dick, the Prince of the Road;* and the anonymous *Frank Reade, the Inventor, Chasing the James Boys with His Steam Train.* From the comparative study of these texts readers gain some perspective on the development of the formula "Western" that emerged from the dime-novel tradition.

Ned Buntline, *Buffalo Bill and His Adventures in the West* (1886; reprinted by Whitefish, Mont.: Kessinger, 2007).

Republication of a classic example of Buntline's work mythologizing the figure of William Cody, which captured the public imagination for years to come. No writer's name is more closely associated with the dime novel than Buntline's.

Zane Grey, *Riders of the Purple Sage* (1912; New York: Penguin, 1990).

Affirming the antimodern ideology of the traditional Western and borrowing heavily from Wister's *The Virginian* for its themes and structure, presents an ideal of gender balance in the romance between the rough and impulsive Lassiter and the nurturing Jane Withersteen.

Owen Wister, *The Virginian* (1902; New York: Penguin, 1988).

The prototype for the modern Western.

Criticism

Blake Allmendinger, *The Cowboy: Representations of Labor in an American Work Culture* (New York: Oxford University Press, 1992).

Bringing together traditional Westerns, dime fiction, music, and "cowboy poetry," explores the shifting image of the cowboy within American popular culture.

Richard Aquila, ed., *Wanted Dead or Alive: The American West in Popular Culture* (Urbana: University of Illinois Press, 1996).

A wide-ranging collection of essays about popular fiction, film, television, music, and live performances that present the iconic imagery and mythology of the Western from the mid nineteenth century to the present.

Christine Bold, *Selling the Wild West: Popular Western Fiction, 1860–1960* (Bloomington: Indiana University Press, 1987).

Analysis of the ways in which the Western form has adapted and evolved, providing a comprehensive overview of the Western genre. It is among the first recent works to present a wide-ranging argument that encompasses both "high" and "low" literature.

John G. Cawelti, *The Six-Gun Mystique Sequel* (Madison: University of Wisconsin Press, 1999).
A revision of Cawelti's 1970 *The Six-Gun Mystique,* provides a thorough genealogy of the development of the Western as a genre, as well as a useful chapter updating the critical debates surrounding the subject. Cawelti deploys a historically grounded notion of myth indebted to the work of Henry Nash Smith and Richard Slotkin.

William Handley, *Marriage, Violence, and the Nation in the American Literary West* (New York: Cambridge University Press, 2002).
A revisionist argument about Westerns centering on the impact that these works have had outside the Western genre itself, particularly in their focus on issues of marriage and family. Handley traces the ways in which notions of race, gender, and religious Otherness are negotiated in Wister's and Grey's best-known novels.

Lee Clark Mitchell, *Westerns: Making the Man in Fiction and Film* (Chicago: University of Chicago Press, 1996).
Responding to contemporary studies of gender and masculinity, asserts that a fascination with the male body is among the defining characteristics of the Western.

Susan Rosowski, "The Western Hero as Logos," in her *Birthing a Nation: Gender, Creativity, and the West in American Literature* (Lincoln: University of Nebraska Press, 1999).
In the context of Rosowski's larger argument about the relationships between aesthetic production, procreation, and gender, a concise argument about the laconic Western hero and nature of language within the traditional Western.

Henry Nash Smith, *Virgin Land: The American West as Symbol and Myth* (1950; revised edition, Cambridge, Mass.: Harvard University Press, 1970).
An early example of the kind of interdisciplinary interpretation that characterizes American Studies. Smith's investigation of the unifying myth of western expansion traces the origins of the Western hero through Cooper's Leatherstocking Tales and the dime novels and offers a substantive analysis of the contradictions behind the central narratives and images of the frontier.

Richard Slotkin, *Gunfighter Nation: The Myth of the Frontier in Twentieth-Century America* (New York: Atheneum, 1992).
The final volume in Slotkin's trilogy of works on the myth of "regeneration through violence" in American literature and culture. This book focuses on the emergence of the formula Western in the late nineteenth century and its development through the twentieth century, particularly in film.

Jane Tompkins, *West of Everything: The Inner Life of Westerns* (New York: Oxford University Press, 1992).
Investigates the "cultural work" performed by the Western. Largely avoiding issues of literary genealogy and historical context, Tompkins instead focuses on several key areas of concern within the Western genre, including landscape, death, and

gender, seeking to explore the ways in which several canonical Westerns respond to ongoing cultural anxieties.

Barbara Will, "The Nervous Origins of the American Western," *American Literature*, 70 (June 1998): 293–316.
Builds on claims about gender made by Mitchell and Tompkins and explores the overlapping discourses of neurasthenia and manhood in *The Virginian*. Will argues that Wister's novel emerges as the product of then-current debates about gender and Wister's association with S. Weir Mitchell, the physician best known for his treatment of nervous disorders.

PEOPLE OF INTEREST

Ned Buntline (aka Edward Z. C. Judson) (1823–1896)
One of the most successful writers of pulp westerns after the Civil War, totaling some four hundred novels, many of them featuring Buffalo Bill Cody.

William F. (Buffalo Bill) Cody (1846–1917)
American soldier, hunter, and showman, founder of the circus-like Buffalo Bill's Wild West in 1883.

James Fenimore Cooper (1789–1851)
Author of the five Leatherstocking Tales published between 1823 and 1841 featuring Natty Bumppo.

Edward S. Ellis (1840–1916)
A prolific writer of dime-novel Westerns best known today for *Seth Jones, or Captives of the Frontier* (1860), published by the New York firm of Beadle and Adams.

Zane Grey (1872–1939)
Was a popular writer of Westerns and other adventure novels and one of the first millionaire authors. He also was instrumental in the adaptation of the Western formula to film.

Edward L. Wheeler (circa 1854–1885)
Sensational dime novelist best known for his "Deadwood Dick" series inaugurated in 1877.

Owen Wister (1860–2938)
A Harvard graduate, began to travel to Wyoming in 1885 to treat his "neurasthenia." His first Western story appeared in *Harper's* in August 1892, and a decade later his novel *The Virginian* established the classic Western formula and became a best seller.

—*John Dudley*

Women's Writing

Although women were actively publishing well into the early nineteenth century, it was not until after the Civil War that their writing took on a more political and social agenda. After the war, women became more familiar with the publishing world and their place within it. Several became writers and editors. Sarah Josepha Hale is credited with largely influencing the shape of the literary marketplace for women. As editor of *Godey's Lady's Book,* Hale refused to reprint British stories as was the custom and chose to publish only original American works that focused on educating a female readership. Even though women's place in the publishing industry had been established in the early part of the century, writers during the latter part clearly extended their influence, bringing to the forefront more progressive ideas. Where their writing had before been more domestic and feminine, the Civil War prompted many postbellum women writers to draw on the motifs of conflict and violence to explore the psychological and political effects of the Civil War and women's place within a patriarchal order. The war marked a shift in focus from sentimental romance to Realism as women authors sought to reflect a changing society. Drawing on themes of power, sacrifice, and independence, female authors such as Rebecca Harding Davis in *Waiting for the Verdict* (1868) and Louisa May Alcott in "My Contraband; or, the Brothers" (1863) explored race and class conflict during the war. Social-protest and reform movements were deeply embedded in women's writing throughout the mid nineteenth and early twentieth centuries as women campaigned for universal suffrage. Much of their writing centered on the tension between the Victorian "angel of the house" and the ambitious artist. For example, Alcott's *A Modern Mephistopheles* (1877) and *Diana and Persis* (written 1873, published 1978), Kate Chopin's *The Awakening* (1899), and Elizabeth Stuart Phelps's *The Story of Avis* (1877), to name just a few, dealt with the incompatibility of marriage and maternity with artistry.

The latter part of the nineteenth century has been typically associated with literary Realism and designated specifically as a male-centered period. Many women writers, however, participated in the tradition of literary Realism and its offshoots, Regionalism and local-color fiction. For these writers, literary Realism's concentration on aspects of everyday life offered ample and familiar material. Reacting against the earlier domestic fiction that ended in marriage, women writers at the turn into the twentieth century explored the conflicts inherent in marital life and in so doing profoundly shaped a distinctive literary form about particular regions. For many women Regionalist writers, marriage was not the sole outcome female characters sought. Rather, what we see is writing that more accurately depicts the thoughts and actions about and between women. For example, Louisa Ellis in Mary Wilkins Freeman's "A New England Nun" (1891) realizes that marriage does not represent the most important event in her life, and she chooses to remain single. Rose Terry Cooke's "Miss Beulah's Bonnet" (1880) focuses on the world of girls and women.

The more prominent regional and local-color writers such as Freeman (*A New England Nun and Other Stories*, 1891), Sarah Orne Jewett (*The Country of the Pointed Firs*, 1896), and Rose Terry Cooke (*The Sphinx's Children and Other*

People's, 1886) wrote about New England and the North Atlantic coastal area, while others sought to represent the Southern region. For example, Chopin's *Bayou Folk* (1894) depicts Creole culture in Louisiana, Mary Noailles Murfree's *In the Tennessee Mountains* (1884) looks toward the rustic men and women who inhabit the Tennessee mountains, and Constance Fenimore Woolson's *For the Major* (1883) paints a world redolent of Southern gentility. Helen Hunt Jackson, a New Englander by birth, is best known for her novel *Ramona* (1884), which details competing property claims in California. All of these writers departed from domestic fiction in their narratives of aging villages inhabited by oddly wise spinsters and matriarchs. Although the terms "local-color" and "Regionalism" were used somewhat derogatorily to depict the types of works these writers authored, this genre nevertheless paved the way for the literary careers of many women writers. Writers such as Freeman, Cooke, and Jewett were able to explore their own regions while earning success in the literary marketplace.

The primary venue for women's publishing was through the periodical, an industry run and managed by such figures as James T. Fields, Louis A. Godey, and William Dean Howells. Some female authors were able to circulate their work in such prestigious magazines as the *Atlantic Monthly, Century, Scribner's,* and *Harper's Bazaar,* while others were content to publish their stories, poems, and advice treatises in American ladies' magazines, which tended to pay three times as much as their high-culture counterparts. With the proliferation of new periodicals, middle-class monthlies, and cheap weeklies, the topics women addressed in their writing ran the gamut from women's rights, dress reform, domestic duties, and divorce. The postbellum era also saw a niche filled by devotional writing, children's literature, and the abolitionist gift book as women navigated the complicated web of writing, editing, and publishing.

Although white women dominated the literary scene and thus much of their writing reflects conflicts experienced from a predominantly white, middle-class perspective, there has recently been an attempt by scholars such as Elizabeth Ammons to reconsider the writings and experiences of nonwhite women writers. Pauline Hopkins, for example, argued for social change in the African American community through her short fiction in the *Colored American Magazine,* which she edited from 1900 until 1909. Non-Anglo female authors such as María Christina Mena, Sarah Winnemucca Hopkins, and Zitkala-Ša experimented with regional topics tied to their own culture and ethnic identity. For Mena, writing for a mostly white, middle-class readership meant that she had to include quaint pictures of Mexican life, but she spoke in a realistic voice that covertly betrayed her condemnation of imperialism and patriarchy. Well aware of the literary constructions of race, Mena used them to her advantage by challenging male dominance and power. Winnemucca's *Life among the Piutes: Their Wrongs and Claims* (1883) includes elements of myth, poetry, biography, and oral tradition that profoundly reveal a Native American culture. Zitkala-Ša's "Impressions of an Indian Childhood" (1900) details the struggles of a nonwhite American girl attempting to achieve a sense of self-worth and equality in a white-dominated culture.

Local-color fiction often incorporated supernatural elements because of the prominence of ghosts within regional folklore. As a result, supernatural stories abound at the turn of the twentieth century, and women writers took advantage of the ghost tale as a means of challenging conventional gender roles. This form allowed women writers more freedom to explore issues of sexuality and victimization than could be asserted in their more realistic fiction. Specifically, American women writing during the age of literary Realism found the ghost story an attractive alternative. Writers such as Wharton, Freeman, Harriet Prescott Spofford, Willa Cather, Gertrude Atherton, and Charlotte Perkins Gilman wrote and published many supernatural tales. Catherine Lundie's *Restless Spirits: Ghost Stories by American Women, 1872–1926* (Amherst: University of Massachusetts Press, 1996) and Alfred Bendixen's *Haunted Women: The Best Supernatural Tales by American Women* (New York: Ungar, 1985) are substantive anthologies of American women's Gothic fiction with introductions that clearly locate the Gothic within a feminist tradition.

Women writing in the vein of Naturalism, an outgrowth of literary Realism, found an appropriate venue to depict their despair in a patriarchal world, a powerful force acting on the world and specifically defining women's place within it. Adhering to the principles of Darwin in *The Descent of Man* (1877) and Gilman's *Women and Economics* (1898), women writers used literary Naturalism to explore women's economic dependence and biological destiny to highlight their lack of choices in a hostile and indifferent world. Three key works that best illustrate this type of literature are Chopin's *The Awakening*, Wharton's *The House of Mirth* (1905), and Cather's *O Pioneers!* (1913). These novels illustrate how societal forces and inherited characteristics determine the fates of female characters, fusing feminism with deterministic elements.

Students seeking to familiarize themselves with late-nineteenth- and early-twentieth-century women writers are encouraged to begin with *American Women Regionalists, 1850–1910* (New York: Norton, 1992), edited by Judith Fetterley and Marjorie Pryse, which includes sixty-four stories by fourteen women as well as biographical and critical headnotes and an extensive bibliography. Elaine Showalter's collection *Scribbling Women: Short Stories by 19th-Century American Women* (New Brunswick, N.J.: Rutgers University Press, 1997) reprints short stories by key women writers and includes brief biographies of the authors.

Students wishing to read criticism on the body of work produced by women writers would benefit by reading the introduction to Elizabeth Ammons's *Conflicting Stories: American Women Writers at the Turn into the Twentieth Century* (New York: Oxford University Press, 1991) and chapters 7 through 12 of Elaine Showalter's *A Jury of Her Peers: American Women Writers from Anne Bradstreet to Annie Proulx* (New York: Knopf, 2009). Other critical sources students will find particularly useful are *"The Only Efficient Instrument": American Women Writers and the Periodical, 1837–1916* (Iowa City: University of Iowa Press, 2001), edited by Aleta Feinsod Cane and Susan Alves; *Nineteenth-Century American Women Writers: A Critical Reader* (Malden, Mass.: Blackwell, 1998), edited by Karen Kilcup; and *The Cambridge Companion to Nineteenth-Century American Women's Writing*, edited by Dale M. Bauer and Philip Gould. These collections offer intriguing approaches to understanding gender, race, and class conflict as seen in the diverse writings by women at the turn into the twentieth century.

TOPICS FOR DISCUSSION AND RESEARCH

1. How do works by women of different ethnicities and from within and outside of the literary canon, such as those by Winnemucca, Hopkins, Mena, Chopin, Wharton, and Zitkala-Ša, sustain or problematize a female literary voice?
2. How are the characters and description in women's realistic and regional writing different from their male counterparts, and what are the continuities?
3. How do these works alter our view of women's writing and the literary tradition in general?

Some possible answers to these questions can also be obtained from a helpful website dedicated to American women's writing at <http://www.wsu.edu/~campbelld/ssaww/index.html> [accessed 9 September 2009].

RESOURCES

Bibliography

Maurice Duke, Jackson R. Bryer, and M. Thomas Inge, *American Women Writers: Bibliographical Essays* (Westport, Conn.: Greenwood Press, 1983).
Fourteen bibliographical essays on individual works by twenty-four major American women writers, with information on editions and manuscripts.

Barbara A. White, *American Women Writers: An Annotated Bibliography of Criticism* (New York: Garland, 1977).
Critical assessments of American women's writing, including such topics as biography, literary history, contemporary analyses, and feminist literary scholarship.

Biography

Denise D. Knight, *Nineteenth-Century American Women Writers: A Bio-Bibliographical Critical Sourcebook* (Westport, Conn.: Greenwood Press, 1997).
An invaluable resource that gives biographical information on representative American women writers, including lesser-known authors. Each entry also discusses the author's major works and central themes and provides an overview of the scholarship pertaining to particular texts.

PEOPLE OF INTEREST

Willa Cather (1873–1947)
While managing editor of the widely read *McClure's,* in New York City, met and befriended Sarah Orne Jewett. She later moved to the Southwest.

Rebecca Harding Davis (1831–1910)
Led a literary career that spanned five decades and included works in the genres of local color, Realism, travel literature, and children's stories.

Pauline Elizabeth Hopkins (1859–1930)
Editor of the *Colored American Magazine,* where she published sentimental fiction that dealt with miscegenation and racial prejudice.

—Cindy Murillo

Part III
Study Guides
on Works and Writers

Ambrose Bierce, "An Occurrence at Owl Creek Bridge"

San Francisco Examiner, 13 July 1890, pp. 11–12; collected in *Tales of Soldiers and Civilians* (San Francisco: Steele, 1891)

Ambrose Bierce (1842–1914?) was a journalist and writer of satire who developed an international reputation as an ironist. At the beginning of the American Civil War, he enlisted as a private in the Ninth Indiana Infantry, and he fought at Shiloh, Murfreesboro, Chickamauga, and Chattanooga. After being discharged as a first lieutenant in 1865, Bierce worked as a night watchman for the U.S. Subtreasury in San Francisco, where he began reading classic authors such as Voltaire, Jonathan Swift, Francis Bacon, and Plato. Soon he was publishing poetry, essays, articles, and pieces of humor in local newspapers. He thereafter embarked on a career in journalism, writing satirical columns for several publications and going on to work for William Randolph Hearst at the *San Francisco Examiner, New York Journal,* and *Cosmopolitan.* In the meantime, Bierce published poems, epigrams, fables, and short stories. Book-length collections of his essays first appeared in 1873; his first collection of stories appeared in 1891. Shortly before Bierce disappeared in Mexico in 1913 during the Mexican Revolution, his twelve-volume *Collected Works* appeared in print.

"An Occurrence at Owl Creek Bridge" is Bierce's most highly regarded and widely reprinted short story. It was published in *Tales of Soldiers and Civilians* (1891), a collection that received enthusiastic reviews and gave Bierce nationwide fame as a story writer. The stories in this collection are tales of horror that use coincidence to create ironic, ghastly situations that unnerve the bravest of individuals. Bierce's war stories are radically different from the romantic, sentimental Civil War stories in vogue at the time; they reveal that war is not an arena for duty, sacrifice, and glory, but an absurd, horrifying mess that ends in death of the loneliest and most undignified kind. Although "An Occurrence at Owl Creek Bridge" has these qualities, it is not a war story in the strictest sense; it is mainly a piece of speculative fiction on the subjective nature of human perceptions, especially concerning the passage of time, and the wartime setting could just as readily be made into a civilian one.

Nonetheless, the background of "An Occurrence at Owl Creek Bridge" does have its origins in Bierce's experiences as a soldier. The story is set in northern Alabama, a region that Bierce knew intimately from the war. Evidence suggests that he modeled the Owl Creek Bridge after a bridge called the Sulphur Creek Trestle, which was on the Tennessee and Alabama railway and which was guarded by Union troops stationed in a nearby blockhouse and stockade. Bierce knew of an actual Owl Creek in Tennessee, but he apparently transposed it to northern Alabama because the real creek had no railroad near it and he wanted to maintain the story's verisimilitude. He probably also wanted to take advantage of symbolic connotations in the name of "Owl Creek"; according to this view, the owl is an omen of mortality and an emblem of wisdom, and the reader of the story certainly comes to a better understanding of war as the protagonist dies on Owl Creek Bridge in the end.

The main character in the story is Peyton Farquhar, a civilian planter who ardently supports the Southern cause. Enticed by a disguised Union scout into taking action on behalf of the Confederacy, Farquhar tries to burn down the Union-held bridge on Owl Creek. He is hanged for his attempted crime, but he appears to have been given a reprieve when the rope apparently breaks and he plunges into the creek. Most of the rest of the story takes place in Farquhar's imagination as he makes his grueling but exhilarating escape. The stress of flight heightens his perceptions so that he sees his surroundings with an almost hallucinatory intensity. As he makes his way back home to his wife and children, his once-familiar environs become strange and nightmarish. Finally, just as Farquhar is about to embrace his wife, he feels a blow on his neck and the reader finds out that he has indeed been hanged.

Readers have quibbled over the surprise ending, debating whether it is a cheap trick or a legitimate device, but most critics find that Bierce prepares his readers for the ending through the skillful use of foreshadowing. In fact, critics generally praise "An Occurrence at Owl Creek Bridge" as a masterful demonstration of technical skill, one that reveals Bierce's command of the short story. It has even been called a work of genius, if only on a small scale. It has also been acknowledged as an influence on stories by Stephen Crane, Ernest Hemingway, William Golding, and Jorge Luis Borges, and it is one of the few works by Bierce that has survived and made its way into the literary canon.

Any study of "An Occurrence at Owl Creek Bridge" would be enhanced by some familiarity with Bierce's Civil War experiences and his outlook on life. An excellent introduction to the man and his career may be found in Carey McWilliams's *Ambrose Bierce: A Biography*. Other insightful biographies include Richard O'Connor's *Ambrose Bierce: A Biography* and Paul Fatout's *Ambrose Bierce: The Devil's Lexicographer*. Students needing information on the biographical origins of the story as well as its historical and geographical backgrounds are well advised to consult David M. Owens's *The Devil's Topographer: Ambrose Bierce and the American War Story*. Before seeking out other works of criticism, students would benefit from perusing Robert C. Evans's *Ambrose Bierce's "An Occurrence at Owl Creek Bridge": An Annotated Critical Edition*, which contains an annotated version of the story in addition to a wide range of analyses written from multiple critical perspectives.

TOPICS FOR DISCUSSION AND RESEARCH

1. "An Occurrence at Owl Creek Bridge" can be studied from several different angles. One is to consider Bierce's literary Impressionism, which involves the idea that perceptions of reality are affected by one's state of mind. Illustrations of this concept abound in the story; the most obvious one is the time dilation that Farquhar experiences as he is being hanged. From his point of view, he lives out the rest of the day after supposedly escaping, but to the soldiers hanging him, his execution lasts for only a few seconds. Moreover, Farquhar's perceptions become preternaturally acute during his experience, so much so that the ticking of his watch sounds like a hammer banging on an anvil and,

while in imaginary flight, he sees the sand of the creek bed as "diamonds, rubies, emeralds" and the trees as "giant garden plants." Many more examples of what has been called Farquhar's "postmortem consciousness" may be found to examine Bierce's use of Impressionism.

2. Another major approach to analyzing the story is to view it as a satire of the human capacity for fantasy and self-delusion. In making a distinction between external events and subjective experience, Bierce exposes the human tendency to favor wishful thinking over reason and careful observation. He juxtaposes lofty human aspirations with the cold facts of war and shows that Farquhar is as bound by his romantic notions as he is by the noose around his neck. Bierce mocks the overblown rhetoric of Farquhar's cheap patriotism as well as his heroic fantasies, revealing that Farquhar is guilty of an irrational, foolish pride, a lack of social ethics, and an insufficient understanding of war's seriousness. Bierce also argues through the example of Farquhar that human beings fully appreciate life only when they are threatened with the loss of it, as we see when Farquhar suddenly becomes aware of the natural beauty in his surroundings only during the crisis of escape.

3. The story may also be seen as a literary prank played on inattentive readers who share Farquhar's values and read the narrative as a heroic adventure tale. Bierce uses narrative strategies that cause readers to participate in the mental experiences of Farquhar even as he also provides readers with enough information to piece together what is actually happening. Bierce therefore invites readers to make the same errors that Farquhar makes in interpreting his experiences, and the author assumes that readers will ignore the clues throughout the narrative in favor of a more romantic interpretation of the evidence. For example, readers should recognize that some of Farquhar's sensory impressions are impossibly acute, but they become so caught up in the drama of his escape, desiring it almost as much as he does, that they willingly suspend disbelief and accept his impressions as plausible. Ultimately, the story challenges readers to learn not only from Farquhar's mistakes but also from their own in succumbing to desires instead of facing facts. The ways in which Bierce handles the narration to manipulate the response of readers to the material is a promising area for further investigation.

4. Another fertile area for inquiry is to examine the adaptations of "An Occurrence at Owl Creek Bridge" for other media. This story lives on in American popular culture in the form of audio books, comic books, television shows, and movies. The audio and comic book versions are recent phenomena, but the story has a long history on the screen. It has been made into TV programs at least twice, once as an episode of "Alfred Hitchcock Presents" (NBC, 1959) and once as an episode of "The Twilight Zone" (CBS, 1964). It has also been made into short films at least four times, in 1929, 1962, 1980, and 2005. Other than Gerald R. Barnett's *From Fiction to Film: Ambrose Bierce's "An Occurrence at Owl Creek Bridge,"* however, little has been written on film versions of the story. Studies which consider relationships between the original text and any of its adaptations or among the adaptations themselves have a great deal of scholarly potential.

RESOURCES

Bibliography

Ambrose Bierce Appreciation Society <http://www.biercephile.com/> [accessed 24 August 2009].
Provides a primary and secondary bibliography as well as useful general information about Bierce and Bierce studies.

Biography

Ambrose Bierce, *A Sole Survivor: Bits of Autobiography*, edited by S. T. Joshi and David E. Shultz (Knoxville: University of Tennessee Press, 1998).
The only attempt at autobiography by Bierce, supplemented with first-person selections from published and unpublished writing by the author.

Paul Fatout, *Ambrose Bierce: The Devil's Lexicographer* (Norman: University of Oklahoma Press, 1951).
A reliable study of Bierce and his career.

M. E. Grenander, *Ambrose Bierce* (New York: Twayne, 1971).
An insightful survey of the author and his work.

Carey McWilliams, *Ambrose Bierce: A Biography* (New York: Boni, 1929).
An early but thorough examination of Bierce's life and career, useful for the publication history of Bierce's works as well as their reception by critics and the public. The updated introduction provides a helpful overview of the subject.

Richard O'Connor, *Ambrose Bierce: A Biography* (Boston: Little, Brown, 1967).
An accessible biography of Bierce, containing narrative details not found elsewhere.

Criticism

Gerald R. Barnett, *From Fiction to Film: Ambrose Bierce's "An Occurrence at Owl Creek Bridge"* (Encino, Cal.: Dickinson, 1973).
A pioneering study of Robert Enrico's 1962 film adaptation of the story.

Donald T. Blume, "'A Quarter of an Hour': Hanging as Ambrose Bierce and Peyton Farquhar Knew It," *American Literary Realism,* 34 (Winter 2002): 146–157.
Documents the popular understanding of the physiological effects of hanging, in which the victim dies not by strangulation but from a broken neck.

Robert C. Evans, *Ambrose Bierce's "An Occurrence at Owl Creek Bridge": An Annotated Critical Edition* (West Cornwall, Conn.: Locust Hill, 2004).
A highly recommended resource that examines the story from a variety of angles and summarizes the existing criticism. It is also an experiment in pluralist criticism, including student responses that interpret the text from many critical perspectives.

David M. Owens, *The Devil's Topographer: Ambrose Bierce and the American War Story* (Knoxville: University of Tennessee Press, 2006).
A detailed examination of Bierce's Civil War experiences and the war stories that grew out of those experiences.

—Seth Bovey

Charles W. Chesnutt (1858–1932)

Charles Waddell Chesnutt was the most successful African American fiction writer of the late nineteenth and early twentieth centuries. At a time when most black writers did not have access to mainstream audiences or major publishing houses, Chesnutt's stories appeared in the *Atlantic Monthly*, the period's preeminent literary magazine and champion of such major American Realists as Mark Twain and Henry James; and Houghton Mifflin published his two short-story collections, *The Conjure Woman* (1899) and *The Wife of His Youth and Other Stories of the Color Line* (1899), and two of his novels, *The House behind the Cedars* (1900) and *The Marrow of Tradition* (1901). Chesnutt's final published novel, *The Colonel's Dream*, appeared in 1905. While he was most famous during his career for his stories written in dialect, modern critics have deemed Chesnutt an important figure not just in African American and local-color fiction but also in American Realism more broadly. Because of increasing scholarly interest in his work and the issues he addressed, since the early 1990s most of his unpublished manuscripts, an edition of his journals between 1871 and 1882, two volumes of his correspondence, and an edited collection of his essays and speeches have been published.

THE CONJURE WOMAN (1899)

Until William Dean Howells noted that Chesnutt was "of negro blood" in a review of his story collections, readers of his conjure stories likely assumed that Chesnutt was white because of obvious similarities between the conjure tales and popular stories by Joel Chandler Harris, Thomas Nelson Page, and other writers of the plantation tradition. Like Harris's and Page's works, Chesnutt's stories are written primarily in dialect and feature a former slave storyteller who regales a white outsider (or child in Harris's Uncle Remus stories) with tales of life "befo' de Wah." Chesnutt brought a new element to such stories, however, by focusing on conjure, a Southern-black folk practice typically involving some combination of divination, spells, charms or talismans, homeopathic medicine, and prayer. Even more important, Chesnutt saw his stories as a corrective to those in the plantation tradition that depict former slaves nostalgically, recalling kind, honorable masters and docile, contented slaves peacefully coexisting in a web of mutual dependence, loyalty, and devotion. By contrast, the tales narrated by Chesnutt's trickster-freedman, Uncle Julius McAdoo, feature mean, greedy, and dishonest masters who regard their slaves purely in terms of profit and loss, and slaves who, despite their efforts to cope with or lessen the evils of slavery, frequently are victims.

All of Uncle Julius's stories are framed by a white narrator, John, who, along with his wife, Annie, is the usual audience for Julius's storytelling. John and Annie have moved to Patesville (Fayetteville), North Carolina, from Ohio because of Annie's poor health, and John is trying to establish viticulture on a commercial scale in the New South. John regards Julius's tales as mere self-serving entertainments, and Julius and/or his friends and family members *do* often materially benefit at story's end. Nevertheless, John usually misses what Annie calls "the stamp of truth" in Julius's tales because he is caught up in their factuality. Even on their surface, Julius's tales ought to remind John and Annie that slavery was a brutal and oppressive system whose effects continue into the present, not the benevolent patriarchal arrangement depicted in nostalgic tales of the plantation tradition. Through John, Chesnutt illustrates Northern capital's tendency to forget or disregard this truth in their eagerness to open the South to investment and industrialization following the Civil War.

THE WIFE OF HIS YOUTH AND OTHER STORIES OF THE COLOR LINE (1899)

The celebrated title story of this collection features Mr. Ryder, a former fugitive slave who has turned himself into a cultured and successful member of the mixed-race community in "Groveland" (Cleveland). He chooses to acknowledge his illiterate, aged, and dark-skinned slave wife, though he was about to propose to a woman more suited to his current situation in life. In the context of growing color and class divisions among blacks, Mr. Ryder's decision can be read as a rejection of colorism and an affirmation of upwardly mobile blacks' continuing obligations to their less fortunate brethren. The remaining stories move between the North and the South and range in tone from tragic ("The Sheriff's Children") to comic or satirical ("A Matter of Principle") to sentimental ("Her Virginia Mammy"), but most examine the tragedies, paradoxes, and compromises faced by mixed race individuals who straddle the color line.

THE HOUSE BEHIND THE CEDARS (1900)

Chesnutt's first published novel addresses directly the tragedy of the racial caste system that makes passing seem necessary for some mixed-race individuals. John Walden has assumed the name John Warwick and passed as a white man for a decade when he returns home and offers a similar opportunity to his sister Rena. Passing as Rowena Warwick, Rena falls in love with and is engaged to George Tryon, a white man from a prominent family, but his love cannot withstand the shock of learning Rena's true racial identity. A heartsick Rena seeks solace in teaching and serving the race she had tried to escape. The novel ends with Rena's death after she is caught in a storm while fleeing a villainous mulatto suitor and her remorseful former fiancé.

On the most superficial level, Rena Walden seems the classic "tragic mulatta": sexually imperiled because of her beauty, rejected in her attempt to pass into the white world, and out of place in the black world. Her death is not a judgment on passing, however. Though Chesnutt rejected this option in his own case, he depicts John and Rena in sympathetic terms. No other option is available to them if they wish to make the most of their skills and talents and remain in the South. No one can tell by looking at Rena that she has black blood; she is a "Negro" only because she is known as one in Patesville and its environs. Chesnutt suggests that if racial identity can be so unstable, it must be an absurd fiction.

THE MARROW OF TRADITION (1901)

Chesnutt's most overtly political novel is a fictional treatment of the 1898 Wilmington, North Carolina, massacre in which white supremacists staged a coup, violently forcing Fusion Party (Republican and Populist) elected officials and appointees from office and restoring white Democrats to power. Chesnutt examines this key betrayal of Reconstruction promises and American ideals through several interwoven plots, but the primary characters are the Carterets and Millers. Major Carteret and his wife Olivia are white aristocrats who have lost some of their wealth and power since the war but are still among the leading citizens of Wellington (Wilmington). Janet Miller is Olivia's free-born, near-identical, mixed-race half sister, whom Olivia refuses to acknowledge; Janet's physician husband William is a particular target of Major Carteret's dislike because the Millers now own the old Carteret mansion. Chesnutt builds around these characters several sensational plots involving family secrets, romantic rivals, a murder and near-lynching, and post-Reconstruction racial and class politics. These plots come together in the Wellington "riot," a plan hatched by Major Carteret and coconspirators General Belmont and Captain McBane to provide cover for their seizure of political and economic power. Their show of force quickly devolves into mob violence and murder that Carteret first tries ineffectually to halt and then washes his hands of.

Contemporary newspaper accounts tended to frame the Wilmington massacre as a "race riot," thereby justifying white violence and disregard for the rule of law. One of Chesnutt's primary goals in *The Marrow of Tradition* was to set the record straight and reveal white Democrats' actions for what they were: "a mere vulgar theft of power." Chesnutt does this by returning to the theme that animates much of his fiction: the hypocrisy and folly of appeals to racial purity and white supremacy. The Carterets insist on the moral and intellectual superiority of the white race, but Chesnutt's use of doubles, especially Olivia and Janet, reveals that "white" is a dubious racial category at best and racial purity is a willful delusion. Moreover, various white characters lie, cheat, and steal in order to protect their names or class position and usurp name, power, and property from those to whom they rightly belong. Ironically, Carteret's racism and race-baiting imperil his only child, the long wished for heir to the Carteret name, but the novel bleakly suggests that Carteret's realization of his folly is temporary and that "the veil of race prejudice" will again descend over the community once the crisis is safely past.

TOPICS FOR DISCUSSION AND RESEARCH

1. Chesnutt's concern with the position and plight of mixed race blacks makes him a figure of interest to scholars interested in hybridity. His fiction repeatedly challenges the truth of racial categories. Dean McWilliams notes that Chesnutt during his career "straddled and confounded several important American categories" and periods. As such, his work can be fruitfully studied and taught from various perspectives. For example, Chesnutt's Uncle Julius stories may be contrasted with Joel Chandler Harris's Uncle Remus tales. Did Chesnutt simply rewrite Harris's folktales? Or was his response to them more

complicated? What risks did Chesnutt run in using the tropes of the planta-tion tradition in order to refute it? Did he manage to avoid these pitfalls?

2. Slave narratives were the most important literary form for African Americans before the Civil War, and they continued to appear into the twentieth century. Is it appropriate to think of Uncle Julius's stories as slave narratives? If so, in what ways has the achievement of freedom, at least nominally, changed (or not) the form and purposes of the genre? Making such a comparison also raises questions about literacy and orality—whether and why one might be privileged over the other at a particular historical moment or within particular texts.

3. In his review of *The Wife of His Youth and Other Stories of the Color Line* Howells championed Chesnutt as a literary Realist of the first order. Can the conjure tales also be classified as realistic? Is Realism sufficient to convey the "truth" of slavery?

4. Though he did not practice law, Chesnutt passed the Ohio bar exam, and lawyers are important, though not central characters in *The House behind the Cedars* and *The Marrow of Tradition*. Moreover, Chesnutt was writing at a time when much of the legal framework for Jim Crow (antimiscegenation laws, voting restric-tions, the U.S. Supreme Court decision *Plessy v. Ferguson* sanctioning "separate but equal" public facilities) was erected. What do Chesnutt's novels suggest about the law's role in constructing racial-identity categories? What is the con-nection between the law and lawlessness like that depicted in *The Marrow of Tradition*? Does Chesnutt seem to regard the law as an effective means to redress the wrongs inflicted on black Americans? (The strategy was later adopted by the NAACP, of which Chesnutt was an early member.)

RESOURCES

Biography

Helen M. Chesnutt, *Charles Waddell Chesnutt: Pioneer of the Color Line* (Chapel Hill: University of North Carolina Press, 1952).
A documentary biography by the author's daughter.

Frances Richardson Keller, *An American Crusade: The Life of Charles Waddell Ches-nutt* (Provo, Utah: Brigham Young University Press, 1978).
Largely ignores Chesnutt's fiction to focus on his nonfiction, particularly his autobiographical writing. Keller situates his life in the context of contemporary Cleveland.

Criticism

William Andrews, *The Literary Career of Charles W. Chesnutt* (Baton Rouge: Louisiana State University Press, 1980).
A pioneering study of the whole of Chesnutt's literary career, including his unpublished late novels, with a focus on his racial progressivism.

Charles Duncan, *The Absent Man: The Narrative Craft of Charles W. Chesnutt* (Athens: Ohio University Press, 1998).

Examines the subtlety of Chesnutt's treatment of racial identity in his short fiction to explain his idiosyncratic and ambiguous place in American literary history.

Joseph R. McElrath Jr., ed., *Critical Essays on Charles W. Chesnutt* (New York: G. K. Hall, 1999).
A rich selection of contemporary reviews and recent scholarship, including three previously unpublished essays.

Dean McWilliams, *Charles W. Chesnutt and the Fictions of Race* (Athens: University of Georgia Press, 2002).
A study of the whole of Chesnutt's oeuvre, including his recently-published late novels, short fiction, and nonfiction. McWilliams argues the case for Chesnutt as a literary modernist in his attitude toward race.

Ryan Simmons, *Chesnutt and Realism: A Study of the Novels* (Tuscaloosa: University of Alabama Press, 2006).
Pleads the case for Chesnutt as a literary Realist, particularly in *The Marrow of Tradition,* his most autobiographical novel.

Eric J. Sundquist, *To Wake the Nations: Race in the Making of American Literature* (Cambridge, Mass.: Belknap Press of Harvard University Press, 1993).
Argues for the centrality of African American literature in the American literary tradition, rooted in the period 1830–1930, with Chesnutt one of its central figures.

Matthew Wilson, *Whiteness in the Novels of Charles W. Chesnutt* (Jackson: University Press of Mississippi, 2004).
An analysis of Chesnutt's six novels, including the three that have been recently published for the first time, and his methods in addressing issues of race for his predominantly white readers.

Henry B. Wonham, *Charles W. Chesnutt: A Study of the Short Fiction* (New York: Twayne, 1998).
A solid introduction to Chesnutt's dialect and color-line short stories.

—Kadeshia Matthews

Kate Chopin, *The Awakening*
(Chicago: Herbert S. Stone, 1899)

Katherine O'Flaherty was born on 8 February 1850, in St. Louis and grew up in a slave-owning Southern family dominated by women. Her father, an Irish-Catholic immigrant, died in a railway accident when she was five, and she spent the remainder of her childhood surrounded by her mother, grandmother, and great-grandmother, all of whom were widows. It is this unconventional lifestyle and fierce independence that scholars claim influenced her best-known and most controversial work, *The Awakening*. Published on the cusp of a new century and at the crossroads of a progressively changing nation, *The Awakening*, originally subtitled "A Solitary Soul," dealt unabashedly with marital and maternal oppression as well as infidelity to the extent that even women's-rights reformers did not quite know what to make of such female sexual freedom. Interestingly, though, Chopin's marriage to Oscar Chopin, whom she wed in 1870, in no way seemed an unhappy union, although biographers disagree as to how to characterize her marriage and her reaction to the six children she bore in the span of nine years.

Twelve years after their marriage, Oscar died of malaria, leaving Kate in charge of his cotton business in Louisiana. Shortly afterward, she sold the business, paid off their debt, and returned with her children to St. Louis. Chopin began publishing short stories in such well-known periodicals as the *Atlantic Monthly*, *Century*, and *Vogue* about the Creole culture in Louisiana that established her reputation as a local colorist. Drawing on quaint language and specific customs mined from her memories of years spent in Louisiana and summering in Grand Isle, Chopin appealed to a wide readership, as can be seen in her first story collection, *Bayou Folk* (1894), which had a guaranteed publisher and was well received. However, within this vein of Regionalist writing appear complex issues, specifically as they pertain to women's roles and needs. At the center of this emerges *The Awakening*. Following its publication and controversial reception, Chopin wrote little. Her publisher canceled her third short-story collection, *A Vocation and a Voice*, likely because of the poor sales of *The Awakening*. Chopin died in 1904 of a cerebral hemorrhage.

Upon its release on 2 April 1899, *The Awakening* was met with scathing reviews. The *St. Louis Republic* labeled the novel "poison" and "too strong a drink for moral babes." Willa Cather in the *Pittsburgh Leader* called the novel "trite and sordid," demonstrating that women, as well as men, objected to its subject. Although it was never technically banned, it was censored. The novel received almost no critical attention until scholars such as Cyrille Arnavon (who in 1953 translated the novel into French), Warner Berthoff, Larzer Ziff, Edmund Wilson, George Arms, Louis Leary, and Per Seyersted contributed to a revival of Chopin's work. Seyersted's *Kate Chopin: A Critical Biography* was published in 1969 at the beginning of the second feminist wave. From the 1970s onward *The Awakening* has attracted a great deal of critical attention. There have been four biographies of Kate Chopin, but the best is the most recent, *Unveiling Kate Chopin* (1999) by Emily Toth, which is crucial in placing the novel within its appropriate historical framework. Unlike the other biographers, Toth takes a feminist approach, depicting a more unconventional woman who flouted social expectations.

The Awakening depicts a female protagonist, Edna Pontellier, who embarks upon a journey of self-discovery while vacationing for the summer in Grand Isle. While her husband Léonce travels back and forth to New Orleans on business, Edna befriends Adèle Ratignolle (the ultimate mother-woman), Mademoiselle Reisz (an unmarried musician), and Robert Lebrun (the bachelor son of the resort owner). She learns how to swim, which unleashes a sensuality that facilitates her later affair with Alcée. Moving out of her husband's mansion, Edna establishes her own residence at the "pigeon house," where she takes up painting and manages to earn a small income. After a romantic tryst with Robert, she is called to assist Adèle in childbirth. After witnessing this "scene [of] torture," she returns home to find that Robert has left her a goodbye note. Upset and bewildered, she removes her clothes, and swims out into the Gulf of Mexico until she drowns.

TOPICS FOR DISCUSSION AND RESEARCH

1. The novel may be located at the intersection of several important literary movements, including local color, Romanticism, Realism, Naturalism, Impressionism, and modernism. Chopin's accurate portrayal of Creole culture speaks to its regional character, while the ambiguous ending, absence of a narrative point of view, and lack of linear plot point to modernism. The unifying symbol of water and use of light and color with blurred scenes conform to the tenets of Impressionism. What is even more apparent is the tension between Romanticism and Realism. The romantic elements seem obvious with references to Edna's romantic sensibility and overwrought imagination (for example, the cavalry officer, the tragedian, her reading of Emerson, and the romantic piano compositions by Mademoiselle Reisz and Adèle). Yet, there are just as many elements of Realism in the text. After Edna witnesses Adèle in childbirth, for example, she comments to Dr. Mandalet that she does not wish to "remain a dupe to illusions" for the rest of her life.

2. Chopin was greatly influenced by French writers, particularly Charles Baudelaire, Gustave Flaubert, and Guy de Maupassant, whose short stories she translated from French. The subtitle of *The Awakening*, "A Solitary Soul," is perhaps an allusion to Maupassant's "Solitude" (1895). Edna not only reads Emerson, but she also reads the Goncourt brothers. The theory of literary Naturalism is central to Chopin's message. Chopin was greatly influenced by the works of Charles Darwin and Herbert Spencer, and she appropriated their theories within a specific social context. This influence can be witnessed in a particularly potent scene where Dr. Mandalet says to Edna (regarding motherhood), "It seems to be a provision of Nature, a decoy to secure mothers for the race." In 1899 there was no reliable method of birth control, so Edna was, indeed, biologically trapped.

3. Many of the thematic elements are identified in the opening chapter. Feminist critics have been quick to associate the caged parrot in the first scene with Edna's plight as an oppressed woman who attempts to escape her "cage of domesticity." Edna does escape briefly by committing adultery and moving out of her house, but she ultimately fails. We can perhaps see the fate of such transgressive behavior in the falling bird Edna witnesses before her final swim, which recalls the myth of Icarus. When Mademoiselle Reisz feels Edna's shoulder blades, the implication is that Edna is not strong enough to maintain her flight and will plummet. Although Edna awakens to her limitations, in the process she undergoes four types of awakenings: psychological, emotional, intellectual, and sexual. All of these awakenings speak to the emerging New Woman at the fin de siècle, a figure the patri-

archal establishment excoriates. Both Adèle and Mademoiselle Reisz serve as alternative female models for Edna: whereas Adèle epitomizes the True Woman (she is covered head to toe in white throughout the narrative), Reisz signifies the emerging New Woman.

4. Nature symbols play an important role in how to read the novel. Water, as an archetypal symbol for baptism, represents both death and rebirth. It is the Gulf where Edna feels most alive and awakens to her sensuality and this same body of water contributes to her death. Such imagery becomes problematic in light of the novel's ending which concludes but does not resolve. The manner in which Chopin closes her novel deserves careful consideration. Questions students should ask are: how are we to understand Edna's final swim? Is it triumphant or an indication of defeat? If we read the final scene as redolent of Walt Whitman, then Edna's drowning is life-affirming because it points to a rebirth. Edna's steps are regressive: the water recalls the womb and Edna recollects her childhood. This scene presages Freud, whose *Studies in Hysteria* (1895; translated, 1909) and *The Interpretation of Dreams* (1900; translated, 1913) were contemporaneous with *The Awakening*. Edna's last swim could be seen as a step toward a new beginning. Conversely, we could also read the ending as indicative of self-annihilation and defeat. Along these lines, Edna's regressive behavior is a sign of arrested development, her loss of her mother at an early age contributing to her immaturity and her threatened sense of self. Students should also consider the role of race in the novel since a quadroon cares for Edna's children, but she is never given a name.

5. Although *The Awakening* is clearly concerned with female proscription, Chopin was never intimately involved with the suffragist movement and took very little interest in any organized feminist groups. What can we make of such radical feminism? One way to understand this is to note that Chopin seemed more concerned with the individual than with society and social movements. Her character's condition was not merely a female conflict, but a human one (race withstanding, obviously). Clearly, Chopin knew that marital happiness was possible. After all, she presents Adèle as happy in her mother-woman role. Yet, Edna cannot find happiness as a wife and mother or as a solitary artist, and so the conflict becomes less about the external world and more about Edna's internal self.

6. Students reading *The Awakening* for the first time are encouraged to consult Margo Culley's Norton Critical Edition (1994). Its critical apparatus will open the door to further study. *Kate Chopin's* The Awakening: *A Sourcebook,* edited by Janet Beer and Elizabeth Nolan (London & New York: Routledge, 2004), is an excellent resource tool that includes a contextual overview, contemporary documents, a critical history, illustrations, and modern criticism. Because the extensive scholarship on Chopin can be daunting, students will appreciate this condensed version of significant criticism and key passages on the text. The website of the Kate Chopin International Society (http://www.katechopin.org/society.shtml) may also be helpful to students.

RESOURCES

Primary Work

The Awakening: An Authorative Text, Biographical and Historical Contexts, Criticism, second edition, edited by Margo Culley (New York: Norton, 1994). Originally published in 1976.

Bibliography

Marlene Springer, *Edith Wharton and Kate Chopin: A Reference Guide* (Boston: G. K. Hall, 1976).
A good overview of critical work on Chopin up and through 1976. Includes both primary and secondary sources.

Suzanne Disheroon Green and David J. Caudle, *Kate Chopin: An Annotated Bibliography of Critical Works* (Westport, Conn.: Greenwood Press, 1999).
An excellent book that is clearly organized and provides annotations for Chopin scholarship between 1979 and 1999. It also includes two biblio-critical essays and a critical introduction by Emily Toth.

Biography

Per Seyersted, *Kate Chopin: A Critical Biography* (Baton Rouge: Louisiana State University Press, 1980).
A useful analysis with a checklist of archival sources. Seyersted presents a less radical Chopin than does Toth.

Emily Toth, *Kate Chopin* (New York: Morrow, 1990).
Thorough depiction of Chopin's early and latter years. Toth asserts that *The Awakening* accurately depicts a feminist consciousness during the late nineteenth century.

Toth, *Unveiling Kate Chopin* (Jackson: University Press of Mississippi, 1999).
Explores Chopin's life as a daughter, mother, and wife whose unconventional ways reveal a vastly different person from the one portrayed by Seyersted. Although there is no documented proof, Toth makes a strong case that the widowed Chopin had an affair with a married man who likely was the model for Alcée.

Criticism

George Arms, "Kate Chopin's *The Awakening* in the Perspective of Her Literary Career," in *Essays on American Literature in Honor of Jay B. Hubbell,* edited by Clarence Gohdes (Durham, N.C.: Duke University Press, 1967), pp. 215–228.
Pioneering essay, published two years before Seyersted's biography, that explores Chopin's many literary achievements. Although the essay does not delve into Chopin's personal life, this groundbreaking work paved the way for later Chopin studies.

Phillip Barrish, "*The Awakening*'s Signifying 'Mexicanist' Presence," *Studies in American Fiction*, 28 (Spring 2000): 65–76.
A much overdue analysis of the role of ethnicity in Chopin's novel, specifically as it pertains to the construction of gender and identity.

Nicole Camastra, "Venerable Sonority in Kate Chopin's *The Awakening*," *American Literary Realism*, 40 (Winter 2008): 154–166.
A provocative discussion that examines the composer Frédéric Chopin's influence on Kate Chopin's novel and the romantic elements that resonate.

Lewis Leary, "Kate Chopin and Walt Whitman," *Walt Whitman Review*, 16 (December 1970): 120–121.
Examines Walt Whitman's influence on Chopin, particularly "Song of Myself" and "Out of the Cradle Endlessly Rocking."

Ryu-Chung Eun, "The Negro as a Serious Subject in Kate Chopin's Fiction," *Journal of English Language and Literature*, 36 (1990): 659–678.
Argues that Chopin's dispassionate treatment of race reveals a great sensitivity to the topic and allows for a realistic depiction of Creole culture.

—Cindy Murillo

Kate Chopin, "Desirée's Baby"

Vogue (4 January 1893); collected in *Bayou Folk* (Boston: Houghton, Mifflin, 1894)

Kate Chopin, born Katherine O'Flaherty to Thomas O'Flaherty and Eliza Faris in 1850, was immensely popular during the thirteen years she published fiction. Best known today for her novel *The Awakening*, she began publishing in 1889 as a poet and author of short stories. Forced to support her family by her pen after her husband's sudden death, Chopin, like many other women writers of the period, published in popular magazines, including the *Atlantic Monthly* and *Vogue*. Her first novel, *At Fault* (1890), sold well, but her short stories and later collections of these stories, *Bayou Folk* (1894) and *A Night in Acadie* (1897), boosted her popularity. In her fiction, Chopin continually challenged the limits of what publishers would accept, and she never hesitated to discuss controversial issues such as unhappy marriages ("The Story of an Hour"), miscegenation ("Desirée's Baby"), and adultery ("The Storm"). Though she was successful for many years, the publication of *The Awakening* (1899) offended many readers and her popularity suffered as a result. After her death at fifty-four, her works lapsed from print. Not until the 1950s did scholars begin to reexamine Chopin's works, and by 1970 her critical recovery was complete.

Chopin's story "Desirée's Baby" was one of her most popular works prior to the publication of *The Awakening*. Heavily influenced by Guy de Maupassant, considered by many to be a master of the short story and known for his intense and sometimes snap endings, "Desirée's Baby" has an intricate plot and surprising denouement. Though Chopin does not use real names, places, or events, the story is plausible in every way.

Set on the bayou plantation L'Abri, "Desirée's Baby" gives readers a look into the lives of the newly married Desirée Valmondé, a foundling child, and her slave-holding husband, Armand Aubigny. Desirée is the adopted child of the Valmondés and is of unknown lineage; still, Armand is content to extend his family name to Desirée. Desirée soon gives birth to a son. Armand, who has always been a harsh master to his slaves, becomes gentler and calmer in his behavior toward them. But the bliss Armand and Desirée experience ends when the baby's skin begins to darken. Initially, Desirée says nothing about it, knowing it is an indication that the baby may not be purely white. Once Armand raises the question of the baby's race, however, he becomes cold toward Desirée and finally banishes his wife and child from their home, placing the blame on Desirée for their child's racially mixed appearance. Desirée's adoptive mother offers to take her back, but Desirée disappears into the bayou with her son. The story ends with Armand, who has again begun to treat his slaves harshly, burning everything that reminds him of Desirée and the baby in an attempt to erase all trace of them from his life. In the final moments of the story, however, he finds a letter from his mother that reveals he is a mixed-race child.

Students studying Kate Chopin should read her biographical sketches, as Chopin put much of her own life into her works, but also should be aware that Chopin's life and writings sometimes work in opposition to one another: Chopin grew up on a plantation with slaves, yet she inveighed against slavery; happily married, she wrote stories about troubled marriages. Current critical reception of her works will also be helpful in illuminating her writings.

TOPICS FOR DISCUSSION AND RESEARCH

1. A riveting and shocking story, especially for its time, "Desirée's Baby" addresses topics that were controversial, including miscegenation, patriarchal marriage, and racial bias. Especially for readers unfamiliar with customs and standards in the Old or New South, it was provocative, heart wrenching, and a sharp indictment of social hypocrisy. It treats several hot-button issues for students to question and research, particularly miscegenation. The antebellum Louisiana setting allows Chopin to discuss the sexual exploitation of slave women, a closely related subject students may also choose to investigate. Students interested in this topic should especially look in the story to the character of the slave woman La Blanche, whose name means "white woman." Further, students should question just how La Blanche's son came to be described as a "little quadroon boy" by exploring the possibility of a forced or coercive relationship between Armand and La Blanche, an unfortunate but common occurrence at the time.

2. Another topic for students to research is the role of women in the story, in particular that of Armand's mother, whose letter her son chances to read. What does the letter reveal? In addition to information about Armand's ancestry, what attitude does it reveal about misogyny and the authority of women? Chopin also questions the recklessness of judging someone for a lack

of family history: Desirée may have an unknown background, but she is not the one whose background is mixed. Armand ironically passes for white. How common in American literature was the plot of racial "passing" at the time "Desirée's Baby" was published? How were such stories as "Desirée's Baby" and Mark Twain's *Pudd'nhead Wilson* received by contemporary reviewers?

3. Chopin presents the marriage of Desirée and Armand as initially blissful, which is an unusual depiction of marriage in her works. Why is their happiness short-lived? Because Armand believes it is Desirée's "fault" their baby is racially mixed, she takes the baby and disappears. What alternatives were available to her? Desirée's biracial baby must have been fathered by a slave, or so the skewed logic of the period would insist. What other explanations are possible? After her disappearance, Armand reverts to his old abusive ways. Is Armand personally responsible for his misbehavior, or does Chopin condemn patriarchal marriage as an institution and/or a society that would condone such misbehavior?

RESOURCES

Primary Work
Per Seyersted, ed., *The Complete Works of Kate Chopin* (Baton Rouge: Louisiana State University Press, 2006).
Compiles virtually all of Chopin's writings and includes biographical and bibliographical data.

Bibliography
Heather Kirk Thomas, "Kate Chopin: A Primary Bibliography, Alphabetically Arranged," *American Literary Realism,* 28 (Winter 1996): 71–88.
Includes all of Chopin's writings, excluding personal correspondence.

Suzanne Disheroon Green and David J. Caudle, *Kate Chopin: An Annotated Bibliography of Critical Works* (Westport, Conn.: Greenwood Press, 1999).
A comprehensive bibliography of scholarly publications about Chopin and her works from 1976 to 1997, with introductory essays by Green, Caudle, and Emily Toth.

Biography
Emily Toth, *Kate Chopin* (New York: Morrow, 1990).
An authoritative chronicle of Chopin's life based on all documents available at the time.

Toth, *Unveiling Kate Chopin* (Jackson: University Press of Mississippi, 1999).
A more intimate portrait of Chopin based on recently discovered diaries and manuscripts.

Toth and Per Seyersted, eds., *Kate Chopin's Private Papers* (Bloomington: Indiana University Press, 1998).
Offers a chronology of Chopin's life, her private correspondence, her diary, and a scholarly bibliography and list of Chopin's complete writings.

Criticism

Annetta M. F. Kelley, "French Cherries on Cordon Bleu Cakes: Kate Chopin's Usage of Her Second Language," *Louisiana History*, 34 (Summer 1993). 345–356.

Discusses Chopin's use of French phrases and their relevance to her characterizations.

—Jennifer Nader

Stephen Crane, *The Red Badge of Courage*

(New York: Appleton, 1895)

Stephen Crane (1871–1900) was an unconventional and prolific writer whose life was unsettled and tragically short. The fourteenth child of a Methodist minister who died when Crane was eight, he attended two different colleges before finally leaving school for good to pursue work as a journalist and a writer. He paid for the publication in 1893 of his first novel, *Maggie: A Girl of the Streets,* an unsparing tale of a young woman trapped in prostitution. While the work was not widely read, it attracted the attention of other prominent authors, most notably W. D. Howells and Hamlin Garland, who recognized Crane's talent, even while they expressed reservations about his subject. After reading old copies of *Century* magazine containing its acclaimed 1880s series on the Civil War, Crane began work on *The Red Badge of Courage* in 1893 while continuing to pursue journalism and to write "lines," as he referred to his poems. A shortened version of the novel first appeared in syndication newspapers in 1894. His first book of poetry, *The Black Riders,* was published in 1895, followed later that year by *The Red Badge of Courage.* The book was a critical and popular success, and it established its young author as a literary force and a reluctant celebrity. Crane wrote three more novels during his short career: *George's Mother* (1896), *The Third Violet* (1897), and *Active Service* (1899). He was at work on a fourth novel, *The O'Ruddy* (1903), when he died of tuberculosis. Along with a prodigious amount of journalism, he completed another collection of poetry, *War Is Kind* (1899), and five collections of short stories. He also served as a war correspondent in Greece and Cuba. Despite numerous personal adventures and controversies, Crane was forever identified with his first tale of a young man under fire, *The Red Badge of Courage.*

Crane's novel tells the story of Henry Fleming, a private in the Union army who volunteers in anticipation of heroic scenes of battle and valor. After a long winter in camp, his ardor has cooled, and, as rumors circulate that his regiment will soon be engaging the enemy, he begins to question his courage and grapple with his fear that he will run in the face of the enemy. When finally put to the test, he withstands the first assault but, upon a second charge, his nerve fails him and he runs. What follows is a nightmarish journey behind the lines punctuated by several significant episodes. The first comes as Fleming seeks solace in the quiet of nature, seeking both relief and, in the fleeing of a squirrel from a pinecone he flings, justification for his actions. His hopes for solace are dashed when, upon entering a "chapel" of tree boughs, he is confronted by the corpse of a Union soldier. He later falls in with a group of injured soldiers leaving the battle; there he is reunited with his friend Jim Conklin, who has been seriously injured. Fleming and another soldier, "the tattered man," follow Conklin as he walks off into the woods with single-minded determination before finally succumbing to his injuries. As the tattered man, who continually queries Fleming about his nonexistent injury, begins to fail as well, Fleming leaves the man wandering pathetically in an empty field. After he is struck on the head with a rifle butt by another fleeing soldier, he is finally led back to his regiment by a "cheery man" whom he never sees. While he had feared becoming a "slang phrase" for his cowardice, his fellow soldiers accept his explanation for his absence, and after being nursed by a fellow soldier he returns to the front where he displays an unconscious, animalistic fury in battle, eventually seizing the enemy's colors and winning the attention of his commanding officers. Save for a final pang of guilt for the wounded soldier he abandoned, Fleming leaves the field smiling, pleased with his actions and content in his belief that "he was a man."

At the time of its publication, Crane's readers could have read two different versions of *The Red Badge of Courage:* the shortened newspaper publication of 1894 or the Appleton book publication of 1895. A third version became available when a facsimile of the manuscript was published in 1972, including a great deal of deleted material. Much critical debate ensued, with supporters of the new edition, most prominently Hershel Parker, arguing that the manuscript was more true to Crane's intentions, his published work being compromised by his financial necessity and an intrusive and cautious editor. Opponents argued that the evidence for editorial meddling was circumstantial and that, since Crane had approved of the novel at its publication, the Appleton text should be read as authoritative. (See James Colvert, "Crane, Hitchcock, and the Binder Edition of *The Red Badge of Courage,*" in *Critical Essays on* The Red Badge of Courage, edited by Donald Pizer [1990]). Despite an energetic debate, the manuscript version (known as the "Binder Edition," for its editor) does not seem to have gained acceptance. More recently, the newspaper publication has gained increased attention, including a careful study by Charles Johanningsmeier in *American Literary Realism* (2008).

TOPICS FOR DISCUSSION AND RESEARCH

1. Criticism of *The Red Badge of Courage* has inevitably centered on the question of how readers are to make sense of Henry Fleming's experience and his final assessment of his actions. Has war truly made him a man, or is this another example of the same naive misapprehension that led him to enlist in the first place? One of Crane's earliest biographers, Robert W. Stallman, argues that Henry Fleming's is a story of Christian redemption, noting the religious symbolism of Jim Conklin's death, most significantly a much-discussed image that

ends chapter 9: "The red sun was pasted in the sky like a wafer." For Stallman, this is a sacramental image, and Fleming is saved through the death of J. C. Other critics, while uneasy with elements of Stallman's religious readings, have nevertheless embraced the notion that Fleming emerges strengthened and transformed by his ordeal. In what some term the "literal" reading, Fleming's assessment of his manhood is taken as accurate, his earlier misunderstandings and bravado replaced with self-assurance. He has passed through a kind of initiation ritual into manhood.

2. Those who see irony in Fleming's assessment of his manhood point out that he has been repeatedly mistaken in his assessments of events throughout the novel. He is inordinately swayed by what he sees, and, as with the squirrel who flees his pinecone, he has a mind that rationalizes his behavior and throws it into the best light. Even when contemplating his desertion of the dying tattered soldier, "gradually he mustered force to put the sin at a distance." Moreover, his bravery, like his flight, seems to be the product more of instinct than deliberate courage. While the majority of recent critics seem to have adopted the ironic reading of Fleming's views of his manhood, the debate persists.

3. Related to these questions is the novel's relation to Naturalism, a movement in literature commonly associated with European authors Émile Zola and Leo Tolstoy, whose war novel *Sebastopol* (1856; translated, 1888) is cited as an inspiration for *The Red Badge of Courage*. In the commonly understood definition of Naturalism, human events are seen as insignificant in the face of an uncaring, often destructive, natural world. Proponents of reading the novel in terms of Naturalism cite Fleming's confrontation with the corpse in the "chapel" of trees as one of many examples that demonstrate how Crane eschews a more Romantic view of nature. One of the earliest critics to offer this view is Charles C. Walcutt in *American Literary Naturalism, a Divided Stream* (1956). More recently, in a tribute to Donald Pizer, James Nagel has argued that reading the text solely in terms of Naturalism tends to reduce rather than enlarge our understanding and appreciation of the novel ("Donald Pizer, American Naturalism, and Stephen Crane" [2006]).

4. Given the paucity of formal names, the absence of any discussions of ideology or causes for conflict, *The Red Badge of Courage* has been seen by some as less a historical novel than a meditation on war in general and the human psyche. However, the historical accuracy of Crane's depiction of battle has long been a topic of discussion. In 1963 Harold R. Hungerford first documented the historic parallels between the novel and the battle of Chancellorsville. More recently, Perry Lentz has argued in a book-length study that Crane conducted much more research than has generally been acknowledged (*Private Fleming at Chancellorsville:* The Red Badge of Courage *and the Civil War* [2006]). In addition to reading *Century* magazine, Lentz asserts, Crane likely read the expanded versions of these articles in the four-volume collection *Battles and Leaders of the Civil War* and may even have read the official government report on Chancellorsville. While much of Lentz's argument regarding Crane's

sources is conjectural, he is meticulous in pointing out the accuracy of Crane's description of the battle and martial details of the story.

5. Other critics, notably Amy Kaplan, have read the novel more for what it suggests about the 1890s than for its depiction of the 1860s. For Kaplan, the novel is caught up in a rhetoric regarding "strenuous" action and masculinity and a culture that emphasizes spectacle as a means of representing conflict (Norton Critical Edition, third edition, pp. 269–294). More recently, Andrew Lawson has argued that the novel needs to be read in the context of the economic upheaval of the late nineteenth century ("The Red Badge of Class: Stephen Crane and the Industrial Army" [2005]). While Lawson's reading is suggestive and points toward the kind of creative work that can still be done in considering the context of the novel's creation, a great deal of critical attention continues to be paid to the accuracy of Crane's portrayal of war and to questions of theme.

RESOURCES

Primary Works

The Red Badge of Courage: A Facsimile Edition of the Manuscript, two volumes, edited by Fredson Bowers (Washington, D.C.: NCR/Microcard Editions, 1972, 1973).
Includes material deleted from the 1895 edition of the novel.

The Red Badge of Courage: An Authoritative Text, Backgrounds and Sources, Criticism, edited by Donald Pizer, third edition (New York & London: Norton, 1994).
A critical edition of the text, with bibliographies and critical essays.

Bibliography

Patrick K. Dooley, *Stephen Crane: An Annotated Bibliography of Secondary Scholarship* (New York: G. K. Hall, 1992).
An informative guide to scholarship on Crane and his works, including relevant biographies, through 1991.

Donald Pizer, "Crane and *The Red Badge of Courage:* A Guide to Criticism," in *The Red Badge of Courage: An Authoritative Text, Backgrounds and Sources, Criticism,* edited by Pizer, third edition (New York: Norton, 1994), pp. 120–145.
A thorough and readable survey of major works of criticism and central areas of scholarly debate through 1992.

Biography

John Berryman, *Stephen Crane: A Critical Biography,* revised edition (New York: Cooper Square, 2001).
First published in 1950, when Crane was reentering the American literary canon. Critics have taken exception to some of Berryman's psychoanalytic interpretations, as he concedes.

Robert W. Stallman, *Stephen Crane: A Biography* (New York: Braziller, 1968). One of the earliest biographies of Crane. Stallman argues for a religious interpretation of *The Red Badge of Courage.*

Criticism

Charles Johanningsmeier, "The 1894 Syndicated Newspaper Appearances of *The Red Badge of Courage,*" American Literary Realism, 40 (Spring 2008): 226–247.

Andrew Lawson, "The Red Badge of Class: Stephen Crane and the Industrial Army," *Literature and History,* 14 (October 2005): 53–68.

Perry Lentz, *Private Fleming at Chancellorsville:* The Red Badge of Courage *and the Civil War* (Columbia: University of Missouri Press, 2006).

James Nagel, "Donald Pizer, American Naturalism, and Stephen Crane," *Studies in American Naturalism,* 1, no. 2 (2006): 30–35.

Donald Pizer, ed., *Critical Essays on* The Red Badge of Courage (Boston: G. K. Hall, 1990).

Charles C. Walcutt, *American Literary Naturalism, a Divided Stream* (Minneapolis: University of Minnesota Press, 1956). Includes the chapter "Stephen Crane: Naturalist and Impressionist."

Stanley Wertheim and Paul Sorrentino, *The Crane Log: A Documentary Life of Stephen Crane, 1871–1900* (New York: G. K. Hall, 1994). A detailed retelling of Crane's life that has become a frequently referenced source of biographical information.

Linda H. Davis, *Badge of Courage: The Life of Stephen Crane* (Boston: Houghton Mifflin, 1998). An engaging and accessible retelling of Crane's life.

—Martin T. Buinicki

Stephen Crane, "The Open Boat"

Scribner's, 21 (June 1897): 728–740; collected in *The Open Boat and Other Tales of Adventure* (New York: Doubleday & McClure, 1898)

Stephen Crane (1871–1900) established his reputation as one of the foremost novelists of his day with the publication of *The Red Badge of Courage* (1895), but his diverse literary output also included tales, sketches, poetry, and journalism. He began writing professionally as a newspaper reporter in his native New Jersey while still in his teens. Crane subsequently attended Lafayette College in Pennsylvania and then Syracuse University where, in 1891, he began drafting an early version of his first novel, *Maggie: A Girl of the Streets,* which he had privately printed in 1893. Living in New York, he completed *The Red Badge of Courage,* which he published to wide acclaim. A subsequent collection of short stories, *The Little Regiment and Other Episodes of the American Civil War* (1896), reinforced Crane's reputation as a writer of war tales. In late 1896, Irving Bacheller, who headed a newspaper syndicate, hired Crane to visit Cuba and report on the Cuban insurrection. "The Open Boat," which many readers consider Crane's finest short story, resulted from his disastrous attempt to reach Cuba.

In late November 1896 Crane found himself in Jacksonville, Florida, with many other journalists searching for a way to reach Cuba. Finally, on New Year's Eve, Crane sailed aboard the *Commodore*, which was loaded with supplies and ammunition for the Cuban insurgents. Sailing in a dense fog, the *Commodore* struck a sandbar less than two miles offshore. After several hours, a revenue cutter towed the *Commodore* off the sandbar and sent it on its way. The night of January 1, 1897, a leak developed, the mechanical pumps proved defective, and the sailors resorted to buckets and handpumps, which were no match for the sea. As the *Commodore* sank, the men took to lifeboats and improvised rafts. Several perished in the effort. Captain Edward Murphy, William Higgins, Charles B. Montgomery, and Crane were the last to abandon ship. The four took the dinghy, a ten-foot open boat. On Saturday morning, January 2, the dinghy neared the coast of Florida, but the men could not summon help from shore. Captain Murphy decided to wait until morning before attempting to beach the dinghy in the heavy surf. The men rowed all night to keep the craft outside the breakers. On Sunday morning, January 3, they attempted to land the dinghy, but it overturned. Crane, Montgomery, and Murphy survived, but Higgins perished.

Crane initially wrote up their perilous experience as a newspaper report, "Stephen Crane's Own Story." Relating his personal account, Crane had little choice but to tell it in the first person, but in "Stephen Crane's Own Story" he seems reluctant to accept the first person. The report begins by describing the appearance of the *Commodore* at the dock in Jacksonville prior to its departure. Though Crane would sail aboard the vessel, it is unclear over the course of the first several paragraphs whether he is aboard or simply reporting its departure from shore. Not until the *Commodore* pulls away from the dock and blasts its whistle does it become clear that Crane is a passenger headed to sea. Though "Stephen Crane's Own Story" is factual, it is a carefully shaped account that makes use of different literary devices and narrative techniques.

Crane knew that his story of survival gave him the stuff for a fine short story, and he later recast his adventure as "The Open Boat." Significantly, he changed the narrative point of view in the transfer from truth to fiction. The first person of "Stephen Crane's Own Story" gives way to an omniscient, third-person narrative, and "The Open Boat" begins after the ship has foundered and the survivors have escaped in the lifeboat. Though "Stephen Crane's Own Story" begins with an obvious reluctance to admit point of view, "The Open Boat" flaunts its third-person, omniscient narrator from its famous opening sentence: "None of them knew the color of the sky."

"The Open Boat" offers many opportunities for study. Since Stanley Wertheim and Paul Sorrentino exposed Thomas Beer's 1923 biography of Crane as a fraud in 1990, Crane studies have burst open. So much earlier scholarship and criticism was based on Beer's fraudulent information that previous work must be scrutinized and, in many cases, scrapped entirely. Christopher Benfry's biography, the first since Beer was discredited, makes a good start. The finest biographical work is a documentary biography, not a narrative one. *The Crane Log,* edited by Wertheim and Sorrentino, contains the fullest gathering of facts available about Crane's life and work. For further critical studies, see the secondary bibliographies by Patrick K. Dooley and R. W. Stallman.

TOPICS FOR DISCUSSION AND RESEARCH

1. Readers can approach "The Open Boat" in many ways. A historical approach can help put the work in context. Warner's essay is the best place to go for understanding the Cuban insurrection and American attitudes toward it. Elizabeth Friedmann's 1987 discovery of the wreck of the *Commodore* confirms much of Crane's physical detail. George Monteiro's article, a model of its kind, situates "The Open Boat" within the context of contemporary popular literature.

2. Similar studies could enhance the appreciation of "The Open Boat" significantly. This short story can also be appreciated in terms of its literary style. Crane has alternatively been labeled a Realist, a Naturalist, and an Impressionist. P. Adams identifies Naturalist elements in the story. Charles R. Metzger demonstrates Crane's use of Realist techniques. Stefanie Bates-Eye takes a different look at its style, identifying its affinity with Crane's journalism.

3. With "The Open Boat" Crane anticipated techniques that would be developed by the New Journalists of the 1960s and 1970s. Crane's sophisticated use of narrative point of view offers many opportunities for study. Kevin J. Hayes compares the point of view in this story with that in other Crane stories. James Nagel provides the fullest treatment of the subject. Sura P. Rath and Mary Neff Shaw apply the critical theory of Mikhail Bakhtin to look at how Crane's third-person narrative incorporates multiple voices.

4. "The Open Boat" also lends itself to different philosophical approaches. Oliver Billingslea and Christopher Metress situate the story in terms of epistemology. Peter Buitenhuis examines its ties to existentialism. Ideas that Buitenhuis suggests briefly in his notes, such as the comparison between Crane and Albert Camus, deserve to be elaborated. Others, including Rath and Shaw, regard the story as an expression of Darwinism.

RESOURCES

Bibliography

Patrick K. Dooley, *Stephen Crane: An Annotated Bibliography of Secondary Scholarship* (New York: G. K. Hall, 1992).

Divided into sections treating biography, general criticism, and criticism focused on individual works or groups of works. Supplement Dooley with reference to the periodical bibliographies in *Stephen Crane Studies* (1992).

R. W. Stallman, *Stephen Crane: A Critical Bibliography* (Ames: Iowa State University Press, 1972).
While superseded by Dooley's list of modern criticism of "The Open Boat," still useful for its list of reviews of *The Open Boat and Other Tales of Adventure*.

Biography

Christopher Benfey, *The Double Life of Stephen Crane* (New York: Knopf, 1992).
This thesis-driven study elaborates Willa Cather's idea that Crane lived a double life, first writing about subjects that interested him and then attempting to live what he had written.

Stanley Wertheim and Paul Sorrentino, *The Crane Log: A Documentary Life of Stephen Crane, 1871–1900* (New York: G. K. Hall, 1994).
Excerpts of Crane's writing, contemporary reviews, letters, and diary entries from friends and family, newspaper articles, and photographs.

Criticism

P. Adams, "Naturalistic Fiction: 'The Open Boat,'" *Tulane Studies in English,* 4 (1954): 137–146.
Finds that Crane applies the basic tenets of Naturalism inconsistently.

Stefanie Bates-Eye, "Fact, Not Fiction: Questioning Our Assumption about Crane's 'The Open Boat,'" *Studies in Short Fiction,* 35 (Winter 1998): 65–76.
Suggests parallels between "The Open Boat" and New Journalism, claiming that it deserves consideration as a factual report.

Sharon Begley, "Found: Crane's 'Open Boat,'" *Newsweek,* 5 (January 1987): 52.
Reports Elizabeth Friedman's discovery of the wreck of the *Commodore*.

Oliver Billingslea, "Why Did the Oiler Drown?: Perception and Cosmic Chill in 'The Open Boat,'" *American Literary Realism,* 27 (Fall 1994): 23–41.
Combining literary and philosophical approaches, uses Crane's literary Impressionism as a springboard to show how Crane plays with the meaning of perception in the story.

Peter Buitenhuis, "The Essentials of Life: 'The Open Boat' as Existentialist Fiction," *Modern Fiction Studies,* 3 (1959): 243–250.
Identifies how the story anticipates many of the central tenets of existentialism.

Kevin J. Hayes, *Stephen Crane* (Tavistock, Northumberland: Northcote House in association with the British Council, 2004).
A general survey of Crane's career, which includes a chapter on Crane's use of point of view in his short fiction.

Christopher Metress, "From Indifference to Anxiety: Knowledge and the Reader in 'The Open Boat,'" *Studies in Short Fiction,* 28 (Winter 1991): 47–53.

Charles R. Metzger, "Realistic Devices in Stephen Crane's 'The Open Boat,'" *Midwest Quarterly,* 4, no. 4 (1962): 47–54.
Analyzes Crane's use of description and irony to show how the story exemplifies the practice of literary Realism.

George Monteiro, "The Logic beneath 'The Open Boat,'" *Georgia Review,* 26 (Fall 1972): 326–335.
Identifies some new sources for Crane's story, showing how they clarify his depiction of human behavior.

James Nagel, "The Narrative Method of 'The Open Boat,'" *Revue des Langues Vivantes,* 39 (1973): 409–417.
Demonstrates Crane's sophisticated use of perspective to portray shifting attitudes toward nature.

Sura P. Rath and Mary Neff Shaw, "The Dialogic Narrative of 'The Open Boat,'" *College Literature,* 18 (June 1991): 94–106.
Applies Mikhail Bakhtin's notion of dialogic heteroglossia to show how Crane's narrator articulates multiple perspectives.

Robin O. Warren, "The Cuban Insurrection and Northeast Florida in 'Stephen Crane's Own Story' and 'The Open Boat,'" *Stephen Crane Studies,* 8 (Spring 1999): 8–19.
Presents a finely detailed description of the historical, political, and cultural background of the insurrection as it pertains to Crane's writings.

Stanley Wertheim and Paul Sorrentino, "Thomas Beer: The Clay Feet of Stephen Crane Biography," *American Literary Realism,* 22 (Spring 1990): 2–16.
Reveals that Beer fabricated facts about Crane's life and even invented Crane letters.

—*Kevin J. Hayes*

Emily Dickinson, *Poems*

3 volumes, edited by Thomas H. Johnson
(Cambridge, Mass.: Harvard University Press, 1955)

Though only ten of her poems were published during her life, Emily Dickinson (1830–1886) has emerged as one of the most prolific and original poets of the nineteenth century. Born in Amherst, Massachusetts, at a time when religious revivals were sweeping New England and into a culture where young, educated women of her upper-middle-class background were expected to marry and have children, Dickinson rejected the structures of both church and marriage to devote her life to writing. She composed more than eighteen hundred poems, some of which she copied into homemade manuscript books (also known as her "fascicles"), some of which she sent to her many correspondents, and some of which she wrote on loose sheets of paper and household scraps.

Emily Elizabeth Dickinson was the second child of Edward and Emily Dickinson, a couple with strong ties to the Amherst community in which they lived and to the Puritan tradition from which her father descended. Dickinson, who had an older brother, Austin, and a younger sister, Lavinia, maintained a fierce loyalty to her family, only leaving Amherst on short trips (the longest of which was a year and a half spent at Mount Holyoke Female Seminary) and living in the Dickinson homestead until her death. Regardless of what seems a provincial and cloistered existence (it is rumored that she rarely left the house during her last twenty years, sometimes even refusing to leave her room when visitors called), Dickinson fostered friendships with many people, including public figures such as Samuel Bowles, the editor of the *Springfield Republican,* and Thomas Wentworth Higginson, an influential literary man and reformer.

While biographies of Dickinson often mark her correspondence with Higginson after his 1862 article "Letter to a Young Contributor" appeared in the *Atlantic* as the moment when Dickinson took herself seriously as a poet, she had been writing for many years and had found conversation about that writing with her closest friend and sister-in-law, Susan Dickinson. She also sent poems in letters to many of her regular correspondents, including her cousins Frances and Louisa Norcross and family friends Josiah and Elizabeth Holland, displaying quite publicly the fact that she was a writer. When asked by Higginson which writers she best liked to read, she answered: "For Poets—I have Keats—and Mr and Mrs Browning. For Prose—Mr Ruskin—Sir Thomas Browne—and the Revelations." While these authors might have been Dickinson's favorites, she read much more widely than this short list reflects—in her letters she refers to works by, among others, William Shakespeare, William Wordsworth, Ralph Waldo Emerson, Alfred Tennyson, Henry Wadsworth Longfellow, and the Bible—and could quote lines from poems and novels from memory.

When Dickinson died in 1886, Lavinia burned her sister's correspondence (as Dickinson had instructed her to do); but when she came upon the box containing her poems, she took the opposite tack and sought to have them printed. After first giving them to Susan, and then becoming restless with her slow pace on the project, she turned to Mabel Loomis Todd, a young woman who, despite never having met Dickinson, was connected to the literary community. Todd and Higginson edited *Poems,* which was published just in time for the Christmas holiday in 1890. Although this book was met with mixed reviews, Todd and Higginson produced two more editions of *Poems* in 1891 and 1896, and Todd edited the first edition of Dickinson's *Letters* in 1894.

Dickinson's poems had many editions over the first half of the twentieth century, but not until 1955, when Thomas H. Johnson compiled *The Complete Poems of Emily Dickinson,* were they all printed together. Further research has challenged previous editors' transcriptions and analyses of her writing. Most recently, Ralph Franklin edited a three-volume variorum, *The Poems of Emily Dickinson* (1998), which most scholars regard as the most comprehensive edition of Dickinson's poems.

TOPICS FOR DISCUSSION AND RESEARCH

1. The 1890, 1891, and 1896 collections of Dickinson's poems separated them into four thematic categories: "life," "love," "nature," and "time and eternity." It can be interesting for students to look at the poems included in these categories and to think about why her early editors put them there. For example, how do we know a Dickinson poem is about love? How, exactly, does Dickinson define "Eternity"? Does the accumulation of poems in the "Life" section actually project some philosophy on living? While it is true that many of Dickinson's poems can be made to fit under these very general headings, her poems also defy simple attempts at categorization. For instance, while some read "After great pain, a formal feeling comes—" as a poem about heartbreak, others read it as a poem about religious crisis. Some read the final line as a description of dying, while others read it as a release back into life. Because Dickinson often leaves out the main topic or subject of her poems, the question of what a poem is "about" is often hard to answer. For this reason, identifying poems that fit into more than one category or those that avoid categorization altogether can be a fruitful exercise.

2. One way to study Dickinson's often dense and confusing poems is to start with those that take their readers on a journey. "I started Early—Took my Dog—" is a poem that, in many ways, tells a very simple story: the "I" starts early, takes her dog, and visits the sea. We hear what happens when she gets there, who greets her, and how the "Tide" acts when she approaches. Then, when she turns from the tide, we learn that it follows her to the town, at which point it goes back to where it came from. Because we can follow the speaker of the poem on her journey to the sea and back, the poem is accessible to even the novice reader. What other poems provide visual roadmaps? What is the significance of having this kind of guide through a Dickinson poem? Where do these journeys often lead the reader? Once comfortable with the parameters of Dickinson's journeys students are more likely to see that embedded in these simple stories are more complicated ones. In the case of "I started Early—Took my Dog—," students might come to wonder about the seduction story present here or the one about the country versus city. What other complications lurk within Dickinson's seemingly most simple poems?

3. Once comfortable with the mappable poems, students can move onto the slightly more complicated fractured journey poems, such as "Because I could not stop for Death—." Who are the figures on this journey? What are they doing in the same carriage? Where do they go and why do they go there? It quickly becomes clear to any reader that this poem is not a depiction of a simple carriage ride, but is the narration of how the speaker is grappling with her memory of how both space and time were ordered in her own death scene. How does Dickinson move from what seems like a simple declaration about the situation of the "I" in the present to this complicated reflection on death, eternity, and time?

4. While some poems begin and end a journey ("I started Early—Took my Dog—") and others begin and disrupt a journey ("Because I could not stop for Death—"), still other poems have no stake at all in the movement a jour-

ney requires. Instead, many of Dickinson's poems capture the still moment of looking and hearing. "There's a certain Slant of light," for example, situates its reader at a certain time of day (afternoon) and at a certain time of year (winter), a moment when that "certain slant of light" can be both seen and felt. Each reader imagines some kind of light, and the poem evokes this light without revealing anything about it. What are the different senses that Dickinson employs to describe this light? If this light leaves "no scar" and is unteachable, what is Dickinson doing writing a poem about it? Is there any narrative to follow in this poem?

5. One might say that the complicated nature of the light that Dickinson is describing demands a complicated explanation, and this would hold true for many of her poems. Whether she is describing watching a bird ("A Bird came down the Walk—"), imagining the specific sound a fly makes ("I heard a Fly buzz—when I died"), or describing her life in metaphorical terms ("My Life had stood—a Loaded Gun—"), Dickinson finds some unexpected and startling ways of describing her experience in language so rich and with turns so abrupt. While most of her poems are written in short alternating lines of iambic tetrameter and iambic trimeter, their rhyme schemes are almost always a-b-c-b, she rarely includes a title, and she breaks with standard uses of punctuation (including, most dramatically, unconventional capitalizations and dashes); no two Dickinson poems work exactly the same way. In order to see this, students can take two poems that are ostensibly about the same thing and note all of the different formal tactics that Dickinson uses to render them unique.

6. Because many of Dickinson's manuscripts are accessible, there are also several approaches that looking at the materials themselves makes available to students. For instance, look at the manuscripts that Franklin reproduces in *The Manuscript Books of Emily Dickinson* (1989) or online at the *Dickinson Electronic Archives* (<www.emilydickinson.org> [accessed 25 August 2009]), and grapple with the variant words and phrases that Dickinson often copied at the bottom of her poems, analyze the different choices that her editors have made when publishing her poems, and look at drafts of the same poem that Dickinson made sometimes years apart. This allows students to engage in the collaborative endeavor that is Dickinson scholarship and to see that no authoritative edition or reading of her poems can exist.

RESOURCES

Primary Work

Open Me Carefully: Emily Dickinson's Intimate Letters to Susan Huntington Dickinson, edited by Ellen Louise Hart and Martha Nell Smith (Ashfield, Mass.: Paris, 1998).

Presents the correspondence (letters, poems, and what Hart and Smith call "letter-poems") sent from Dickinson to her sister-in-law, arguing that this relationship constituted the most sustained, creative, and intimate relationship of Dickinson's life.

Biography

Alfred Habegger, *My Wars Are Laid Away in Books: The Life of Emily Dickinson* (New York: Random House, 2001).
Presents the most recent and detailed research on Dickinson's life, offering particularly rich descriptions of her family history.

Richard B. Sewall, *The Life of Emily Dickinson* (New York: Farrar, Straus & Giroux, 1974).
The first major study of Dickinson's life, with chapters largely organized around her relationships with individual family members, friends, and correspondents.

Criticism

Sharon Cameron, *Choosing Not Choosing: Dickinson's Fascicles* (Chicago: University of Chicago Press, 1992).
Explores how reading poems in relation to the others bound into the same fascicle can shift our sense of what a poem is about.

Jack L. Capps, *Emily Dickinson's Reading: 1836–1886* (Cambridge, Mass.: Harvard University Press, 1966).
Offers description and analysis of the books found in Dickinson's library, the periodicals to which her family subscribed, Dickinson's marginalia, and any mention of what Dickinson was reading that appears in her letters.

Virginia Jackson, *Dickinson's Misery: A Theory of Lyric Reading* (Princeton: Princeton University Press, 2005).
Complicates Dickinson studies by arguing that twentieth-century criticism has turned Dickinson into the lyric poet she is considered to be today, as critics have engaged in a "lyric reading" of Dickinson's highly eclectic texts and purified her poems for the purposes of literary analysis.

Mary Loeffelholz, *Dickinson and the Boundaries of Feminist Theory* (Urbana: University of Illinois Press, 1991).
Examines the fraught relationship between feminist and deconstructionist studies of Dickinson's life and works.

Marietta Messmer, *A Vice for Voices: Reading Emily Dickinson's Correspondence* (Amherst: University of Massachusetts Press, 2001).
Suggests that Dickinson's letters and poems exist in a tightly bound and intergeneric exchange with one another and therefore must be studied in relation to each other.

Martha Nell Smith, *Rowing in Eden: Rereading Emily Dickinson* (Austin: University of Texas Press, 1992).
Exposes the ways in which Dickinson took herself seriously as a writer, "publishing" her work in what critics have tended to regard as private contexts, most notably her correspondence with her sister-in-law.

Marta L. Werner, ed., *Emily Dickinson's Open Folios: Scenes of Reading, Surfaces of Writing* (Ann Arbor: University of Michigan Press, 1995).
Looks closely at Dickinson's understudied late scraps, which were often written on pieces of household paper, including the backs of kitchen lists, advertisements, and bills.

—Alexandra Socarides

Paul Laurence Dunbar (1872–1906)

Paul Laurence Dunbar is regarded as one of the most significant African American writers. He was born in Dayton, Ohio, on 27 June 1872, the son of Matilda (a former slave) and Joshua (a former slave, plasterer, and soldier), who married six months before his birth and divorced by the time he was three. Raised by his mother, he had three siblings: two older brothers from his mother's first marriage and a younger sister, who died at age three of malnutrition. Like his sister he was sickly and his mother took every precaution and spared no expense, despite their overwhelming poverty, to maintain his health and ensure his education. Unlike his brothers, who had to leave school to work and support the family, Dunbar completed high school. His mother's efforts paid off, as Dunbar earned high marks and evidenced a bright intellect and artistic ability. He presented his first original poem ("An Easter Ode") at thirteen; had his first published poem ("Our Martyred Soldiers") appear in the *Dayton Herald* at seventeen; and started the short-lived *Dayton Tattler*, an African American newsletter printed by Orville and Wilbur Wright, at eighteen.

Though he is mostly noted for poetry, Dunbar's works span several other genres—short fiction, letters, nonfiction, reviews, essays, plays, musicals, lyrics, librettos, and novels. Moreover, they address a wide range of multicultural, social, and political themes and issues affecting Americans of all stations in the post-bellum, post-Reconstruction era. Consequently, from his first published writing Dunbar painted America "for better or worse, richer or poorer, in sickness and health" with a broad brush, which in retrospect has been seen as an experiment with forms of literary masking. During his short life he produced twelve books of poetry, four novels, more than one hundred short stories, numerous librettos and lyrics, as well as numerous essays, articles, and lectures.

His experience as the only black student in his class at the integrated Central High in Dayton was a surprisingly positive one, given the troubled racial times. He was senior class president, was editor in chief of the school newspaper, was elected to the prestigious Philomathean Literary Society, was named class poet, won two literary awards, and composed the school song for his 1891 graduating class. Without the means to afford college and unable to gain employment as a journalist because of racial discrimination (despite his publications in the *Dayton Herald*, his excellent educational background, and his reputation as a writer), Dunbar took a job as a janitor and shortly thereafter (due to his unsuitability for physical labor) as an elevator operator. Thus employed, Dunbar made good use of both the time and money afforded him. He purchased a home for himself and his mother, spent time reading literature and composing works, gave public recitals, and sold his first short story ("The Tenderfoot," 1891). During this time he also made important connections that would lead to the publication of his first two books of poetry: *Oak and Ivy* (1893) and *Majors and Minors* (1895). Invited by a former teacher, he gave a well-received recitation of a welcome poem—before a predominately white audience—at the meeting of the Western Association of Writers in Dayton in 1892, which marked a turning point in his career. The audience was intrigued by the incongruity of the talent and tincture of this black poet.

James Newton Matthews met the man he described that day as "the rising laureate of the colored race." Reflecting on the despondency in the poet's voice that accompanied requested samples of his poetry, Matthews lamented the racism that kept a literary gem like Dunbar "chained like a galley slave to the ropes of a dingy elevator at starvation wages." Encouraged by Matthews's personal correspondence and public recognition in his letter to the *Indianapolis Journal* (1892); his newfound friendship with one of the most popular poets of the time, James Whitcomb Riley; and prompted by his longtime friend Orville Wright, who suggested United Brethren Publishing House for binding and printing of his book, Dunbar assembled *Oak and Ivy* (1893). It was purchased by people on his subscription list, former classmates, elevator patrons, and curiosity seekers for $1.00 each. In three weeks time he had earned enough to repay the $125.00 production costs and to buy Christmas gifts for his mother. Rather than immediate substantial financial gain, the publication of *Oak and Ivy* garnered the poet recognition and increased public-speaking opportunities.

Traveling with copies of his new publication for sale, in 1893 he moved to Chicago, securing employment as a hotel waiter, janitor, and, most important, as Frederick Douglass's personal assistant at the World's Columbian Exposition. During this time Dunbar met many of the best and brightest of the black men and women of this era, among them Mary Church Terrell, Ida B. Wells-Barnett, and Alexander Crummell. Upon his return to Dayton and his elevator job, Dunbar found the years from 1893 to 1895 some of the most difficult financially as he struggled to maintain a home for him and his mother. He worked briefly as a court page and as temporary editor of the *Indianapolis World*, applied unsuccessfully for several teaching positions, depended on friends for financial assistance, and at his most despondent moment contemplated suicide. Fortunately, friends such as Dr. H. A. Tobey not only provided financial support that enabled him to keep his home but also recommended him for public presentations and recitations and backed his second book of poems, *Majors and Minors*.

The years that followed (1895–1898) were bittersweet ones for the poet. He suffered the loss of his friend and mentor Frederick Douglass, but William Dean Howells glowingly reviewed his dialect poetry. He courted Alice Moore almost entirely in letters between 1895 and 1897 before they secretly wed in 1898. Ultimately, they separated in 1902 after a troubled marriage. After their divorce and his relocation to Dayton, Dunbar spent the rest of his life writing prolifically, lecturing nationally and internationally, and dealing with his failing health. He died on 9 February 1906, of tuberculosis.

TOPICS FOR DISCUSSION AND RESEARCH

1. Given that Dunbar's fame is acknowledged as having come on the heels of Howells's review of his dialect poetry rather than any significant praise for his standard English verse, the poet's work can be studied from a perspective that considers the cultural contexts within which his work was first received. Students might want to consider how the caste of color prejudice, racism, and post-Reconstruction ideas about what a new American identity and literature should represent may have impacted nineteenth-century white and black American views of early black poetry. One important topic to explore along these lines is how the "color line" that W. E. B. Du Bois had so carefully articulated and the "double consciousness" he assigned to the black American psyche challenged the conventions of regional, local color, and vernacular American literature. Questions concerning American concepts of what constitutes black authenticity (from Dunbar's time to ours) are important ones to consider: What, for example, makes Dunbar a more authentically black poet than say Phillis Wheatley or Jupiter Hammon? Why are the subjects and themes in Dunbar's work both applauded and denounced? What is most appreciated, and what is most problematic, about Dunbar's use of the plantation tradition in his poetry and fiction?

2. Other topics for research and discussion might consider Dunbar's use of signifying (playful goading) in his depiction of Negro and white characters. Specifically, students might approach Dunbar's use of stereotypes from multiple perspectives—as an expression of the poet's ambivalence, accommodation, or concession about political race issues in post Reconstruction, or perhaps as his attempt to creatively transcend (through his work) the racism of his era.

3. An alternative view of reading his writing is to analyze Dunbar the man as a key element, or extension, of his works. That is, Dunbar might be considered within a context that sees him as being caught between the proverbial rock and a hard place. On the one hand, he might be viewed as one whose success as a poet depended on the patronage and support of such influential men as Howells and white readers who harbored certain expectations of black people. On the other, he might be read in light of those expectations of him as a man of "race" whose job it was to confront the very stereotypes his work sometimes appeared to endorse. Students might want to research the contradictions inherent in his relationship and attitude toward his contemporaries as a way of understanding the complicated nature of his works. For instance, how do we explain his simultaneous reverence for Frederick Douglass, his respect and admiration for Booker T. Washington's organizational and administrative skill, and his fundamental agreement with the goals and ideals advanced by W. E. B. Du Bois?

4. One of the most recent and provocative perspectives on Dunbar comes from research in the intersecting areas of gender and race. In particular, scholars such as Eleanor Alexander have called into question the extent to which Dunbar's own troubled marriage and his relationship with women in general might serve as a model for understanding not only his work, but also black male/female relationships in the nineteenth century. Students interested in pursuing this topic will want to consider the many critical questions that

emerge. One vital question should not be overlooked: given that both his womanizing and his violence toward women—Alice Dunbar-Nelson, in particular—was well documented, why has this issue been largely ignored by critics (during and immediately after his life and in recent scholarship)? Research that considers Dunbar's work from this perspective will necessarily guide students into research that considers the less-than-celebratory aspects of this nineteenth-century iconic figure. It may also suggest connections between Dunbar and such contemporary celebrities as Chris Brown.

The cultural influences, formal aesthetics, and his personal history are only a small sampling of the many ways of studying and exploring Dunbar's work. Clearly, they unearth many questions and point to avenues of research that support the need for modern readers to further probe the complexities of this poet's life and work.

RESOURCES

Primary Works

The Collected Poetry of Paul Laurence Dunbar, edited by Joanne M. Braxton (Charlottesville: University Press of Virginia, 1993).
The "largest, most authoritative collection of Dunbar's poetry ever published." This book does important work of contextualizing and reclaiming his work "for a new generation of lovers of verse." It includes the lost poems, previously not in other editions of collected works of Dunbar's poetry. Moreover, Braxton's introduction unpacks and critically surveys the most heated controversies surrounding Dunbar's work.

The Complete Stories of Paul Laurence Dunbar, edited by Gene Andrew Jarrett and Thomas Lewis Morgan (Athens: Ohio University Press, 2005).
Provides 103 previously uncollected short stories that, as Shelley Fisher Fiskin puts it, enable readers to "watch the author develop as a professional writer increasingly aware" of cultural limitations of his work and how those obstacles impacted his writing.

In His Own Voice: The Dramatic and Other Uncollected Works of Paul Laurence Dunbar, edited by Herbert Woodward Martin and Ronald Primeau (Athens: Ohio University Press, 2002).
A valuable anthology of Dunbar's drama, poetry, essays, short fiction and nonfiction, including previously unpublished and uncollected works.

Biography

Eleanor Alexander, *Lyrics of Sunshine and Shadow: The Tragic Courtship and Marriage of Paul Laurence Dunbar and Alice Ruth Moore* (New York: New York University Press, 2001).
The most important contribution to recent Dunbar studies, as it deals with the significant controversies in his life and marriage to Alice Dunbar-Nelson. It fills a gap left by earlier biographers, who gave little more than a nod to their "troubled" relationship.

Criticism

African American Review, Special Issue, Paul Laurence Dunbar, 41 (Summer 2007). Twenty-five essays taken from the 2006 Paul Laurence Dunbar Centennial Conference at Stanford that "uncover neglected aspects . . . challenge [existing] assumptions" and analyze "forms and genres [he] helped to pioneer, such as epistolary dialect poetry."

—*April Langley*

Alice Dunbar-Nelson, *The Goodness of St. Rocque and Other Stories*

(New York: Dodd, Mead, 1899)

Alice Moore (1875–1935), later known as Alice Dunbar and Alice Dunbar-Nelson, was the younger of two daughters born in a Creole household with a mixed African American, European American, and Native American heritage. She spent the first twenty years of her life in New Orleans, where she received a comprehensive education with courses in the classics department, the law school, and the printing department of Straight University (now Dillard University). She also received academic training at Cornell University, the Pennsylvania School of Industrial Art, and the University of Pennsylvania. A student with many talents, she became a teacher in 1892, an occupation she practiced with only a few interruptions for almost forty years at schools in different cities of the United States. She was married three times, including a short-lived (1898–1902) marriage to poet Paul Laurence Dunbar, which acquainted her with the world of professional authorship, and in 1916 to Robert J. Nelson, a journalist, politician, and civil-rights activist, with whom she coedited and published the Wilmington *Advocate,* a progressive black newspaper.

Dunbar-Nelson led an active life that, in addition to her teaching, was filled with activities ranging from literary and journalistic work to social and political activism. She wrote poems and fiction, contributed literary, art, and film criticism to various newspapers, and reviewed some of the most prominent writers of the early 1920s. With her energy and skills as a writer, public speaker, and organizer, she became involved in feminist and racial politics. She was active in the women's club movement, helped found the Industrial School for Colored Girls in Delaware, and was a prominent voice in the fight for the Dyer Anti-Lynching Bill, which passed in the House of Representatives but failed to become law owing to a Senate filibuster in 1922. The wide range of her activities in the decade between 1921 and 1931 is documented in her diary, the surviving portions of which were published in 1984.

Throughout her life, Dunbar-Nelson's poems, nonfiction, and fiction appeared in a variety of newspapers and periodicals. *Violets and Other Tales* (as

Alice Moore, 1895) and *The Goodness of St. Rocque and Other Stories* (as Alice Dunbar) collected her literary work in book form. She also edited two volumes of African American speeches (*Masterpieces of Negro Eloquence: The Best Speeches Delivered by the Negro from the Days of Slavery to the Present Time* [1914] and *The Dunbar Speaker and Entertainer* [1920]). She died in Philadelphia in 1935.

The Goodness of St. Rocque and Other Stories is regarded as Dunbar-Nelson's finest literary work. Whereas her first book contained poems, reviews, essays, and short fiction, this collection is devoted to short stories. Since most of them are set in New Orleans and focus on Creole culture, scholars have pointed out stylistic and thematic resemblances with the work of her contemporaries George Washington Cable and Kate Chopin and tend to categorize her as a Southern local Regionalist writing in the local-color tradition. By identifying street names, local buildings, and institutions Dunbar makes explicit references to specific locations in the city of New Orleans and its surroundings and frequently draws on the region's local practices, customs, and events. She also inserts instances of linguistic code-mixing and code-switching into the speech of her characters, thus drawing particular attention to the multilingual and multicultural atmosphere of the region. Her repertoire of mimetic techniques lends an air of authenticity to the stories and anchors them solidly in the culture from which they emerged. Despite the manifold references to the cultural specifics of the region, it would be reductive to consider the stories only in their regional dimension. The social, political, psychological, and moral issues addressed in her fiction clearly transcend the regional limits of Creole culture in Louisiana.

Taking their cue from its deceptively simple diction, scholars have traditionally described her writing style as aesthetically pleasing but conventional. More-recent readers, however, have drawn attention to the complexity that lies beneath the surface of her muted narratives. To experience the full effect of her writing, readers need to pay attention to the subtleties in her descriptions of scenes and characters. A single reference to a specific detail, and sometimes individual words, may turn out to provide the only clue necessary for an adequate understanding of a given story. This is particularly important in a narrative style in which individual scenes often follow upon each other in straight cuts with no transition. Frequently, her stories fail to provide key pieces of information or introduce peculiar perspectives and evasions, leaving the reader wondering what to make of the text. Although most stories are told from the perspective of an omniscient narrator, the narrative voice rarely if ever helps to clarify the situation. More often than not, it complicates the matter by undermining seemingly obvious conclusions by introducing unexpected perspectives or a finely tuned irony. One critic described the effect of these strategies as "an increasing skepticism about our ability to settle on a perspective that will manage the multiple perspectives these stories generate" (Strychacz).

TOPICS FOR DISCUSSION AND RESEARCH

1. All fourteen stories assembled in Dunbar's second anthology exhibit more or less similar features. The title story presents the rivalry between two women for the affection of a man. The contest is resolved when Manuela, dark-eyed,

graceful, and beautiful, emerges as Theophilé's bride at the end of the story, but the reason she prevailed over "blonde and petite" Claralie remains unclear as the narrative voice offers five different explanations of the final outcome. Students might identify these perspectives and judge the reliability of each of them. As in this story, several others in the collection are constructed around male-female relationships motivated by a love interest expressed by young women hoping to realize their romantic notions. None of these relationships is problem-free, however. How does Dunbar complicate them? In "The Fisherman of Pass Christian," why does Annette, an aspiring singer, abandon her plans to pursue an education in Paris when she learns that the man she loves has married someone else? Is her decision reasonable? Why does Odalie, the young and innocent protagonist in a story with the same title, choose confinement in a convent as a way to escape from disappointment in love? Is her decision more reasonable than Annette's? In a rare exception to this generally sad and depressing pattern in Dunbar's depiction of mostly one-sided love relationships, the young couple in "La Juanita" manages to overcome the opposition of a strict and stern Creole grandfather, the patriarch of a family "that had held itself proudly aloof from 'dose Americain' from time immemorial." How is the American suitor in this story able to win the respect and admiration of the Juanita's family? How explain this happy ending in contrast to the conclusions of the other stories? Does Nelson indulge in sentimentality here, or is "La Juanita" in the same realistic vein as the other stories in the collection? In a fictional world elsewhere dominated by a sense of loss and futility, what circumstances permit Juanita, "the pride of Mandeville, the adored, the admired of all," and her suitor to escape the disappointment, entrapment, or death suffered by the characters in the other tales? Is the success of this mixed marriage merely a chance event, or is Dunbar's depiction of it ironic?

2. In several of the stories, the protagonists become victims of circumstances over which they have no control. In an intellectual atmosphere that resembles Stephen Crane's view of an indifferent universe in "The Open Boat," Dunbar's characters suffer and die for reasons that are incomprehensible to them and to the readers. Moreover, her detached narration offers neither consolation nor rationalizations regarding the fatal consequences of her stories. Despite the ubiquity of allusions to faith and religion, the stories refuse to provide an explicitly moral perspective, a sense of fairness and justice, or a reason for hope. Do their fates seem fated? Put another way, are these tales fairly described as "Naturalistic"? Waiting for their son and prospective husband to return from a prolonged work stay in Chicago, for example, a mother and a prospective fiancée are shocked to learn that the young man died from consumption three hours before the train arrived at its destination ("When the Bayou Overflows"). Is he portrayed as a victim of blind chance, or does Dunbar hint at another explanation? Another story dramatizes the death of a poor old man who is caught in a violent labor struggle pitting striking Irish laborers and African American strike breakers against each other ("Mr. Baptiste"). Again, is he a victim of circumstances beyond his control, or does he simply make bad decisions and so is responsible for his predicament? The same questions may

be asked about "A Carnival Jangle," in which a young girl is a victim of mistaken identity. Dunbar actually heightens the effect when she allows Sylves ("When the Bayou Overflows") and Sophie ("Little Miss Sophie") to come very close to their goals only to deny them their realization. "Tony's Wife" ends on a similarly depressing note when the reader learns that a dying man refuses to acknowledge as his legitimate wife the woman with whom he has lived. Why does he refuse to deny her legitimacy? Does Dunbar's emotionless narration provide a clue? The student may also wish to consider whether his cold and harsh decision to leave her destitute is the unavoidable result of an abusive relationship. What about the ethnic differences between the two? Is it relevant to a reading of the text that the man is Italian and his consort is German?

3. The impact of a dramatic turning point in a person's life also lies at the heart of "M'sieu Fortier's Violin," in which an elderly musician loses his job at the French Opera in New Orleans partly because he has gradually lost the dexterity needed to handle a violin and partly because the new management of the opera house hires younger talent from France. Is this drama of an aging artist also set in a Naturalistic world, his fate determined by uncontrollable circumstances? Or does Dunbar criticize the greed of the opera house managers? The old musician is forced by poverty to sell his violin to a young man who wants it as a souvenir. Though he manages to recover the instrument, is this ending a happy or triumphant one? Or will this sentimental moment will have any effect on his personal fate?

4. The problem of identity is posed in other stories in the collection. In "A Carnival Jangle" and "Odalie," Dunbar chooses a carnival setting with its attending masquerade to demonstrate how disguising one's face and body may lead to painful or fatal results. Perhaps the most intense deliberation on personal identity occurs in "Sister Josepha," where the young and beautiful title character struggles with fundamental questions about her life. Raised in a convent since the age of three, she has been sheltered from all conflict. Is this the reason she has become "a child without an identity"? How critical is Dunbar of the "miniature world" of the convent? Does she suggest that conflict or struggle is crucial to the development of personality? How does such a message square with the Naturalistic themes in some of the other stories in the collection? In the end Sister Josepha resigns herself to a life within the convent walls. Is her decision commendable or expedient?

5. A pair of stories illustrate Dunbar's refusal to oversimplify her plots and her tendency to show both the virtues and the flaws of her characters as in "Titee," a story about a problem child, who sacrifices himself in order to feed a poor old man. These techniques are also apparent in "The Praline Woman," technically the most unconventional story in the collection, mostly narrated in monologue and in the native idiom of a female street vendor. How effective is this narrative device? What do her comments reveal about her life?

6. Perhaps surprisingly, among the many engaging themes and topics addressed in Dunbar's work, the problem of race does not figure prominently. Does the apparent lack of racial consciousness mar her fiction? Certainly a lively debate over the issue has erupted among critics. While some of them have criticized her

for apparently ignoring racial themes (Hull), others have praised her complex representations of race (Strychacz) and the subtleties involved in the depiction of her Creole characters (Brooks). Students may wish to weigh these arguments for themselves. Does Dunbar really ignore race, or is her treatment of racial themes ambiguous and provocative? Do her tales transcend their regional setting?

RESOURCES

Bibliography

Lori Leathers Single, "Alice Moore Dunbar-Nelson (1875–1935)," in *African American Authors, 1745–1945: A Bio-Bibliographical Critical Sourcebook,* edited by Emmanuel S. Nelson (Westport, Conn.: Greenwood Press, 2000), pp. 139–146.
A comprehensive list of Alice Dunbar-Nelson's publications.

Biography

Eleanor Alexander, *Lyrics of Sunshine and Shadow: The Tragic Courtship and Marriage of Paul Laurence Dunbar and Alice Ruth Moore* (New York: New York University Press, 2001).
Draws on the almost five hundred letters she and her husband exchanged during their short marriage; the book comments broadly on their relationship.

Alice Moore Dunbar-Nelson, *Give Us Each Day: The Diary of Alice Dunbar-Nelson,* edited by Gloria T. Hull (New York: Norton, 1984).
Covers only the years 1921 and 1926–1931; accompanied by Hull's concise and well-documented introduction, notes, and chronology.

Ora Williams, "Alice Moore Dunbar Nelson," in *Dictionary of Literary Biography,* volume 50: *Afro-American Writers Before the Harlem Renaissance,* edited by Trudier Harris and Thadious M. Davis (Detroit: Bruccoli Clark Layman/ Gale, 1986), pp. 225–233.
Provides condensed information in a widely available reference work.

Criticism

Kristina Brooks, "Alice Dunbar-Nelson's Local Colors of Ethnicity, Class, and Place," *MELUS,* 23 (Summer 1998): 3–26.
A perceptive reading of many of the stories in the collection, with many enlightening insights into the cultural contexts and the literary techniques applied by Dunbar.

Robert C. Clark, "At the Corner of Bourbon and Toulouse Street: The Historical Context of Alice Dunbar-Nelson's 'M'sieu Fortier's Violin,'" *American Literary Realism,* 41 (Winter 2009): 163–179.
A perceptive study of the historical sources of Dunbar-Nelson's tale.

Gloria T. Hull, "Alice Dunbar-Nelson (1875–1935)," in her *Color, Sex, and Poetry: Three Women Writers of the Harlem Renaissance* (Bloomington: Indiana University Press, 1987), pp. 33-106.

One of the earliest extensive studies of Dunbar-Nelson's short fiction by the scholar who recovered the author's work, edited her diary, and wrote an introduction to a modern reprinting of her writings in the Schomburg Library of Nineteenth-Century Black Women.

Thomas Strychacz, "'You . . . Could Never Be Mistaken': Reading Alice Dunbar-Nelson's Rhetorical Diversions in *The Goodness of St. Rocque and Other Stories*," *Studies in American Fiction*, 36 (Spring 2008): 77–94.

Argues that Dunbar's strategy of "rhetorical diversion" has led some readers to believe that her stories are conventional and romantic whereas an awareness of her technique reveals the full range of her literary achievement; contains several insightful readings of the stories collected in the anthology.

—*Holger Kersten*

T. S. Eliot, "The Love Song of J. Alfred Prufrock"

Poetry, 6 (June 1915): 130–135; collected in *Prufrock and Other Observations* (London: The Egoist, 1917)

Thomas Stearns Eliot (1888–1965) was among the most important writers of the twentieth century and the most widely recognized of the literary modernists. A member of a prosperous family from St. Louis, Missouri, Eliot graduated from Harvard University in 1909, then began spending extensive periods of time in Europe—first Paris, then Oxford and London. This trend culminated in his permanent relocation to England, marriage to an Englishwoman (Vivienne Haigh-Wood), eventual conversion to the Anglican church, and English citizenship. In 1910–1911 he composed "The Love Song of J. Alfred Prufrock."

The poem was not published until 1915, when, thanks in large part to the efforts of Eliot's eventual friend and rival, Ezra Pound, "The Love Song of J. Alfred Prufrock," appeared in the important journal *Poetry* (Chicago). Eliot's other major poetic works include *The Waste Land* (1922), his masterpiece and arguably the most important single poem written in English in the twentieth century, and *Four Quartets* (1943). He was also the author of verse dramas, including *Murder in the Cathedral* (1935), *The Family Reunion* (1939), and *The Cocktail Party* (1950); his *Old Possum's Book of Practical Cats* (1939) was the basis for the long-running Broadway musical *Cats* (1982–2000).

Despite Eliot's growing reputation as an innovative poet, his daily life during this time was quite stable after his employment by Lloyd's Bank and assumption of the editorship of *The Egoist*. His transformation from avant-gardist to premier poet of the establishment was completed by 1932, with his acceptance of the Charles Eliot Norton professorship at Harvard and confirmed by his winning of the Nobel Prize in 1948. He died in 1965, survived by his second wife, Valerie.

TOPICS FOR DISCUSSION AND RESEARCH

1. One initial approach to "Prufrock" is suggested by the contrast between the title, with its invocation of the traditional "love song," and the epigraph from Dante's *Inferno* (XXVII, 61–66):

   > If I believed that my answer were to a person who should ever return
   > to the world, this flame would stand without further movement;
   > but since never one returns alive from this deep, if I hear true,
   > I answer you without fear of infamy. (trans. Robert Scholes)

   The speaker, Guido da Montefeltro, continues to fear infamy on earth even while condemned to hell. He is willing to address Dante truthfully because he fails to realize that Dante is human and still able to return to the living. What is suggested by the epigraph, the overwhelming concern with reputation, how one is perceived, will become one of the key themes of the poem. But how does this concern for reputation fit with the traditional concept of a "love song"? What type of "love song" could the speaker of the poem be planning on singing with an epigraph whose imagery is so dark?

2. The opening line of the poem, "Let us go then, you and I," may initially return readers to their first notion of the poem as a traditional "love song," with the speaker as the (male) lover and the addressee as the (female) beloved. But, again, the parameters of a traditional love song seem quickly to fall to the side as the invitation is modified by the following lines: "When the evening is spread out against the sky / Like a patient etherized upon a table." Eliot's use of juxtaposition in these lines will become another key feature of the poem. A reader might profitably consider how the unusual imagery used here (clinical/surgical/urban) helps to develop or resists the notion of a "love song." This can also be used to extend the first question, which asks what type of love song this can be?

3. As the poem progresses, it becomes less clear whether the speaker is addressing a (female) beloved, the reader of the poem, or, in fact, anyone at all. A related approach to this poem could therefore attempt to determine the status of the addressee. Though the "you" makes several reappearances (at lines 10, 27, 30, 31, 56, 78, 89, and 95), the forms of address and the subjects on which the speaker meditates become increasingly bizarre if the addressee is a beloved. At lines 37–46, the speaker repeatedly questions his own ability to take action:

   > And indeed there will be time
   > To wonder, "Do I dare?" and, "Do I dare?"
   > Time to turn back and descend the stair,
   > With a bald spot in the middle of my hair—
   > (They will say: "How his hair is growing thin!")
   > My morning coat, my collar mounting firmly to the chin,
   > My necktie rich and modest, but asserted by a simple pin—
   > (They will say: "But how his arms and legs are thin!")
   > Do I dare
   > Disturb the universe?

Who exactly is the speaker addressing? Consider the multiple settings, which include a grimy urban street scene, as well as one or more sophisticated social gatherings, and the final walk on the beach. Does the speaker in reality visit these places or do they too exist only in his mind (and the reader's)?

4. Another potential, but not necessarily related, approach to the poem would entail an analysis of the themes of failed communication, especially those between men and women. For instance, in lines 87–98, the speaker speculates about what is at stake in these moments of failed communication:

> And would it have been worth it, after all,
> After the cups, the marmalade, the tea,
> Among the porcelain, among some talk of you and me,
> Would it have been worth while,
> To have bitten off the matter with a smile,
> To have squeezed the universe into a ball
> To roll it towards some overwhelming question,
> To say: "I am Lazarus, come from the dead,
> Come back to tell you all, I shall tell you all"—
> If one, setting a pillow by her head,
> Should say: "That is not what I meant at all;
> That is not it, at all."

Prufrock shares his fantasies of heroic action—and they do remain, fundamentally, fantasies—with his beloved, but her reaction seems to indicate utter incomprehension. How is this theme related to the overall structure of a poem that purports to be a "love song"?

5. One of the most important aspects of the structure of this very strange, "modern" love song is the way in which Eliot has adapted the form of the dramatic monologue, a concept popularized by the nineteenth century poet Robert Browning, through his own concept of the "persona." That is to say, Eliot is *not* Prufrock, though they may appear to share some similarities, at least superficially (Eliot was at one point well-known for wearing his hair "part[ed]... behind," in what was considered a fashionable style). The dramatic monologue is a poetic form not unlike the monologue in a play, where the speaker speaks uninterrupted to another, usually silent, interlocutor (who may be named or, as in "Prufrock," implied). Readers are "listening in" on this one-sided conversation, becoming aware through the performance of the speaker of information that he often inadvertently reveals—and may not even fully realize himself. The dramatic monologue in the Browning tradition tended to direct heavy irony toward characters who were criminal, insane, unsavory, or possibly all three. For Eliot, this new notion of the person *as* persona becomes an integral part of the subject of the poem as well as the form.

6. An approach to the poem that attends to the notion of the modernist dramatic monologue might assess what type of speaker Eliot has created for the poem, and why? That is, what kind of person is Prufrock? Is the

reader meant to admire him, sympathize with him, despise him, or some tenuous combination of these reactions? The dramatic monologue form allows the reader insight into Prufrock's mind even while it ensures a kind of ironic distance from him. What insights does this notion of the "persona" provide for this speaker? This approach could be extended to reveal the way the poem represents the "persona" as theme as well as form: Prufrock, the persona, admits repeatedly that his "self" is propped up, if not wholly supported, by such surface niceties as clothing, hair style, and social graces.

7. Though Eliot adapted Browning's use of blank verse (unrhymed iambic pentameter) in the dramatic monologue into what is purportedly free verse in "The Love Song of J. Alfred Prufrock," he uses other formal effects to structure his poem. A formal approach to this poem could focus on any of these. One of the first of these is his use of repeated sound structures and rhyme. Though "The Love Song of J. Alfred Prufrock" does not have a regular rhyme scheme, the use of rhyme within the poem remains important. Why would a poet who chooses to eschew both meter and a traditional rhyme scheme retain the use of such structured sounds? What effects do these patterns of sound add to the poem?

8. Eliot's use of end rhymes exemplifies a principle that is repeated in different ways throughout the poem: repetition with a difference. This can be found in the series of rhyming words from lines 87–98, including "ball" and multiple uses of the word "all." In other instances, the repetition of certain key phrases, which are shifted slightly from line to line, is one of the ways in which this notion of "repetition with a difference" works to organize the poem. How do these changes influence the reader's impression of the speaker? Is he a typical romantic hero? Or is Prufrock someone else entirely? A reader can think about any of the repeated and varied features to make an argument about how the "poetic" use of language informs "meaning" of free verse.

9. The poem employs a type of repetition without a difference in the refrain, "In the room the women come and go / Talking of Michelangelo." This refrain is repeated after the first and second verse paragraphs, and, as refrains go, it seems a strange one. Rather than tying together or summarizing ideas put forward in the previous lines, it seems to come from out of nowhere; it emphasizes pointless movement and phatic speech in two lines of pentameter, the first characterized by rising rhythm, the second by falling rhythm. What is the meaning of this refrain? And what is its structural purpose within the poem? Who are these "ladies" and where are the "rooms" in which they "come and go"? It may be that the "present" of the poem takes place in the "rooms" in which the ladies come and go, and the opening invocation and street scene occurs only in the speaker's mind—or the reverse may be true. Or both settings could be fantasies of sorts. The interpretive option the reader chooses helps to determine the ultimate "meaning" of the poem.

10. A final approach to "Prufrock" would consider the conclusion of the poem, which is marked by a very striking extended image, in relation to the poem as a whole:

> I grow old . . . I grow old . . .
> I shall wear the bottoms of my trousers rolled.
> Shall I part my hair behind? Do I dare to eat a peach?
> I shall wear white flannel trousers, and walk upon the beach.
> I have heard the mermaids singing, each to each.
>
> I do not think that they will sing to me.
>
> I have seen them riding seaward on the waves
> Combing the white hair of the waves blown back
> When the wind blows the water white and black.
> We have lingered in the chambers of the sea
> By sea-girls wreathed with seaweed red and brown
> Till human voices wake us, and we drown. (lines 119–131)

While Prufrock's ruminations on aging seem to lead to a renewed assurance of risk-taking, the next three lines, unusually suffused with color, describe the speaker's vision of the mermaids, "Combing the white hair of the waves blown back." Curiously, in the next line, the first-person singular pronoun shifts to the first-person plural with the final lines 129–131. The pronoun "we" has not been used in the poem until these final lines, and readers are left to wonder, who is this "we"? Is it the speaker and his listener, the "you and I" from line 1? If so, how can the reader reconcile the image of the relationship that is created here, which is vastly different from the one given earlier? Likewise, how can one account for the change in tone between the earlier lines and the conclusion? One clue to the meaning of the conclusion to this poem may lie with lines 73–74, which is another blank-verse couplet in iambic pentameter that weighs against the refrain:

> I should have been a pair of ragged claws
> Scuttling across the floors of silent seas.

The speaker's own estimation of his worth, that he would have been better off as a scavenging crab underneath the ocean, is the only other moment of such imagery in the poem, but it resonates with the "mermaid" section, invoking very different reactions to and depictions of a dramatically dark solitude. This imagery and affect offer additional opportunities for thematic analysis and close reading.

11. The mermaid section, unlike the silent and solitary crab fantasy, involves communion between human and nonhuman beings as well as between beings and nature. How should a reader understand this communion, and what impact can it have on the speaker's life? And how is a reader to interpret the role of the "mermaids"? Is it viable to characterize the closing lines

of the poem as a statement on art, and art's efficacy to intervene in the daily human world? "We"—perhaps humanity? the speaker and his beloved? or the reader and the poet?—have been engaged in a beautiful dream, engaged fully with a work of art, but when daily life interrupts that dream, what happens to it?

RESOURCES

Bibliography

Jewel Spears Brooker, "Eliot Studies: A Review and a Select Booklist," in *The Cambridge Companion to T. S. Eliot,* edited by A. David Moody (New York: Cambridge University Press, 1994), pp. 236–246.
The most definitive, accessible, and recent of many bibliographies.

Biography

Ronald Schuchard, *Eliot's Dark Angel: Intersections of Life and Art* (New York: Oxford University Press, 1999).
The most current and authoritative study of Eliot's life, which interprets his literary contributions in order to generate insights about his career, relationships, and times.

Criticism

John Xiros Cooper, *The Cambridge Introduction to T. S. Eliot* (New York: Cambridge University Press, 2006).
Offers an approachable, jargon-free overview of Eliot's life and work that is specifically intended for an audience of readers with little background in modernist literature.

James Longenbach, *Modernist Poetics of History: Pound, Eliot, and the Sense of the Past* (Princeton: Princeton University Press, 1987).
Provides background on the "historical sense"—or complex attempts to understand the past in the present—which both animated Eliot's work and made it possible.

Louis Menand, *Discovering Modernism: T. S. Eliot and His Context,* revised edition (New York: Oxford University Press, 2007).
Assesses from an analytical and evaluative perspective Eliot's place in literary history, focusing on questions of reputation, influence, and "consequentiality" for popular as well as high culture.

Marjorie Perloff, "Avant-Garde Eliot," in her *21st-Century Modernism: The "New" Poetics* (Malden, Mass.: Blackwell, 2002).
Makes fresh claims for Eliot's status as a meaningfully innovative poet whose early work (including "The Love Song of J. Alfred Prufrock") uses qualities of "instability" and "dislocation" in ways that are finally compatible with postmodern writing.

—Scarlett Higgins

Sui Sin Far, *Mrs. Spring Fragrance*
(Chicago: A. C. McClurg, 1912)

The Asian American author Sui Sin Far was named Edith Maude Eaton at birth in England in 1865. Her father was an English merchant who had met her mother in Shanghai. Edith Eaton was the second of fourteen children. Her family immigrated to the United States, where they lived briefly, before moving to Montreal, Quebec. She left school at the age of ten to work and help support her family. Eaton wrote articles for newspapers in Canada about the Chinese before moving first to Jamaica and then to San Francisco and Seattle, where she lived in the Chinatowns. She later wrote fiction about the experience of the Chinese who had settled in North America during the period of the so-called "Yellow Peril." Her short-story cycle *Mrs. Spring Fragrance,* a seminal text in the history of Asian American writing, appeared in 1912, and she died from heart disease two years later.

Other Asian American writers had published before Sui Sin Far, a pseudonym referring to the narcissus flower popular in Chinese culture. The earlier writers, however, set their tales in Asia or wrote in Asian languages. Sui Sin Far's fiction is the first to explore the Chinese experience in North America and in English. The writer's mixed-blood perspective and international experience allowed for a range of insights into the struggle between East and West at a time China was the target of colonization by European, North American, and Japanese interests.

Mrs. Spring Fragrance begins with the introduction of the title character as she arrives in Seattle. She speaks no English. Within five years, however, she has a complete knowledge of "American" vocabulary. One of her friends, so thoroughly Americanized that her parents call her Laura, is in love with a young native-born American of Chinese descent, Kai Tzu, whose assimilation is represented by his skill at baseball. Laura's parents live in an American house and dress in American fashion, but they adhere to some Chinese customs and honor the ideals of their Chinese ancestors. As a result, they have arranged a marriage between their fifteen-year-old daughter and the son of a Chinese Government teacher in San Francisco. As Laura's confidante, Mrs. Spring Fragrance is the only person who knows of the young woman's relationship with her American-born beau. She comforts Laura with the words of the "American" poet, Alfred Tennyson: "'Tis better to have loved and lost, / Than never to have loved at all." Mrs. Spring Fragrance's mistake—Tennyson was English, not American—underscores her assimilation into American society.

Mrs. Spring Fragrance chats with Laura for a long time, and when the conversation ends Laura is much happier. The story shifts at this point to a visit Mrs. Spring Fragrance makes to her family and friends in San Francisco. From there she writes to Laura to say that the man she had expected to marry but did not love will in fact marry Ah Oi, whose name is clearly Chinese and who is given no "American" name. The son of the government teacher will marry according to tradition, leaving Laura free to marry with Kai Tzu.

In the next section Mr. Spring Fragrance reads two letters: one from his wife, the other from a cousin in San Francisco. The latter reports his wife's frequent company with the government teacher's son, adding an admonition that women who are allowed to stray from under their husbands' mulberry roofs become butterflies. Although Mr. Spring Fragrance concludes that his cousin is old and cynical and in America men and women might converse without an evil purpose, he harbors a small kernel of doubt. That kernel takes root as he considers compliments he and his wife have received for her assimilation into American society, leading him to worry that his wife might decide "to love as an American woman—a man to whom she was not married." He decides not to give her the jade pendant he has purchased for their fifth anniversary. His worry grows as he thinks of the Tennyson lines again; he telegraphs his wife that she may stay the additional time in California that she desires, but adds the Tennyson quote as a kind of cryptic warning. Mrs. Spring Fragrance is delighted to think her husband had been reading her American poetry books in her absence, musing that it was necessary that she be discreet in helping Laura, given her husband's "old-fashioned notions concerning marriage." She remembers how they had fallen in love with one another simply by seeing the other's photograph.

Part 4 opens with Mr. Spring Fragrance speaking with Mr. Chin Yuen, Laura's father, who observes that as the old order passes away a new one is taking its place, even with the Chinese. His consent to his daughter's wish to marry Kai Tzu, a man of her own choosing, surprises Mr. Spring Fragrance, and Chin Yuen's explanation further nourishes the doubt growing in his mind. When his wife returns, she is delighted to be back in Seattle, but her husband is unresponsive, orders the servant boy to make her comfortable, then leaves, ostensibly to attend to business at the store. However, he returns quickly, to his wife's surprise. She never learns of her husband's doubt. When she says she suspects he has been reading her poetry books, he dismisses the notion "fiercely," saying that "American poetry is detestable, *abhorrable!* [sic]." She exclaims "Why! why!" Her husband's reply is simply to give her the jade pendant he had purchased for the anniversary that had passed.

TOPICS FOR DISCUSSION AND RESEARCH

1. Sui Sin Far's stories focus on the issues of immigration and assimilation. How do they handle notions of cultural transplantation? What is the purpose of Sui Sin Far's floral imagery? How does the author treat the idea of romantic love? How does she contrast arranged Asian marriages with marriages based on courtship and romance? How does Sui Sin Far portray Asian femininity and Asian masculinity transplanted to the New World?
2. Much as Henry James is well known for his treatment of the "international theme," Sui Sin Far contrasts the social codes of the Asians and Asian Americans with the customs of Euro-Americans in the New World. Why does Mr. Spring Fragrance finger a "li-chi" in his pocket and touch the little box containing the jade pendant he has purchased as a fifth-anniversary gift? Do Mrs. and Mr. Spring Fragrance express nostalgia for their homeland? Why does Mr. Spring Fragrance denounce the sentiment expressed in the Tennyson poem?

How do the repeated references in the story to "American" language, in which the Chinese characters conflate the dialects of America and England, critique Western caricatures and stereotypes of Asians and Asian Americans?

3. Asians have often been the target of racial prejudice in the West, as in the Chinese Exclusionary Act of 1882, which was renewed in 1892 and again in 1902. In what ways does Sui Sin Far satirize Western bias against the Chinese? Why does Mrs. Spring Fragrance describe the "magniloquent" lecture she attended with an American friend and why is the description ironic? In what ways does *Mrs. Spring Fragrance* contrast the customs of East and West in the lives of Chinese immigrants in America? How do these stories present Westerners as different or "Other," their ways mysterious and strange to the Chinese who sometimes mimic them?

RESOURCES

Biography

Annette White-Parks, *Sui Sin Far/Edith Maude Eaton: A Literary Biography* (Urbana: University of Illinois Press, 1995).
A useful introduction to the life and work of the author.

Criticism

Mary Chapman, "A 'Revolution in Ink': Sui Sin Far and Chinese Reform Discourse," *American Quarterly,* 60 (December 2008): 975–1001.
Examines the work of Sui Sin Far as a response to contemporary suffragists. Contends that Sui Sin Far's writing was not "anti-progressive" or "anti-suffragist," claims made by some recent scholars, but rather transnational and modern.

Xiao-Huang Yin, "Between the East and West: Sui Sin Far, the First Chinese-American Woman Writer," *Arizona Quarterly,* 47 (Winter 1991): 49–84.
Notes that Sui Sin Far was nearly alone among immigrant writers of Chinese descent in writing imaginative literature. Reviewing her favorable contemporary reception, this important essay places it in context as part of an effort to improve the image of Asian Americans in the West.

—Rick Waters

Mary E. Wilkins Freeman, "A Church Mouse"

Harper's Bazaar (28 December 1889): 952–954; collected in *A New England Nun and Other Stories* (New York: Harper, 1891)

Mary E. Wilkins was born 31 October 1852, in Randolph, Massachusetts, to Warren Wilkins and Eleanor Lothrop Wilkins. Her parents were orthodox Congregationalists, and Mary and her siblings were brought up with intense religious instruction. Her father was a carpenter, but financial circumstances forced him to abandon that trade. The family moved to Brattleboro, Vermont, when Mary was still a young child, and Warren Wilkins opened a dry-goods store there. Mary graduated from high school in Brattleboro in 1870 and then attended Mount Holyoke Female Seminary. The religious indoctrination at the seminary was too intense for her, and she came home a "nervous wreck" at the end of a year and concluded her formal education. She taught for a brief time at a girls' school. In 1873 she met and fell in love with Hanson Tyler, who was at home on leave from the navy. Tyler did not return the affection, but her fondness for him remained throughout her life. Apart from the emotional disappointment, there must have been a great deal of discomfort when the Wilkins family moved into the home of Reverend Thomas Pickman Tyler, Hanson's father. The dry-goods store had failed, and Eleanor entered into domestic service there; Mary's father did lawn work in exchange for a place for the family to live. Such circumstances were made all the more humiliating by the feeling that poverty was considered a moral and spiritual failing. When Eleanor Wilkins died at the age of fifty-three, the Wilkinses were compelled to leave the Tyler household. It was at this time that Mary began to write in earnest in order to supplement the family's meager income.

Out of necessity, Mary Wilkins turned to the business of writing with a will and a purpose, and during the course of her career she published fifteen volumes of her collected stories, as well as another fifty or more stories that were not collected during her lifetime. She also wrote three books of poetry, three plays, and fourteen novels. Her early works were for children, but soon she began to write fiction for adult readers. Her first collection of adult short stories, *A Humble Romance and Other Stories* (1887), was published by Harper and Brothers. That collection, along with *A New England Nun and Other Stories* (1891) and the novel *Pembroke* (1894), form the principal foundation for her reputation. She had become an established writer, but her father did not live to see her success; he died in 1883, and Mary moved back to Randolph, where she lived in the residence of her childhood friend Mary Wales for the next twenty years. Spared household duties so that she could write, Mary Wilkins worked constantly and produced some of her best work during that time. Though financial necessity required her to produce fiction to earn her keep, she was at the same time developing her craft. In 1882 she won a literary prize for "The Shadow Family," published in a Boston newspaper. Thereafter, her reputation grew, and she published regularly in some of the better magazines of the day, most frequently in *Harper's Bazaar,* and her books were issued by established publishing houses.

In 1892 she met Dr. Charles Freeman, and they became engaged in 1897. Mary Wilkins evidently was unsure of the match, for she broke off the engagement at one point and postponed the wedding day at another. Her desire for a home of her own was strong, and eventually they were married in 1902 and moved to Metuchen, New Jersey. In leaving Randolph, Freeman was thus cut off from the source of her best literary material. Though the marriage was apparently good in the beginning, it turned out the reasons for her hesitation were well founded. Already a hard drinker, Dr. Freeman became an alcoholic, and, in addition to her household duties, he pressed his wife to write more and more fiction for the money needed to support his addiction. In 1919 Freeman had him committed to the New Jersey State Hospital for the Insane to be treated for his drinking. They were legally separated in 1922, and he died the next year. Now in her seventies, Mary Wilkins Freeman was recognized for her achievement as a writer, winning the William Dean Howells Gold Medal for Fiction in 1926. The same year, along with Edith Wharton, Margaret Deland, and Agnes Repellier, she was inducted into the National Institute of Arts and Letters, the first time the Institute had accorded that honor to a woman. Freeman died in 1930.

TOPICS FOR DISCUSSION AND RESEARCH

1. As a "local color" writer, Freeman wrote about what she knew best—the farms and villages of New England; very rarely do her narratives take place in urban settings. She confidently rendered the speech, customs, and values of her imagined characters, but she did so with both an ironic detachment and a comic sympathy. To the degree that Freeman brings something more to her picture of New England character than its quaint habits and dialect, but keen psychological insight into its manners and motives and a social purpose as well, some have preferred to label her a "Regionalist" or Realist writer. Students should attempt to answer the question of whether this is a local-color or Regionalist story because their answers may affect how they read the work. For example, is Hetty Fifield essentially a type, a representative of the poor, homeless old woman helpless in the face of circumstances, or is she shrewd, determined, and even calculating in her actions? "A Church Mouse" is likely to be seen as more comic if read as a local-color tale, and Gregg Camfield's essay is helpful in this regard. Dominant critical opinion of Freeman after she received the Howells medal, for some forty years, cast her as an acute but rather pessimistic chronicler of New England life in decline. She gave unsparing pictures of the restrictive life lived out under the inheritance of an imperfectly understood but still pervasive Puritan inheritance. Her characters often lacked intellectual curiosity or a love of beauty, were uncommunicative and stubborn, and accepted their bitter portion as best they could. Perry Westbrook's book on Freeman emphasizes the Puritan elements in Freeman's work and is a good starting point for research into this aspect of the tale. The Puritans, for example, did not celebrate religious holidays, and Hetty's ringing the church bell on Christmas day is startling to the townspeople for that reason. Beginning in the 1960s feminist critics began to detect more positive features in her tales. The women characters particularly demonstrated a fierce resoluteness and desire for change, autonomy, and freedom. In them Freeman dramatized a more powerful and hopeful sense of future and affirmation. These two views are not necessarily in conflict; one can act valiantly and defiantly even when the rewards are small. One of Freeman's most widely anthologized stories, "A Church Mouse" illustrates these qualities, and it is leavened with a sense of humor that relieves the stark and diminished possibilities of life it presents. Feminist treatments of Freeman are abundant. Glasser's biography

and Reinhardt's book, *A Web of Relationship*, provide a foundation for critical examination of the story as feminist.

2. "A Church Mouse" begins with the elderly, impoverished, and now homeless Hetty Fifield applying for the job of church sexton. As the titles indicates, she is as poor as a church mouse; it will turn out that she is the mouse that roared. The deacon, Caleb Gale, is stubbornly resistant to the idea, for no woman has ever been a sexton, and makes a series of lame excuses why she cannot occupy the position. Hetty has nowhere to stay that night and proposes to sleep in the church. Caleb objects until Hetty proposes that she could sleep in his house; he relents. Hetty becomes the sexton, moves into the meeting house, dutifully cleans it, and just as dutifully rings the bell at the appointed times. Clearly, Hetty Fifield poses a problem for this community: no one wants to take her because they know that she does not bend to voice of authority, nor is there a poorhouse in the village, and with some perplexity alongside the voice of their "Puritan consciences" the villagers accept the situation, for a while. Hetty moves her small store of belongings into the church, cordons off a space beside the chimney with her bright, sunflower quilt, and takes up residence. Hetty Fifield is a feisty New England woman, but she may also be shrewd and she senses she is the "propounder of a problem," but she knows too that so long as the exact nature of that problem remains unguessed by the village, she has the advantage.

3. But what sort of problem does she pose? Is it a moral or religious one, or is it social and political in nature? More important, perhaps, does the solution to the problem have long-lasting and transformative effects on the village? For three months things go well enough until she overplays her hand and cooks turnips and cabbage for Saturday dinner, and the odor lingers in the church on Sunday morning. Caleb Gale decides that Hetty must leave the church, and on her part she feels like a "little animal driven from its cover, for whom there is nothing left but warfare and death." Hetty slyly bolts herself inside the church, and makes her "sacred castle impregnable except to violence." Befuddled, Mr. Gale hands the situation over to the authority of his wife, and thus there is a quiet transfer of power from the patriarchs to the matriarchs of the village. It is from the gallery window that Hetty pleads her case, mostly to the women of the village, in a direct, homespun dialect, and it is Mrs. Gale who makes a judgment. Hetty can move into the little room beside the pulpit, where the minister hangs his hat; that will be her new home.

4. Is it possible that Freeman is making an oblique and wry comment on the widespread anti-Catholic hysteria in the country at this time? On Christmas Eve, Hetty is filled with joy for her "little measure full of gifts." She awakes the next morning with the promise from Mrs. Gale of some turkey and plum pudding. So grateful is she that, without knowing why, she rings the church bells to awaken the town. Hetty, who had earlier been suspected of "popery" for putting a wax cross on the pulpit, has now violated an unspoken taboo, for never before had the church bell been rung on Christmas; it gladdens the villagers nonetheless. This simple little tale subtly dramatizes the

change of gender roles, the loosening up of orthodox religious sensibility, and implicitly asks the question that is plaguing the nation at large—what are we to do with our poor, homeless, and elderly? At the same time, it creates in Hetty Fifield something of a village hero (fearless, determined, and in her own fashion eloquent) out the most unlikely materials. Students of this story might want to investigate how villages dealt with the problems Hetty presents to them, whether the comedy of the situation detracts from or enhances the feminist qualities in the story, and perhaps whether this piece of local color had broader reference to the social problems of the nation at large during this time period.

RESOURCES

Biography

Edward Foster, *Mary Wilkins Freeman* (New York: Hendricks House, 1956).
Somewhat dated but straightforward account of Freeman's life. Foster is more interested in the writer's craft and the influences upon her than in providing a psychological portrait of the woman.

Leah Blatt Glasser, *In a Closet Hidden: The Life and Work of Mary E. Wilkins Freeman* (Amherst: University of Massachusetts Press, 1996).
A solid, scholarly charting of Freeman's development as a writer, and essentially feminist in its approach. Benefits from Kendrick's editions of Freeman's letters in describing the writer's development and her acquaintance with and sympathy for the struggles of single and elderly women as well as with difficult marital and economic circumstances. Discusses Freeman's novels as well as her short fiction.

Brent L. Kendrick, ed., *The Infant Sphinx: Collected Letters of Mary E. Wilkins Freeman* (Metuchen, N. J.: Scarecrow Press, 1985).
The letters are annotated and provide useful insights into the life of Freeman.

Criticism

Gregg Camfield, "'I never saw anything at once so pathetic and funny': Humor in the Stories of Mary Wilkins Freeman," *American Transcendental Quarterly,* 13 (September 1999): 215–231.
Argues that the humor in Freeman's work is often overlooked and that the combination of humor and pathos do not contradict but enhance one another.

Kate Gardner, "The Subversion of Genre in the Short Stories of Mary Wilkins Freeman," *New England Quarterly,* 65 (September 1992): 447–468.
Identifies the ways Freeman introduces variations on conventional characterization and plots lines and thereby wins sympathy for her otherwise odd heroines.

Shirley Marchalonis, ed., *Critical Essays on Mary Wilkins Freeman* (Boston: G. K. Hall, 1991).
A collection of sixteen essays on Freeman, ranging from older pieces by such scholars as F. O. Matthiessen to more recent ones by critics such as Josephine Donovan and Mary R. Reichardt.

Mary R. Reichardt, *Mary Wilkins Freeman: A Study of the Short Fiction* (New York: Twayne, 1997).
Includes Freeman's statements on her craft, letters, an autobiographical essay, a bibliography of primary works and criticism, and an analysis of a substantial number of her short stories.

Reichardt, *A Web of Relationship: Women in the Short Stories of Mary Wilkins Freeman* (Jackson: University Press of Mississippi, 1992).
A comprehensive study of Freeman's short fiction, showing that the author's portrayal of strong-willed women is not limited to a few stories but is an overarching theme concerned with women struggling toward selfhood.

Perry D. Westbrook, *Mary Wilkins Freeman*, revised edition (Boston: Twayne, 1988).
A capable critical biography. Emphasizes the lingering Puritan elements in the New England culture that Freeman depicts and compares her favorably to Nathaniel Hawthorne. Argues that Freeman is more than a local colorist; she is often a psychological Realist.

—Tom Quirk

Hamlin Garland, "Under the Lion's Paw"

Harper's Weekly (7 September 1889): 726–727; collected in *Main-Travelled Roads* (Boston: Arena, 1891)

Hamlin Garland (1860–1940) grew up on farms in Wisconsin, Iowa, and the Dakotas before moving to Boston in 1884 to begin his writing career. A prolific writer and active social reformer, Garland published books, stories, articles, and pamphlets on a variety of topics: contemporary social and political issues, including *The Book of the American Indian* (1923); historical and cultural analysis of the American West, including *The Westward March of American Settlement* (1927); literary criticism, including *Crumbling Idols: Twelve Essays on Art* (1894); a presidential biography, *Ulysses S. Grant: His Life and Character* (1898); plus several narrative memoirs, including the highly respected *A Son of the Middle Border* (1917) and the Pulitzer Prize–winning *A Daughter of the Middle Border* (1921). His first major literary success was *Main-Travelled Roads* (1891), a collection of short sketches, including "Under the Lion's Paw," that describe the harsh realities of Midwestern farm life. Garland's mentor William Dean Howells immediately praised the book and later wrote an introduction to the 1922 edition that emphasized its importance to American literary Realism. Garland devoted his final years to investigating psychic phenomena.

An influential work of regional literature, *Main-Travelled Roads* challenged the nineteenth-century romantic myths about the Midwest: the farmer as a Jeffersonian archetype and the countryside as a lush garden paradise where farming was easy, relaxing, and highly lucrative. In his preface to the book Garland explained that these stories of "historical fiction" record "[t]he ugliness, the endless drudgery, and the loneliness of the farmer's lot." His farmers are determined, but failure and misery cause some to become pessimistic and bitter. Their struggle for survival traps them in a life determined by outside forces: an indifferent, often hostile environment and an unjust, competitive society. As a result, contemporary critics categorized Garland's fiction as Naturalistic, a label Garland himself rejected. In a 1939 letter he called himself an impressionist, a veritist, rather than the Darwinian Realist who used "sexual vice and crime in the manner of Émile Zola and certain German novelists." His goal: portray the commonplace daily experiences of decent, ordinary people in the rural Midwest.

Garland, like other local-color authors, was influenced by Romanticism, as well as Realism; many of his narratives have an optimistic tone or color. Thus, his descriptions of desolate environments and the tremendously hard work necessary to farm them are truthful but not hopelessly bleak. Garland's cruel landscapes have a rugged beauty, and his provincial, stubborn, petty farmers also express wisdom, strength, generosity, and psychological complexity. Garland's farmers are heroes of the everyday, facing incredible hardship and deprivation often without complaint. In fact, a few characters, such as the Councils in "Under the Lion's Paw," are relatively content and adopt an optimistic approach to farm life. Furthermore, a handful of discontented characters—such as Agnes Dingman in "A Branch Road," Howard McLean in "Up the Coulee," and Nellie Sanford in "A 'Good Fellow's' Wife"—break free from their assigned roles, grasping control of their lives to achieve some success and personal happiness.

"Under the Lion's Paw" is a slice-of-life story of tenant farmer Timothy Haskins's struggle to overcome natural and institutional obstacles. Haskins is an honest, self-reliant, hardworking family man who inspires the reader's sympathy and respect. After drought and grasshoppers destroy his crop and drive him from his farm in Kansas, Haskins takes his wife and three small children to Iowa to look for a new home. Exhausted and starving, the homeless and penniless family appeals to the kindness of strangers: farmer Stephen Council and his wife. The Councils, who would not think of turning away someone in need, share their home until the Haskins family finds one of its own. As Mrs. Haskins sits before the Councils' fire and watches her children eat their first full meal in days, she weeps with joy that "The world was not so desolate and cold and hopeless, after all."

The next day, Council helps Haskins barter for a run-down farm owned by Jim Butler, a selfish and greedy land speculator. Council and Butler represent sharply different approaches to American individualism. Council is a democrat who treats Haskins as a fellow human being, selflessly helping him become self-sufficient. Council's values, his "religion," are built upon generosity and respect for human dignity; he gladly shares everything—his home, money, knowledge, personal toil—with a stranger without wanting any compensation. Butler, on the other hand, is an aristocrat who disregards Haskins's dignity and humanity, only seeing him as a means to acquire more wealth and power. Butler is an opportunist, a taker and hoarder who buys up mortgages throughout the region and reduces self-respecting, independent farmers to serfdom. He has become a lord, spending his days in leisure and living off the labor of others.

Haskins agrees to lease Butler's land, and with Council's financial help and moral support he begins to farm it. After a year of desperately hard work—the result of a strong work ethic and a fear of homelessness and starvation—Haskins's farm is moderately successful, and he is able to make fifteen hundred dollars' worth of improvements to the property. However, these improvements cause Butler to double the purchase price of the land in line with its increased value. Haskins complains that he's being charged twice for his own materials and labor. He reminds Butler that he trusted the speculator not to increase the price, to which Butler replies, "Never trust anybody, my friend." Haskins raises his pitchfork with the intention of murdering Butler, but the sight of his two-year-old daughter stops him. Needing to support his family, Haskins must remain at the mercy of the land speculator: "He was under the lion's paw. . . . and there was no path out." The story ends with Haskins holding his head in his hands, distraught at having to sacrifice his independence and self-respect.

TOPICS FOR DISCUSSION AND RESEARCH

1. Although "Under the Lion's Paw" addresses broad sociopolitical themes, its small details underpin Garland's veritism. The story begins with a description of farmers plowing their fields in the snow and mud. The narrator focuses on one farmer, Council, as he struggles with his plow and horses, continuing to work even after nightfall. Snow covers Council's "ragged greatcoat" and mud clings to his heavy books while wild geese honk and the wind howls. Students should research whether he is a typical farmer of that region.

2. Soon the Haskins family arrives, and the wives immediately begin discussing common domestic concerns over tea while watching the children. One of these children, Haskins's nine-year-old son, will literally step into his father's boots once they move to their new farm, laboring "in his coarse clothing, his huge boots, and his ragged cap, as he staggered with a pail of water from the well." Garland writes that although a "city-bred visitor" might see this as child abuse, Haskins loves his son and would save him from this life if he could. Students might research what farm life was like for children during Garland's time and today.

3. Students might also discuss Garland's use of local color, particularly dialect. The story features regional dialects, a standard convention in local-color fiction. Council, the first character in the story to speak, says to his horse: "None o' y'r tantrums, Kittie. It's purty tuff, but gotta be did. *Tchk! tchk!*" How does Garland's use of the Midwest farmers' voices reflect his own populist politics? Are his yeoman farmers politically engaged? What does Council read and discuss after a day of exhausting manual labor?

4. Students might also examine the animal imagery in the story. How does the oppressive "paw" in "Under the Lion's Paw" symbolize selfish, ruthless speculators? How does it represent the entire American economic and political system? Students should research the Grange movement and populist politics of this time period. Garland campaigned for Populist candidates during the

1890s, often reading "Under the Lion's Paw" aloud at campaign rallies and public lectures to arouse support for farmers, land speculation, urban labor, and the populist movement. How does the story discourage the speculation in land values in particular?

5. Finally, students might research the other progressive movements at the time. In addition to writing and speaking on behalf of farmers, Garland advocated other progressive social reform, including preservation of Indian land and women's rights. Many of Garland's stories, including "Under the Lion's Paw," feature a capable, hardworking farm woman. Do such portrayals promote gender equality between husband and wife?

RESOURCES

Primary Work
Joseph B. McCullough and Keith Newlin, *Selected Letters of Hamlin Garland* (Lincoln: University of Nebraska Press, 1998).

Biography
Keith Newlin, *Hamlin Garland: A Life* (Lincoln: University of Nebraska Press, 2008).
The most comprehensive Garland biography. Donald Pizer, author of *Hamlin Garland's Early Work and Career* (New York: Russell & Russell, 1969), calls the book "a significant contribution toward the understanding both of Garland and his times."

Bibliography
Jackson R. Bryer, Eugene Harding, and Robert Rees, *Hamlin Garland and the Critics: An Annotated Bibliography* (Troy, N.Y.: Whitston, 1973).
A comprehensive, annotated bibliography of Garland criticism. Must be supplemented by the MLA annual bibliography.

Criticism
Robert Gish, *Hamlin Garland: The Far West* (Boise, Idaho: Boise State University, 1976).
An analytical study of Garland's writing and the development of his literary voice, including a major section on *Main-Travelled Roads*.

Quentin E. Martin, "Hamlin Garland's 'The Return of a Private' and 'Under the Lion's Paw' and the Monopoly of Money in Post–Civil War America," *American Literary Realism,* 29 (Fall 1996): 62–77.
An insightful essay about the origins and contemporary sociopolitical influence of "Under the Lion's Paw."

Joseph B. McCullough, *Hamlin Garland* (Boston: Twayne, 1978).
A critical study of Garland's life and works.

—*Matthew Teorey*

Charlotte Perkins Gilman, "The Yellow Wallpaper"

New England Magazine, 5 (January 1892): 647–656

Charlotte Perkins Gilman (1860–1935), born Charlotte Anna Perkins, was descended from a distinguished family of American rhetoricians, advocates, and writers. Her great-aunt was Harriet Beecher Stowe, with whom Gilman spent time as a child. Gilman's father, Frederick Beecher Perkins, was a rare presence after a physician instructed Gilman's mother to have no more children. Her parents permanently separated in 1869. Gilman, her mother, and her brother were left destitute and largely dependent upon the charity of relatives. Gilman received only four years of formal education, but she read prolifically and largely educated herself. Frederick Perkins learned that his daughter had some talent for drawing and paid for Gilman to attend the Rhode Island School of Design where she became skilled enough to support herself financially. Throughout her childhood and early adulthood, Gilman had enjoyed a great degree of independence.

On 2 May 1884, Gilman, despite her reservations, married Charles Walter Stetson. The ensuing mundane domestic routine caused her mental anguish, and shortly after the birth of their daughter Katherine, Gilman suffered a mental breakdown. She was treated by S. Weir Mitchell, who championed a rest cure in order to treat nervous disorders or "neurasthenia." Mitchell advocated six to eight weeks of complete bedrest whereby the patient could not sit up, feed herself, read, or write. She was also to be completely isolated from familiar human contact, including her family. The patient was to be fed excessively, especially on milk. Finally, she was to receive massages and electricity in order to keep her muscles from atrophying. Freud approved of this regimen, and Virginia Woolf underwent its strictures. Mitchell also treated Jane Addams, Edith Wharton, and Winifred Howells, daughter of William Dean Howells.

Some women benefited from the validation and respite that Mitchell's diagnosis brought. Gilman, however, needed to give expression to her inner life. Mitchell allowed her to engage in only two hours of intellectual work a day, which almost caused her to go completely insane. In 1913 Gilman published an article entitled "Why I Wrote the Yellow Wallpaper" in which she explains that her tale was intended to convince Mitchell to change his treatment of nervous disorders.

Gilman had some difficulty getting "The Yellow Wallpaper" published. She sent a copy to *Scribner's,* which rejected it. She sent the story to Howells, who forwarded it to Horace Scudder, editor of the *Atlantic Monthly.* In his cover letter, Howells called the tale "strong, blood curdling, and worth reading." Scudder, however, rejected the piece due to its troubling content. Gilman was not discouraged by the lack of interest. She hired a literary agent, who placed it with the *New England Magazine.* Howells may have also had a hand in its publication, although Julie Bates Dock surmises that it was actually Edward Everett Hale, Gilman's uncle by marriage, who made the story's publication possible. "The Yellow Wallpaper" finally appeared in January 1892. Though Gilman published the equivalent of two dozen volumes during her career, the story remained her best-known fictional work at her death in 1935.

Although "The Yellow Wallpaper" was republished at least twenty-two times prior to 1973, it largely escaped scholarly attention until that year, when it appeared in a Feminist Press edition. This publication included an afterword by Elaine Hedges, who decried the story's neglect. Since then, it has been elevated to the canon, republished throughout the world, and adapted to opera, film, and television.

TOPICS FOR DISCUSSION AND RESEARCH

1. Elaine Hedges, along with other scholars, views "The Yellow Wallpaper" as autobiographical. Gary Scharnhorst notes that Gilman warned against such a reading due to discrepancies between her experiences and those of her protagonist, who is named Jane. Gilman's story can also be understood as an example of American Realism. Gilman stated that the tale was about a woman's "nervous breakdown." Loralee MacPike examines the story as an example of Realist symbolism. The room's wallpaper represents the state of Jane's mind as a result of her imprisonment in a nursery that works to keep her in a state of childish dependence. Beate Schöpp-Schilling praises the tale for its realistic documentation of Jane's decline into mental illness. Hedges calls it a true account of the sexual politics between men and women. Denise Knight concludes that the story is a psychologically accurate portrayal of the effects of the rest cure and inequitable marriages. Knight also posits that the narrator may not be insane but rebelling as a result of the tremendous anger that she feels toward John.

2. "The Yellow Wallpaper" incorporates Gothic elements. In her autobiography, Gilman speculates that Scudder rejected her story because it was similar to the tales of Edgar Allan Poe. Juliann Fleenor argues that the Gothic has long been a genre by which women voice rebellion and anger at their second class status. According to Sandra Gilbert and Susan Gubar, the disturbed doppelgänger helps the female protagonist escape from male-dominated houses and texts in order to imagine what health and freedom would be like.

3. Important contributions have been made in recent years to a better understanding of the story. Susan Lanser incorporates cultural fears of racial impurity to explain it. The yellowness of the wallpaper is evocative of the "yellow peril" and represents societal anxieties about race, class, and ethnicity. Leading intellectuals, including Gilman, were not impervious to such fears. Knight compares "Through This" with "The Yellow Wallpaper" and connects the two tales, the former being a comment upon the latter. The Jane of "Through This" experiences firsthand the dismal life of women who sacrifice their lives entirely to the care of others. Catherine Golden believes that the dual texts within the story operate to depict the wallpaper as palimpsest. According to Golden, Jane's actions comprise the dominant text while her journals operate as a muted text. The subversive journal allows Gilman's protagonist to fictionalize herself as the audience of her own story. Paula Treichler observes that the

male linguistic order imprisons women, and the wallpaper represents feminine linguistic innovation. Judith Fetterley argues that Gilman's tale exposes the pernicious implications of male textual control. This dominance is a primary cause of madness in women. The feminine becomes a fictitious construct, whereby women are forced to deny their own reality.

RESOURCES

Primary Work

The Living of Charlotte Perkins: An Autobiography (1935; reprinted, Madison: University of Wisconsin Press, 1991).
Based on Gilman's diaries.

Bibliography

Julie Bates Dock, ed., *Charlotte Perkins Gilman's "The Yellow Wallpaper" and the History of Its Publication and Reception: A Critical Edition and Documentary Casebook* (University Park: Pennsylvania State University Press, 1998).
Provides a detailed historical account of Gilman's story. This study includes details surrounding the tale's publication history, changes that it underwent with each new printing, the correspondence related to the story, its initial reviews, and a catalogue of the reprinting history.

Gary Scharnhorst, *Charlotte Perkins Gilman: A Bibliography* (Metuchen, N.J.: Scarecrow Press, 1985).
Provides a reliable and comprehensive listing of Gilman's publications, and a selected list of biographical sources and criticism.

Biography

Mary A. Hill, *Charlotte Perkins Gilman: The Making of a Radical Feminist 1860–1869* (Philadelphia: Temple University Press, 1980).
Charts the early evolution of Gilman's feminism.

Ann J. Lane, *To Herland and Beyond: The Life and Work of Charlotte Perkins Gilman* (New York: Pantheon, 1990).
Concentrates on the development of Gilman's inner life through the central personal attachments that shaped her personality.

Criticism

Elizabeth Ammons, "Writing Silence: 'The Yellow Wallpaper,'" in *The Yellow Wallpaper: Charlotte Perkins Gilman,* edited by Thomas L. Erskine and Connie L. Richards (New Brunswick, N.J.: Rutgers University Press, 1993), pp. 257–276.
Postulates that Gilman's protagonist achieves agency as she writes her body on the walls of the nursery. Gilman anticipates Hélène Cixous's arguments for women to write themselves into the world and history.

Juliann E. Fleenor, "The Gothic Prism: Charlotte Perkins Gilman's Gothic Stories and Her Autobiography," in her *The Female Gothic* (Montreal: Eden, 1983), pp. 227–241.
Observes that the Gothic has been used to voice rebellion and anger over the status of women.

Sandra Gilbert and Susan Gubar, *The Madwoman in the Attic: The Woman Writer and the Nineteenth-Century Literary Imagination* (New Haven: Yale University Press, 1979).
Argues that the "mad double" is a recurring theme in fiction by women, whereby the writer works to escape male houses and texts.

Catherine Golden, ed., *The Captive Imagination: A Casebook on The Yellow Wallpaper* (New York: Feminist Press, 1992).
An essential anthology for a comprehensive understanding of the story and its ensuing body of scholarship. In two sections Golden treats the story's background material and subsequent critical canon.

Janice Haney-Peritz, "Monumental Feminism and Literature's Ancestral House: Another Look at 'The Yellow Wallpaper,'" *Women's Studies,* 12 (1986): 113–128.
Argues that the reader should feel sympathy for Jane and not identification with her. Identification has the consequence of making feminism purely imaginary. Gilman, as active social reformer, is the appropriate feminist model.

Elaine Hedges, "Afterword" to *The Yellow Wallpaper* (New York: Feminist Press, 1973), pp. 37–63.
Asserts that Gilman's story is autobiographical and directly confronts the "sexual politics of the male-female, husband-wife relationship."

Denise Knight, *Charlotte Perkins Gilman: A Study of the Short Fiction* (New York: Twayne, 1997).
Provides an account of Gilman's sources of influence, an extended discussion of "The Yellow Wallpaper," Gilman's own reflections on her famous story, and some critical approaches to this and some of her other works.

Knight, "'I am getting angry enough to do something desperate': The Question of Female 'Madness,'" in *The Yellow Wallpaper by Charlotte Perkins Gilman: A Dual-Text Critical Edition,* edited by Shawn St. Jean (Athens: Ohio University Press, 2006), pp. 73–87.
Argues that the narrator's behavior may not be insanity but an act of rebellion brought about by the rage that she feels toward her husband.

Knight, "The Reincarnation of Jane: 'Through This'—Gilman's Companion to 'The Yellow Wallpaper,'" *Women's Studies,* 20 (1992): 287–302.
Argues that the Jane of "Through This," the alter ego of Jane in "The Yellow Wallpaper," is a warning about what happens to obedient women who devote their strengths solely to domestic concerns.

Knight and Cynthia J. Davis, eds., *Approaches to Teaching Gilman's "The Yellow Wallpaper" and* Herland (New York: MLA, 2003).
Reminds teachers of Gilman's didacticism and guides pedagogical approaches to "The Yellow Wallpaper" and *Herland*.

Annette Kolodny, "A Map for Rereading: Or, Gender and the Interpretation of Literary Texts," in *New Feminist Criticisms: Essays on Women, Literature, and Theory,* edited by Elaine Showalter (New York: Pantheon, 1985), pp. 144–167.
Argues that the exclusion of "The Yellow Wallpaper" from the canon meant that generations of women could not, in accord with Harold Bloom's dialectical theory of influence, revise and perfect the ideas contained within the story.

Loralee MacPike, "Environment as Psychopathological Symbolism in 'The Yellow Wallpaper,'" *American Literary Realism,* 8 (1975): 286–288.
Illuminates the story as an example of Realist symbolism. The room that the narrator inhabits represents her status in society, and the wallpaper contained therein represents the state of her mind.

Gary Scharnhorst, *Charlotte Perkins Gilman* (Boston: Twayne, 1985).
Integrates Gilman's life and work into a chronological and thematic narrative. The text is interwoven with relevant poetry, aiding the reader's empathic response to the events of Gilman's life.

Beate Schöpp-Schilling, "'The Yellow Wallpaper': A Rediscovered 'Realistic' Story," *American Literary Realism,* 8 (1975): 284–286.
Uses Adlerian depth-psychology to interpret "The Yellow Wallpaper" as an example of psychological Realism.

Conrad Shumaker, "Too Terribly Good To Be Printed: Charlotte Gilman's 'The Yellow Wallpaper,'" *Arizona Quarterly,* 47 (Spring 1991): 81–93.
Argues that through her main characters, Gilman illumines how and why the fear of the female imagination has been institutionalized though assigned gender roles.

Paula A. Treichler, "Escaping the Sentence: Diagnosis and Discourse in 'The Yellow Wallpaper,'" *Tulsa Studies in Women's Literature,* 3 (Spring–Fall 1984): 61–77.
Postulates that the story is a metaphor for women's linguistic innovation in a phallocentric symbolic order.

—*Heidi M. Silcox*

O. Henry (1862–1910)

For a few years in the early twentieth century O. Henry was the most famous writer in America. "O. Henry" was the pen name of William Sydney Porter, whose path to success was circuitous. Porter was born in Greensboro, North

Carolina, where he spent his teen years as a drugstore clerk. At twenty he went to Texas to help out on the ranch of some family friends. He later wrote for the Houston *Daily Post* and other newspapers, finally settling in Austin, Texas, where he took a job as teller at First National Bank. He also wrote, illustrated, and published a humorous weekly called the *Rolling Stone,* which failed after only a year. When he was accused of embezzlement at the bank, he fled to Honduras but returned in several months to be at his wife's deathbed. He was convicted and served three years in the Ohio Penitentiary at Columbus. His job in the prison dispensary left him much time to read and write, and after his release in 1901 he went to New York City to write for magazines. Employing a variety of pen names to conceal his criminal record as well as his unnatural productivity, he settled on "O. Henry" when that name began to command editors' attention and higher prices.

The decisive event in his career was an offer from the New York *Sunday World* of a contract for a story a week. Until then his fiction had drawn largely on his experiences in Central America and the western and southern United States. But the *World* wanted tales of New York, and the teeming life of the city, combined with continual deadlines, drove him to produce what is widely considered his best work. The *World,* with a circulation of half a million, was the most popular newspaper in the country, and his New York stories made him nationally famous. From late 1903 through 1906, O. Henry published 113 stories in the *World,* while continuing to write for *Ainslee's, McClure's,* and other magazines.

In 1904 O. Henry stitched together his magazine stories set in Honduras to create a continuous narrative. The resulting book, *Cabbages and Kings,* sold poorly, but his next collection extended his fame around the world. The stories in *The Four Million* (1906), nearly all from the *World,* depict the impoverished lives of shop girls, the serial occupants of rented flats, and other members of New York's working class as well as of the leisure class. Other New York–themed collections followed: *The Trimmed Lamp* (1907), *The Voice of the City* (1908), and *Strictly Business* (1910). *Heart of the West* (1907) collects tales of cowboys, lawmen, and outlaws, and *The Gentle Grafter* (1908) takes up the con man types that O. Henry met in prison. In all, he published nine books during his life; and his uncollected stories filled several posthumous collections.

O. Henry's eccentric work habits influenced the shape and even the content of his stories. Despite his popularity, his casual handling of money often left him strapped for cash. Too impatient to wait for royalties, he sold his manuscripts outright to publishers and badgered editors for advances against final payment. He alternated between procrastination and periods of intense work when he attempted to fulfill his many commitments. He rarely delivered an entire manuscript, instead dispatching his stories in what one editor called "propitiatory fragments." His distinctive style, rambling and discursive, was well suited to this propensity for working close to deadline. Many of the stories begin with miniessays on broad subjects such as adventure or destiny, providing just enough information for an illustrator to begin work while buying the writer more time to work out the details of his plot.

O. Henry saw himself more as pieceworker than litterateur. In 1908, however, critical approval was added to popular acclaim with an appreciative essay about his stories in the prestigious *North American Review*. O. Henry began to take his work more seriously and developed plans for a novel. But, drinking heavily and in worsening health, his facility had already deserted him and he found it increasingly difficult in his final years even to produce short stories. He died destitute.

More critical appreciation followed his death—he was called "the American Maupassant" and "the Bret Harte of the City." The first biography of O. Henry, which appeared in 1916, claimed him as a major American short-story writer who had built on the tradition of Washington Irving, Edgar Allan Poe, and Nathaniel Hawthorne. That same year, however, a backlash set in, begun by "The Journalization of American Literature," an essay by F. L. Pattee, who saw in O. Henry's technical skill only superficiality. The Canadian writer Stephen Leacock counterattacked with "O. Henry and His Critics," and the battle over O. Henry's literary stature continued to be fought throughout the 1920s. With the rise of modernism and the "new" fiction, O. Henry came to seem passé and the argument over his reputation moot.

It did not help matters that even his supporters did not bother to read him closely. One early essay, according to Eugene Current-Garcia, "set the pattern for such critical analysis by skimming rapidly through each collection, synopsizing action, situation, and/or personae in a succession of stories." Critics who subjected the stories to close readings did so in order to identify their shortcomings: "thin and sketchy characterization," a "mawkish and wheedling tone," "far-fetched coincidence," and an ending that is "a shabby trick" was the verdict of Cleanth Brooks and Robert Penn Warren in their study of "The Furnished Room" in *Understanding Fiction* (1943).

Though O. Henry's work lived on in anthologies, and some of his characters—such as the Cisco Kid ("The Caballero's Way") and the safecracker Jimmy Valentine ("A Retrieved Reformation")—gained new life through dramatic adaptations, many surveys of American literature took no notice of him. O. Henry scholarship picked up somewhat in the 1960s and at intervals since but is always at low ebb compared to the attention paid to his contemporaries Stephen Crane, Frank Norris, Theodore Dreiser, and Jack London.

TOPICS FOR DISCUSSION AND RESEARCH

1. O. Henry was one of the several American short-story writers who began as journalists in the late nineteenth century. Trying to find his place in the magazine and newspaper market, he took as his models Crane, London, Ambrose Bierce, and Richard Harding Davis. Newspapers competed for their kind of exotic short fiction, and O. Henry's peripatetic life provided him with material that he could exploit in the same fashion. Other influences were the tradition of humor from the Old Southwest and the local-color genre, which was still popular. Students might consider what effect

O. Henry's target market—periodical publications and their readers—had on the shape and content of his fiction. His first biographer, C. Alphonso Smith, gives details on his voracious reading, and Current-Garcia is a useful resource for a discussion of the genres on which he drew.

2. Consider Smith's argument that O. Henry's worth resided not in his trademark surprise endings—skillful as they are—but in the fact that he "enlarged the area of the American short story by enriching and diversifying its social themes." Smith was the first to attempt to catalog those themes: "turning the tables" (rich folks masquerading as poor and vice versa, as in "While the Auto Waits" and "Lost on Dress Parade"); attempts to conquer deeply rooted habits or attachments ("From the Cabby's Seat," "The Romance of a Busy Broker"); the lure of adventure and "what's around the corner" ("The Green Door," "The Enchanted Kiss"); shop girls and others struggling to make their way in the city ("A Lickpenny Lover," "An Unfinished Story"); the city as a collective entity with a distinct personality ("A Cosmopolite in a Café," "The Making of a New Yorker"); and contrasts between different regions of the United States ("The Duplicity of Hargraves," "The Pride of the Cities"). Subsequent critics have suggested other useful frameworks for grappling with O. Henry's three-hundred-odd stories. Karen Charmaine Blansfield, for instance, examines the formulas used to generate their plots. Some useful areas for research are the social and intellectual developments that O. Henry responded to in his stories: How does his treatment of habit, for example, compare with writings on the subject by his contemporary William James?

3. O. Henry's curiosity and sympathetic nature led him throughout his life to go "slumming" in the poor sections of town; he found his material in the streets. In so doing, he not only created the myth of New York City as a modern-day land of Arabian Nights—"Bagdad-on-the-Subway," as he called it—but also tapped into the major currents of change that transformed the country in the years between the Civil War and World War I: "Rapidly increasing wealth, the rise of the city, expanding immigration, a widened spirit of reform, mass education, a new scientific point of view, and the acceptance of technology" (Jay Martin, *Harvests of Change*). O. Henry's stories, especially the New York stories, touch on all of these to some extent. Students are advised to choose one of these currents of change and investigate how O. Henry treated it in one or more of his stories.

4. *The Four Million* in its range of protagonists casts a wider net than the typical local-color collection. The title of O. Henry's breakthrough book was his response to Ward McAllister, who coined the phrase "the Four Hundred" to define the number of people in fashionable New York society. An author's note explains that a "larger estimate of human interest has been preferred in marking out the field of these little stories." O. Henry stressed the individuality of the oppressed; in showing how they counted their pennies and parceled out their small luxuries in stories such as "The Gift of the Magi," he revealed the human dimension behind social statistics in a way that even Jacob Riis's famous photographs of tenement dwellers could not. His aims, in fact, were similar to those of his contemporary John Sloan and other painters of the New York Realist

school. See David E. Shi's *Facing Facts* for a discussion of how Sloan found his material in the same streets that O. Henry frequented. Students might compare an O. Henry story and a painting by a New York Realist and discuss the effect the author's and painter's medium has on their artistic expression and the reader/viewer's perception of it.

5. O. Henry was a champion in particular of the shop girl and her sisters in the workforce, and it was for his series of workingwoman stories in the *World* that he was most renowned in his time. His factory workers, typists, and waitresses are more often depicted on the street or in their rooming houses than at work. "It's not the salesgirl in the department store who is worth studying, it is the salesgirl out of it," O. Henry said. His portrayals of the poor and exploited have led some critics, especially in Russia, to see him as a critic of capitalism. Students might consider whether they find a political message in O. Henry's stories and, if one is found, identify the means by which it is related.

6. The famous "O. Henry twist," or trick ending, seems less important now than his unique style. O. Henry peppered his stories with puns, dialects, arcane words and allusions, and unexpected digressions. His style was baroque yet playful and confiding, prefiguring humorists and metafictionists such as S. J. Perelman and Donald Barthelme. There was a performance or "stunt" aspect to his stories in the *World:* they demanded endless invention, and O. Henry no less than his readers took pleasure each week in discovering how he would manage to pull it off yet again. He loved to pull back the curtain and share the tricks of the writer's trade, as when he second-guessed his own choices: "It was a day in March. Never, never begin a story this way when you write one" ("Springtime à la Carte"). Identify examples of O. Henry's verbal trickery and discuss its effect on the reader. For a focus on this aspect of his work, see the formalist critics B. M. Ejxenbaum and Cesare Pavese as well as Margaret Cannell's "O. Henry's Linguistic Unconventionalities," in which she argues that "O. Henry's language is as surprising as his plots."

RESOURCES

Bibliography
Paul S. Clarkson, *A Bibliography of William Sydney Porter (O. Henry)* (Caldwell, Idaho: Caxton, 1938).

Biography
Be warned: these books contradict each other on key points, and one should be careful about accepting any statement at face value.

Gerald Langford, *Alias O. Henry: A Biography of William Sidney Porter* (New York: Macmillan, 1957).
Still the most thorough and dependable biography, this was the first to address the discrepancies between earlier accounts. Langford includes a detailed discussion of the question of O. Henry's guilt or innocence of embezzlement.

C. Alphonso Smith, *O. Henry Biography* (New York: Doubleday, Page, 1916). Superseded in many ways by Langford and others, but an excellent starting point.

William Wash Williams, *The Quiet Lodger of Irving Place* (New York: Dutton, 1936).
A memoir by one of O. Henry's friends and colleagues.

Criticism

Karen Charmaine Blansfield, *Cheap Rooms and Restless Hearts: A Study of Formula in the Urban Tales of William Sydney Porter* (Bowling Green, Ohio: Bowling Green State University Popular Press, 1988).
A solid scholarly introduction to O. Henry's short fiction.

Eugene Current-Garcia, *O. Henry: A Study of the Short Fiction* (New York: Twayne, 1993).
A good critical overview of the stories and their reception.

—Gary Kass

William Dean Howells, "Editha"

Harper's Monthly, 110 (January 1905): 214–224; collected in *Between the Dark and the Daylight* (New York: Harper, 1907)

"Editha" is the best-known short story by William Dean Howells (1837–1920), a leading figure in post–Civil War American letters. Born in Ohio, Howells began his career as a journalist, writing a campaign biography for Abraham Lincoln in 1860 that helped him to gain a diplomatic position in Venice as the Civil War erupted. While his early writings brought him notice, he first truly rose to prominence with the publication of *Venetian Life,* a collection of his travel writings, in 1866; in the same year he became assistant editor of the influential *Atlantic Monthly*. He became editor in 1871, cementing his position in the New England literary establishment and as an arbiter of American literary taste. His book *Literary Friends and Acquaintance* (1900) documents some of his many relationships with famous American writers. *My Mark Twain* (1910) tells the story of his lengthy and close friendship with the writer whose fame would outlast and surpass his own. A prolific writer even as his book sales began to lag during the early twentieth century, he produced countless reviews and essays, short stories, poems, and novels during his long career. He is perhaps best known now for his novels *The Rise of Silas Lapham* (1885) and *A Hazard of New Fortunes* (1890) and for his thoughtful, even passionate, defense of Realism in fiction. Howells opposed sentimental or idealistic narratives in favor of true depictions of daily life and the internal struggles of men and women. His interest in representing the lived experience of everyday citizens dovetailed with what were seen as his progressive social positions, including his defense of the Haymarket anarchists sentenced to death in 1886 and his opposition to the Spanish-American War in 1898. Although periodically plagued with poor health beginning in his youth, Howells lived to be eighty-three before succumbing to pneumonia in 1920.

"Editha" is told largely from the perspective of its title character, a young woman carried away by wartime excitement and patriotic fervor. Although the war is never explicitly named, most critics agree that the story is set on the eve of the Spanish-American War. Editha is engaged to George Gearson, a young man who once considered becoming a minister, and shows little interest in the drumbeats of war. Editha, however, longs for George to enlist and "win" her affections through courageous deeds in battle. She combines her romantic notions with catchphrases from the jingoistic press to urge the young man to take up arms. Swayed by Editha's encouragement, combined with the patriotic mood of his fellows and strong drink, George volunteers. While it is evident the next day that he is less than convinced of the virtue of this path, the young man commends his aging mother to Editha's care and departs for the war. A short time later, George is killed in the first "skirmish." Editha, abruptly transformed from the role of heroine to grief-stricken lover, takes up her new romantic ideal with a will and sets off to keep her promise. Rather than let the young woman continue playing her part, however, George's mother angrily confronts Editha for being so eager to send her son off to kill other mothers' sons, going so far as to exclaim, "I thank my God he didn't live to do it! I thank my God they killed him first, and that he ain't livin' with their blood on his hands!" Mrs. Gearson then threatens to rip the mourning clothes from Editha's body. The encounter leaves the young woman truly shaken for the first time in the story, a condition that persists until an artist painting her portrait proclaims the elderly woman's actions "vulgar," a judgment that frees Editha "to live again in the ideal."

TOPICS FOR DISCUSSION AND RESEARCH

1. Most of the early criticism of "Editha" centers on the story's indictment both of the war and Editha's romantic notions of warfare and courtship. Early on, the narrator reports that their courtship "was contemporaneous with the war feeling." George appears indifferent to the public furor, while Editha literally pants as she contemplates sending him off to battle. She parrots the papers, and George speaks in tones that confuse Editha but are clearly ironic, as when he remarks, "Our country—right or wrong." Why does his mother condemn Editha, her views, and the patriotic fervor at the end of the story? How is Editha ultimately able to recover from her confrontation with Mrs. Gearson? An influential article on the story by William J. Free will help students evaluate the ending of the story, particularly Editha's conversation with the artist ("Howells' 'Editha' and Pragmatic Belief," *Studies in Short Fiction*, 3 [Spring 1966]: 285–292).

2. While these readings tend to present Editha as ignorant and naive at best and villainous at worst, some critics argue that George is also culpable in his downfall (*The Portable American Realism Reader*, edited by James Nagel and Tom Quirk [New York: Penguin, 1997], p. 412). To what extent is George complicit

in the events that lead to his undoing? In an interesting counterpoint to this argument John W. Crowley argues that the story reveals Howells's own guilt and ambivalence regarding his decision not to take part in the decisive event of his generation ("Howells's Obscure Hurt," *Journal of American Studies,* 9 [August 1975]: 199–211). In this reading George's death serves as an attempt at self-vindication for Howells's failure to volunteer during the Civil War. Is there additional evidence for a biographical reading of the story? Is such a biographical reading persuasive?

3. The story poses some fundamental questions about Editha: is she a villain who shows callous disregard for the life and safety of her lover, who uses her charms to convince him to join a fight in which he doesn't believe? Or is she a woman who has few opportunities to act independently in her world and so uses the only means at her disposal to effect change and to take part in events? Are Editha and George active participants in what unfolds, or are they simply victims of circumstances beyond their control? Among the critics who address these questions are Crowley and Philip Furia ("'Editha': The Feminine View," *American Literary Realism,* 12 [Autumn 1979]: 278–282). Susan K. Harris offers the most sophisticated reevaluation of the title character ("Vicious Binaries," *College Literature,* 20 [June 1993]: 70–83). More recently, two scholars have read "Editha" in a broader historical context: Rosalie Murphy Baum ("Editha's War: 'How Glorious,'" in *War and Words,* edited by Sara Munson Deats, Lagretta Tallent Lenker, and Merry G. Perry [Lanham, Md.: Lexington, 2004], pp. 145–164) and Julie Goodspeed-Chadwick ("Howells's 'Editha': A Reevaluation," *Short Story,* 12, no. 2 [2004]: 63–70). Is the story a period piece, its significance specific to the period, or does it also speak to modern controversies over the morality and purpose of war?

4. Critics have yet to explore the regional issues raised in the tale. How does geography influence the opinions of the characters? How does Howells link the setting to the views expressed in the story? Editha must travel to western Iowa from New York to see George's mother; it seems that George, like Howells, left his Midwestern family to travel east. There are also clear class divisions present in the story. Editha's family's wealth, highlighted by at least three references to "Balcom's Works," her father's business, is brought into stark contrast with Mrs. Gearson's "little house." Is Howells linking his critique of war and jingoism to a critique of the bourgeoisie? Is this another example of a "rich man's war, a poor man's fight," as was often said of the Civil War?

RESOURCES

Bibliography
Ruth Bardon, *Selected Short Stories of William Dean Howells* (Athens: Ohio University Press, 1997).
A concise introduction to much of the criticism of "Editha." While a few studies have been published in the years since, Bardon's introduction to the story still provides an effective entry to most of the scholarship on the story.

Biography

Edwin H. Cady, *The Road to Realism, 1837–1885* (Syracuse, N.Y.: Syracuse University Press, 1956) and *The Realist at War: The Mature Years, 1885–1920* (Syracuse, N.Y.: Syracuse University Press, 1958).
The "first interpretive biography" of Howells, telling the story of his life and, in the second volume, detailing his rise to prominence in the literary world.

Everett Carter, *Howells and the Age of Realism* (Philadelphia: Lippincott, 1954).
An important early biography that treats Howells's life as it pertains to the development of the literary movement most associated with his name and career.

Susan Goodman and Carl Dawson, *William Dean Howells: A Writer's Life* (Berkeley: University of California Press, 2005).
A thorough and well-written biography focusing on events of the author's life rather than on his literary works. The discussion of "Editha," for example, is quite brief.

—*Martin T. Buinicki*

Henry James, "Daisy Miller"

Cornhill, 37 (June 1878): 678–698; 38 (July 1878): 44–67; collected in *Daisy Miller: A Study* (New York: Harper, 1878)

Born into a socially prominent and wealthy family on 15 April 1843, in New York City, the novelist Henry James grew up around some of the most important figures of the period. Ralph Waldo Emerson, for example, was his father's close friend. As a child his family traveled extensively in Europe, where his father hired private tutors for his five children. At the age of twenty-one young James abandoned formal study in science and law, deciding instead to become a professional writer. He also moved abroad, first to Paris, before settling in London in 1876. A key participant in the intellectual life of his day, he became acquainted with Henry Adams, Henry Cabot Lodge, and Oliver Wendell Holmes. He was a friend of William Dean Howells, and he knew many of the leading European writers of the time, including Ivan Turgenev, Émile Zola, George Eliot, and Matthew Arnold. His brother William James became a prominent Harvard professor of psychology and the leading pragmatic philosopher of his generation. Having lived as an expatriate in Great Britain for most of his life, Henry James became a British citizen in 1916, at least in part to protest the reluctance of the United States to enter World War I on the side of the Allies. He received the Order of Merit from King George V in 1916 and died of pneumonia later that year. His ashes are buried in Cambridge, Massachusetts.

James first submitted "Daisy Miller" to *Lippincott's* in Philadelphia, but the story was declined because the editors deemed it an affront to American womanhood. He next sent the manuscript to the *Cornhill* in London, where it was first published. The story was soon pirated in the United States in the absence of international copyright laws. It proved to be a critical, if not entirely a commercial, success. Several reprints of the novella were published, some with extensive illustrations, and James later even converted the story into a play. The script, published privately in 1882 in England and in the *Atlantic Monthly* the following year, is quite different from the original, especially in its happy ending. In 1909 James substantially revised the story for the New York edition of his works.

Daisy Miller and the vacationing Winterbourne meet in Vevey, Switzerland, when Daisy's younger brother introduces them. While the boy is convinced that New York surpasses anything found in Europe, Daisy is fascinated with high society, to which she aspires. An American living abroad since childhood, Winterbourne is unsure what to make of his young countrywoman's attitude and initially regards her as a mere flirt. He pursues his interest in Daisy despite the efforts of his Aunt Costello to discourage it. Her primary objection is the relationship the Millers have with Eugenio, their courier, a servant whose function is to lead the family on their tour of Europe. Eugenio's apparent intimacy with the family prompts the disapproval of the American expatriate community, who consider it vulgar. Mrs. Costello refuses to meet Daisy and studiously avoids her throughout the story. Despite these objections, Winterbourne tours the Château de Chillon with Daisy—significantly, without a chaperone.

The two young people inadvertently meet again in Rome when he visits the parlor of his American friend Mrs. Walker, who submits to the rules and fashions of European high society. When Daisy persists in behavior Mrs. Walker considers risky or "unsafe," such as meeting a man alone in the middle of the afternoon, Mrs. Walker also criticizes her. Mrs. Walker invites the Millers to a party, but, as if to demonstrate how little she understands, Daisy asks to bring a friend, the "third-rate" Italian Mr. Giovanelli, who apparently is her suitor. Both unaware of and unconcerned with the way she is seen by other expatriate Americans in Rome, Daisy behaves as she pleases. Following the lead of Mrs. Walker, Winterbourne tries to convince Daisy of the need for caution and discretion in her public activities, particularly her casual attitudes about her frequent rendezvous with men. She is dismissive, refusing to take any advice seriously, and insists on her right to do precisely as she pleases, regardless of the opinions of others.

When Daisy arrives at Mrs. Walker's salon with Giovanelli, she becomes something of a spectacle. Mrs. Walker turns her back on Daisy and promises Winterbourne she will ostracize her in the future. Throughout the story Winterbourne has persisted in defending Daisy, suggesting she is merely "uncultivated," but walking through the Colosseum one night he sees her and Giovanelli there together in the darkness. He decides that the "riddle" that is Daisy had become "easy to read," that she is common, if not compromised. Warning of the dangers of "Roman fever," or malaria to her health, he convinces her to return to her hotel, although she insists that she does not care. She returns too late, however, and falls ill. While Daisy is dying, Winterbourne visits her family regularly; Giovanelli, not at all. At her burial Winterbourne learns from Giovanelli how innocent Daisy truly was. Winterbourne realizes he has "misread" Daisy's character and admits to his aunt that he has "lived too long in foreign parts." Nevertheless, he returns to Geneva and a "very clever foreign lady" there.

TOPICS FOR DISCUSSION AND RESEARCH

1. The fiction of Henry James is best known today for its treatment of the so-called international theme. The clash between groups is sometimes a difference of age, class, or culture. How does "Daisy Miller" contrast the different social codes observed by old money and the nouveau riche as well as by Europeans and Americans? See Pahl and Wadsworth for ideas about approaching this topic.
2. James is sometimes regarded as a writer with a comic sense. Can "Daisy Miller" be read as a burlesque, or parody, of a sentimental romance with its standard plot of love triumphant? Or consider the different meanings the characters assign to such terms as "intimate," "flirt," "society," and "cool." Even though "Daisy Miller" ends on a sorrowful note, can it be regarded as a comic novella of manners? Read and evaluate Ohmann's argument in this regard.
3. James also selected suggestive names for many of his characters. How is Daisy like the flower and what does her surname suggest? How is Winterbourne an appropriate name? Does it suggest reasons he fails to understand Daisy? Why does James refer to Geneva as a "little metropolis of Calvinism"? Why does he return to Geneva at the close of the story? Does Mrs. Walker's name suggest anything about her character? Or Giovanelli's name, which means "little Giovanni"? Read and respond to Montero's article.

RESOURCES

Criticism

Viola Dunbar, "The Revision of 'Daisy Miller,'" *Modern Language Notes*, 65 (May 1950): 311–317.

An analysis of James's revision of the novella for the New York Edition and his more-carefully nuanced characterization of the heroine.

Lisa Johnson, "Daisy Miller: Cowboy Feminist," *Henry James Review*, 22 (Winter 2001): 41–58.

Summarizes much of the feminist criticism on the story, emphasizing Daisy's activities in the middle of the story rather than the approbation she receives in its beginning or her untimely end. Johnson regards Daisy as a free agent in control of her life, an admirable figure who makes her own decisions.

Paul Lukacs, "Unambiguous Ambiguity: The International Theme of 'Daisy Miller,'" *Studies in American Fiction,* 16 (Autumn 1988): 209–216.
Argues that from its first publication James's novella has always invited two distinct readings: that Daisy's innocence is a virtue or that it is willful ignorance.

George Montero, "What's in a Name? James' 'Daisy Miller,'" *American Literary Realism,* 39 (Spring 2007): 252–253.
Discusses character names and their thematic significance.

Carol Ohmann, "Daisy Miller: A Study of Changing Intentions," *American Literature,* 36 (March 1964): 1–11.
Argues that the novella is a comedy of manners, "of different ways of living," and Daisy is nothing if not ignorant.

Philip Page, "Daisy Miller's Parasol," *Studies in Short Fiction,* 27 (Fall 1990): 591–601.
An analysis of James's narratological technique in the novella.

Dennis Pahl, "'Going Down' with Henry James's Uptown Girl: Genteel Anxiety and the Promiscuous World of Daisy Miller," *LIT,* 12 (June 2001): 129–164.
Reads James's work as an effort to understand the complexities of class difference between the uptown elite and the downtown nouveau riche.

Kimberly C. Reed and Peter G. Beidler, eds., *Approaches to Teaching Henry James's* Daisy Miller *and* The Turn of the Screw (New York: MLA, 2005).
A valuable resource for students and teachers, with background readings and several critical essays. As the title indicates, this text emphasizes pedagogical approaches to two of James's novellas. Three of the essays treat issues of gender and sexuality in "Daisy Miller."

William T. Stafford, "Henry James the American: Some Views of His Contemporaries," *Twentieth Century Literature,* 1 (July 1955): 69–76.
A compilation of early responses to the fiction of Henry James, and hence a helpful guide to understanding how "Daisy Miller" was first received by readers and scholars.

Sarah A. Wadsworth, "Innocence Abroad: Henry James and the Re-Invention of the American Woman Abroad," *Henry James Review,* 22 (Spring 2001): 107–127.
Notes similarities between "Daisy Miller" and Mary Murdoch Mason's *Mae Madden,* suggesting that James designed his story around a popular literary theme at the time, that of the American woman abroad.

—*Rick Waters*

Sarah Orne Jewett, "A White Heron"

In *A White Heron and Other Stories*
(Boston: Houghton, Mifflin, 1886), pp. 1–21

Sarah Orne Jewett (1849–1909) was a popular writer in the late nineteenth century, when literary Realists and local-color writers were in vogue. Jewett came from a prestigious family in South Berwick, Maine, and much of her writing is about life in this area and in New England generally. As a child she suffered from rheumatoid arthritis and, as a consequence, would often miss school and travel with her father, a prominent doctor, on his calls to local farms. These experiences became the basis for *A Country Doctor* (1884). She seems to have had no serious romantic relationships in her life, and this fact has led to speculation about her sexuality; but as her biographer Paula Blanchard explains, "the choice of serious mates must have seemed rather thin." This scarcity was partly because her family represented a coterie of Maine's gentry in an otherwise rural farm community and partly because she was a teenager during the Civil War when the number of young men was seriously depleted. In any case, many women of the time chose to stay single, and they were respected socially. It is also clear that even as a young girl Jewett had career ambitions and recognized that marriage for women was limiting. Her first short story was published when she was only eighteen, and she managed to publish approximately seven or eight short stories a year for the rest of her life; many of these stories were later reprinted in collections, such as *A White Heron and Other Stories*. As one of the first women in America to support herself by her writing, she was an important role model for later female authors, particularly Willa Cather.

Jewett began her career writing children's stories, often with didactic moral messages. Her early short stories for adults were in the sentimental tradition of Harriet Beecher Stowe, an early influence. Today she is known primarily as a writer of local color—sometimes referred to as Regionalism—which is often seen as a subcategory of nineteenth-century Realism. Mentored by William Dean Howells, then editor of the *Atlantic Monthly,* she began to portray life as she saw it, using the voice of a neutral but sympathetic onlooker. Howells praised her gift for dialogue, writing her that she had "an uncommon feeling for talk—I hear your people." Jewett died of a stroke in 1909.

In the past the term "local-color" often was used as a subtle way to relegate women writers to secondary importance by suggesting that their stories lacked sufficient plot to rise to the level of serious literature. Not surprisingly, this issue has been a perpetual concern in regard to Jewett. For one thing, few of her works have the sustained drama associated with the novel. Even her longer works often seem to be merely collections of related episodes. Some critics, however, have argued that local color is a mode of writing that better reflects women's sensibilities, and therefore Jewett should be credited as a pioneer developing a particularly female style and voice, though many men have written local color, too. In any case, Jewett focuses on character and setting rather than plot. She has an optimistic perspective and avoids life's seedier aspects. Part of her optimism is apparent in that her characters exhibit free will and make moral decisions, as does Sylvia in "A White Heron."

Some recent critics have suggested that works of local color are often racist or elitist in that the descriptions usually involve an upper-class, white narrator describing some other ethnic group or social class from a bemused distance, but this seems a difficult charge to level against Jewett, who is sympathetic, appreciative, and involved with her "rustics."

"A White Heron" comes relatively late in Jewett's career and shows her as a mature writer in control of her material. It is one of her most famous and often anthologized works, and rightfully so. Meticulously crafted and often lyrical, it has a style reminiscent of Nathaniel Hawthorne, another of her early influences. Like much of Hawthorne's writing, however, it is a romance, and as such is uncharacteristic of her work. Though set in Maine, the specific location is purposely vague, suggesting a pastoral Eden outside of place and time.

The plot is straightforward. Nine-year-old Sylvia has been sent to live with her grandmother on a farm because she was unhappy living with her family in the city. Rescued from the modern industrial town, symbolized by the aggressive, red-faced boy who taunted her, Sylvia thrives in her new and isolated environment; the grandmother and the girl live an idyllic life, until a young ornithologist appears, searching for an elusive white heron. He suspects that Sylvia knows how to find the bird and attempts to bribe her (first with the gift of a knife and later with the promise of a ten-dollar reward) if she tells him where it is. Sylvia wants to help, partly because, though only nine, she is attracted to him: "the woman's heart, asleep in the child, was vaguely thrilled by a dream of love." However, she is troubled by his gun. The ornithologist loves nature yet wants to kill the heron as a trophy, a position Sylvia cannot understand. Despite her misgivings, she decides to find the bird's nest so that she can later tell him and earn his admiration. Consequently, at dawn, while the others sleep, she climbs a huge pine and discovers the heron's nest. At that point, she has a transcendent moment in which she feels as if "she too could go flying away among the clouds." When she gets home, she realizes she cannot tell of her discovery after all. She has learned that the rare white bird is sitting on a nest. By refusing to speak, she asserts her independence and, thereby, wins a moral victory.

Through Sylvia, Jewett makes one of the first declarations in literature of the importance of preserving nature. Some critics stop their analysis at this moral victory, but the story is more complex than this reading implies. Jewett ends with a melancholy awareness of the cost of Sylvia's decision. Sylvia seems doomed to remain a lonely and innocent girl, a female Peter Pan, alienated from the modern world and the issues surrounding adulthood.

The characters have obvious symbolic significance. Sylvia (from "Sylvan," meaning wooded) is associated with nature, and the ornithologist represents a modern world dominated by science and reason. Another reading, however, notes biographical similarities between the story and Jewett's life. Sylvia is in many ways similar to Jewett, who as a child preferred walks in the woods to school, and the young ornithologist has surprising parallels to Jewett's own father, who was an amateur naturalist. When the ornithologist goes away, the narrator tells us, she "could have served and followed him and loved him as a dog loves!" Significantly, on at least two occasions Jewett compared her relationship to her father as that of a loving dog to its master. Still another reading sees Sylvia as representing a particularly feminine approach to understanding—intuitive, organic—whereas the young man represents a stereotypically male approach: rational and dispassionate. Another reading sees the story as a feminist remake of the traditional fairy tale: according to this view, Sylvia is the modern woman, strong and independent, and the ornithologist is a rejected Prince Charming.

TOPICS FOR DISCUSSION AND RESEARCH

1. Jewett's stories often dramatize the conflict between older, primarily Christian virtues and "modern" values associated with capitalism and the Gilded Age. How could this dichotomy be applied to "A White Heron"? Not surprisingly, Jewett is particularly interested in the plight of women, and her stories focus on issues stereotypically associated with women, such as marriage, the struggle for independence, and social/community harmony. How does "A White Heron," which is about a nine-year-old girl, address these issues? Paradox and the difference between appearance and reality are also common themes in Jewett's work. Often, seemingly foolish country people prove to be wise while sophisticated city folk are shown to be shallow and self-serving. How does this play out in "A White Heron"? In terms of style, Jewett often uses rhetorical techniques to create a sympathetic attitude toward nature. Examine how Jewett describes the natural world in "A White Heron" and consider how these descriptions affect the reader and advance Jewett's thesis.

2. While the phallic imagery—the gun, the knife, the pine tree, even the red-faced boy who chases Sylvia—is obvious, critics have long speculated about the significance of the white heron. Does it represent nature, purity, the girl's innocence, spiritual transcendence, artistic inspiration, or even a clitoris, to name a few possibilities? Some recent critics have refocused the discussion of Jewett's work to the historical context and questioned her acceptance of social Darwinism, particularly Anglo-Norman superiority, and challenged her portrayal of racial, ethnic, and class stereotypes.

RESOURCES

Biography

Paula Blanchard, *Sarah Orne Jewett: Her World and Her Work* (Reading, Mass.: Addison-Wesley, 1994).
Well-researched, extensive, and fair-minded.

Criticism

Joseph Church, "Romantic Flight in Jewett's 'White Heron,'" *Studies in American Literature*, 30 (Spring 2002): 21–44.
Interprets the story as Jewett's coming to terms with her latent lesbian feelings for her longtime friend and companion Annie Fields.

Colby Library Quarterly, special Jewett issue, 22 (March 1986).
Includes Elizabeth Ammons's "The Shape of Violence in Jewett's 'A White Heron,'" a feminist reading that sees the story as a subversion of the traditional fairy tale and Sylvia's journey as a symbolic resistance to heterosexuality (pp. 6–16).

Karen L. Kilcup and Thomas S. Edwards, eds., *Jewett and Her Contemporaries: Reshaping the Canon* (Gainesville: University of Florida Press, 1999).
A collection of critical essays that includes a review of Jewett criticism in addition to several new critical approaches to her major works.

Karen K. Moreno, "'A White Heron': Sylvia's Lonely Journey," *Connecticut Review,* 13 (Spring 1991): 81–85.
Sees "A White Heron" as "the quest myth in feminist terms." Sylvia "becomes one" with the natural world that the ornithologist attempts, but fails, to master through aggression.

Gwen L. Nagel, ed., *Critical Essays on Sarah Orne Jewett* (Boston: G. K. Hall, 1984).
Includes two essays on "A White Heron": "Heart to Heart with Nature: Ways of Looking at 'A White Heron,'" by George Held and "The Language of Transcendence in Sarah Orne Jewett's 'A White Heron,'" by Gayle L. Smith.

Elizabeth Silverthorne, *Sarah Orne Jewett: A Writer's Life* (New York: Overlook, 1993).
A sympathetic biography with brief biographical readings of the major works, including "A White Heron."

Jules Zanger, "'Young Goodman Brown' and 'A White Heron': Correspondences and Illuminations," *Papers on Language and Literature,* 26 (Summer 1990): 346–357.
Claims to reveal "a series of shared elements: themes, settings, narrative sequences, images" showing Jewett's indebtedness to Hawthorne.

—Richard Randolph

Jack London, *The Call of the Wild*
(New York: Macmillan, 1903)

Jack London (1876–1916) was a man of great contradictions: a worshiper of literature who wrote commercially, a dedicated socialist who saw himself as a Nietzschean superman, and a Spencerian uncertain of his own heritage. Born to Flora Wellman, London's childhood was never what one would call structured. His father, almost certainly astrologer William Chaney, was never present in his life. Instead, Flora's new husband, John London, filled this patriarchal vacancy. After completing grade school London worked various hard-labor jobs, spent time as an oyster pirate, sailed on a sealing ship, and then tramped around the country as a hobo before returning to finish high school at age nineteen. Impatient with the educational system, London briefly attended Berkeley, although he never claimed to be an "educated man." Rather, his strength flowed from the books he read and his ability to capture the proletarian spirit. Following his brief stint of education, London traveled to the Yukon where he gained the background for many of his fifty-one volumes of stories, novels, and political essays.

The Call of the Wild is still London's most popular young-adult story. However, it is this very popularity with the general public and the ease with which the novel can be read that has led to some its harshest criticism. Some critics question the novel's status as a classic, as even its author appeared not to recognize its true significance. "I plead guilty," London reportedly said when others discovered the allegory in his work, "I was unconscious of it at the time." Others point to an apparent lack of artistry in London's work; it seems clear from his easy capitulations to editors and slightly flippant attitude toward his own works (he referred to *The Call of the Wild* as simply a "dog story") that what drove London most was monetary desire and a fear of the social abyss of poverty. London was certainly not the first to view writing as a profession rather than an art, but he was uncommonly skilled at it, making use of the controversy surrounding his socialist exploits to thrust himself into the spotlight. However, this skill also led to the commercial nature of some of his works, which London's harshest critics cite in labeling *The Call of the Wild* as at most a fable or a ridiculous adventure tale. And yet, others find in this "dog story" a deeper meaning. In his combination of Nietzschean and Spencerian ideas, London has created an allegory for the human condition; the struggle against hostile forces and the possibility of escape to an older world.

The Call of the Wild revolves around Buck, a magnificent specimen of the Nietzschean "superman," or in this case "superdog," who believes himself to be a lord of civilization at the novel's beginning. His reign over Judge Miller's California home comes to a sudden end, however, when he is stolen by a gardener in need of money. Despite his inability to comprehend his kidnapping (London takes care to emphasize Buck's animal status in an attempt to garner the objectivity due in a Naturalist work), Buck's destiny becomes apparent to the reader as Buck is thrown into a new world, that of the wild. Born with a natural right to rule, Buck must find a new dominion. Displaying his natural superiority, a result of London's own beliefs in certain racial supremacies, Buck quickly adapts to laws of the wild and life as a sled dog in the North, which allows London plenty of opportunities to make use of his own Yukon travels. Through the still-novel idea of atavism, London has Buck's harsh environment bring out in him his long-repressed instincts. At first Buck struggles simply to survive, but soon his natural right to sovereignty manifests and he attempts to take control of the team. Buck eventually becomes the lead dog through his defeat of Spitz, the treacherous husky, but soon becomes tired of this monotonous life, as he still remains a servant to his human masters. He is eventually freed from the life of "trace and trail" through the ineptitude of new owners, Hal, Mercedes, and Charles, and through the goodness of wilderness man John Thornton, but he remains tied to civilization. Only after Thornton's brutal murder by Yeehat Indians and Buck's revenge is he finally free to answer the call. By murdering those who killed his beloved and tasting of the noblest game, man, Buck becomes the leader of the local wolf pack, assuming the legendary status of the Ghost Dog and gaining a more noble lordship over the wilderness.

For a look at the historical and social settings surrounding the novel, students should refer to Daniel Dyer's reader's companion (1997) to the novel, which includes maps, photographs, and detailed annotations. For an introductory sample of the criticisms surrounding the novel, however, students may turn to the casebook edited by Earl J. Wilcox and Elizabeth H. Wilcox (2004). As Jo Ann Middleton notes in *American Literary Scholarship 1992,* London studies have dramatically changed direction over the last twenty years, from the often replayed examination of London in light of his alleged misogyny and racism to new exploration of his works. Highly recommended are Jonathan Auerbach's *Male Call: Becoming Jack London* (1996), Jacqueline Tavernier-Courbin's The Call of the Wild: *A Naturalistic Romance* (1994), and Andrew Flink's "*The Call of the Wild:* Parental Metaphor" (1974).

Unfortunately, no comprehensive biography is yet available, as London's own habit of embellishment, his inclusion of elements of his own life in his fiction, and certain media myths have persisted in clouding the truth. For a sample of London's personal letters, photographs, and conversations, see *The Book of Jack London,* by his wife, Charmian London, but be advised that there are omissions.

TOPICS FOR DISCUSSION AND RESEARCH

1. For many Naturalist writers, the main goal of their works was to understand the fundamental laws that govern the universe and society. In what ways does London use Buck's situation to this end? Consider in particular the two worlds in which Buck must survive. Are these worlds opposing, or do they simply have a different set of values?

2. Whether London intended it or not, the two systems that Buck must work under, those of civilization and the wild, also seem to apply to the human characters within the book, making *The Call of the Wild* an allegory of the human condition. London makes it clear that the wild and civilization are not opposing forces; rather, they are complementary, two parts of the world with different sets of values. When Buck served under Judge Miller in the civilized world, he "would have died for a moral consideration, say the defense of Judge Miller's riding-whip." Once in the wild and forced to accept the "law of club and fang," however, Buck can only worry about his own survival. In fact, Buck's development is often shown through his successful moral degradation, as when he steals food for the first time. In a human character such moral lapses would be deplored. Why do we not condemn Buck for these moral lapses?

3. How do the lessons Buck learns about survival in these two worlds reflect on the human characters within the story? John Thornton, who is the closest thing to an equal that Buck finds among mankind, also seems to live in the

world of the wild, although he is still limited to some degree by his civility. Despite London's apparent support of his pioneer spirit, Thornton still meets his demise when he turns away from the spirit of the wild and begins the idle process of collecting gold, sacrificing his balance with nature. Similarly, Buck's temporary masters Charles, Hal, and Mercedes are unable to make the transition away from the laws of civilization, and they too pay with their lives when the ice opens beneath them. It seems clear that, for London, the laws of the wild cannot be transcended, and that one must have the ability to operate under these laws in order to survive.

4. Why is it that human characters fail so dismally, while Buck succeeds—not only surviving but also becoming a lord of the wild? What might the appearance of primordial man in Buck's visions by the fire suggest? While few of the human characters within the story are able to make this transition flawlessly, Buck succeeds due to his genetic predisposition to greatness and the powerful influence of nature. The harsh conditions of the North serve to bring out Buck's long-repressed instincts, both in the physical form, as his body adapts to the environment, as well as in a more psychological form, as Buck recalls the racial memories of his ancestors. By tying Buck's memories of the primordial man with Buck's reversion throughout the novel, London narrows the gap between civilization and the wild, suggesting that, just as Buck's instincts quickly surface, perhaps mankind too is closer to his instinctual and wilder self than was previously thought.

5. *The Call of the Wild* may also be considered a story about gold fever. While London may not have been successful in his Yukon travels, he did manage to gain enough material to represent this part of American culture vividly and accurately. How does the novel reflect London's own history in the Yukon? Students will find *Jack London and the Klondike* particularly helpful in researching this topic.

6. Students should also take care to observe the continuing battle for supremacy throughout the novel. If Buck is destined to lead, is his path to mastery an easy one? Students should note that each step in Buck's linear atavistic growth is complemented by his rise in importance, first in the pseudo-wild of the sled team, then in the cultural lore of the miners, and finally in the true wild of the wolf pack.

RESOURCES

Bibliography

Joan R. Sherman, *Jack London: A Reference Guide* (Boston: G. K. Hall, 1977).
An annotated bibliography for London research up to 1975, including historical details and extensive annotations.

Roy Tennant and Clarice Stasz, *The Jack London Online Collection*, Sonoma State University <http://london.sonoma.edu> [accessed 28 August 2009].
An invaluable source for any student beginning London research; includes a bibliography of works on London and primary sources such as letters and other documents.

Biography

Charmian London, *The Book of Jack London* (New York: Century, 1921).
A personal look at the life of Jack London, by his wife. There are some omissions of the more basic details of London's life, but the work is still surprisingly candid in reference to his personality.

Joan London, *Jack London and His Times* (Seattle: University of Washington Press, 1968).
A well-researched guide to the historical and sociological context of London's life, by his daughter. The work is especially informative in reference to London's socialism, although it may be tainted by his daughter's bias.

Irving Stone, *Sailor on Horseback: The Biography of Jack London* (Boston: Houghton Mifflin, 1938).
The most popular biography, based on Huntington Library resources and with help from London's family and friends. What could have been a comprehensive biography with exclusive insight from primary sources is, however, marred by Stone's preoccupation with London's "inherited traits" and his use of London's fictions as a basis for statements of fact.

Franklin Walker, *Jack London and the Klondike* (San Marino, Cal.: Huntington Library, 1966).
A scholarly biography that avoids many of the assumptions made by earlier biographers. This work provides a comprehensive look at London's Klondike travels and their influence on his works.

Criticism

Jonathan Auerbach, *Male Call: Becoming Jack London* (Durham, N.C.: Duke University Press, 1996).
Analyzes London's work in relation to his burgeoning growth as a professional author.

Daniel Dyer, *The Call of the Wild: Annotated and Illustrated* (Norman: University of Oklahoma Press, 1997).
The definitive reader's companion with a scholarly introduction, maps, and photos.

Andrew Flink, "*The Call of the Wild:* Parental Metaphor," *Jack London Newsletter,* 7 (1974): 58–61.
A discussion of the ways in which London's work parallels his life.

Earle Labor, "Jack London's Mondo Cane: *The Call of the Wild* and *White Fang,*" *Jack London Newsletter,* 1 (1967): 2–13.
Views London's dog stories as "beast fables" and attempts to explain the popularity of *The Call of the Wild.*

Jacqueline Tavernier-Courbin, The Call of the Wild: *A Naturalistic Romance* (New York: Twayne, 1994).
Examines London's work as a mythic and romantic novel.

—Anoff Cobblah

Jack London, "To Build a Fire"

Century, 76 (August 1908): 525–534; collected in *Lost Face* (New York:
Macmillan, 1910), pp. 63–98

Jack London (1876–1916) was one of the most popular and respected American authors of his time. He created literary characters who, like himself, were active and adventurous, and many of his stories, including "To Build a Fire," argue that humans must either adapt to the Naturalistic universe or be annihilated by it.

London was born John Griffith Chaney to a working class family in San Francisco. At ten he took menial jobs to help support his family, and at fourteen he dropped out of school to work full-time. At sixteen he bought a boat and harvested oysters illegally, becoming known as the "Prince of the Oyster Pirates." Educating himself with books from public libraries, London discovered socialism and at nineteen began giving fiery street-corner speeches, prompting local newspapers to call him the "Boy Socialist of Oakland." He ran unsuccessfully for mayor of Oakland on the Socialist Party ticket in 1901 and 1905. Admired by Eugene Debs and Leon Trotsky, London championed workers' rights in his novels *The People of the Abyss* (1903), *The Iron Heel* (1908), and *The Valley of the Moon* (1913). He attacked Nietzschean individualism and capitalism in *The Sea-Wolf* (1904) and *Martin Eden* (1909).

Author of some twenty novels, two hundred short stories, and four hundred nonfictional pieces during his twenty-year literary career, London's first published work was a newspaper article based on his experiences aboard the sealing ship *Sophia Sutherland*. He later worked as a war correspondent, reporting on the Russo-Japanese War for the Hearst newspapers in 1904 and the Mexican Revolution for *Collier's* in 1914. The journalistic style of his fiction influenced Ernest Hemingway and George Orwell.

Many of London's fictional works were based on personal experiences. His years as an oyster pirate and subsequent employment by the California Fish Patrol are reflected in *The Cruise of the Dazzler* (1902) and *Tales of the Fish Patrol* (1905). His seven months aboard the *Sophia Sutherland* inspired *The Sea-Wolf*, and his 1907–1908 voyage to the South Pacific aboard *The Snark*, a ship London designed himself, was fictionalized in *South Sea Tales* (1911), *The Cruise of the Snark* (1911), and *The House of Pride and Other Tales of Hawaii* (1912). London also participated in the Klondike gold rush of 1897. His adventures inspired *The Call of the Wild* (1903), *White Fang* (1906), and "To Build a Fire."

London initially wrote "To Build a Fire" as a boy's adventure tale, and it was published in *Youth's Companion* magazine in 1902. He later expanded and revised it, publishing the often anthologized, more Naturalistic version six years later. The story begins with the protagonist and his dog hiking across the unforgiving Alaskan wilderness toward a mining camp. Untroubled by the cold and gloomy landscape, the prospector considers himself master of all he surveys—the entire length of the Yukon Territory. Confident in his independent nature, strong will, and ability to reason, the man believes he, not an unpredictable universe, controls his fate. He consults his watch several times, calculating his speed and planning precise times for meals and his arrival at camp. The man takes care to follow a faint sled trail and avoid thin ice that hides dangerous pools of frigid water, which could soak him and threaten his life. He forces his dog to lead, and when the dog breaks through into the water, it instinctively bites the ice from its forepaws. This reaction contrasts with the man, who initially forgets to build a fire when he stops for lunch, not immediately noticing that his hands are dangerously numb. A little frightened, he quickly lights a fire and eats.

Soon after getting back on the trail, the man himself breaks through the ice, soaking his clothes below the knee. He carefully constructs and lights a fire to dry out his feet, socks, and moccasins. Because he builds the fire beneath a spruce tree rather than in the open, however, the snow on the tree's branches drops on the fire, dousing it. The man frantically builds another fire, but his fingers are so numb that he cannot light it. Remembering a story about a man killing a steer and crawling inside during a blizzard, he attempts to catch and kill his dog, but the dog's superior instincts enable it to evade him. Panicked and fearing death, the man begins to run blindly across the snow, stumbles, and realizes that he is doomed. Defeated by the environment and the flaws in his nature, he falls into "the most comfortable and satisfying sleep he had ever known," the sleep of death. The dog leaves the man for the food and fire of the camp.

TOPICS FOR DISCUSSION AND RESEARCH

1. "To Build a Fire" follows many of the tenets of Realism. Students should research literary Realism as they examine London's stark, journalistic style. Students might discuss the effect of London's verisimilitude, such as the man's spittle crackling sharply and explosively in eighty-below temperatures, the amber colored ice on his beard from his tobacco spit, and his symptoms of frostbite and hyperthermia.

2. London's protagonist takes a cavalier attitude about his journey across the frozen tundra. He is brave and strong; he can reason; and he is observant. Is he abnormal, or are his experiences extraordinary? He begins his journey arrogantly self-confident, unconcerned about traveling alone or his rapidly freezing cheeks: "A bit painful, that was all; they were never serious." Why is he surprised by the cold and its effects on him? Also, why doesn't his technology and talents (the ability to build a fire) protect him from hyperthermia and death in the end?

3. Students should conduct research on Naturalism in literature. "To Build a Fire" follows Émile Zola's instruction on how to construct a Naturalistic literary work: placing the protagonist at the center of a scientific experiment and allowing the reader to observe how heredity and environment shape his character and determine his destiny. Why does London characterize his failure to build a fire as "his mistake" rather than "his own fault"? What is the difference? Why is London's protagonist unnamed? How does his background explain his failure to adapt to a hostile environment?

4. Many literary scholars have cited the man's lack of imagination as a reason for his failure. What kind of imagination would he need to survive? Why is it important for him to "meditate upon his frailty as a creature of temperature, and upon man's frailty in general"? The man is proud of his ability to travel and survive alone, rejecting the "womanish" fears and warnings of the old-timer never to travel in these conditions without a partner. Why is asking for help or taking advice gendered female? London's protagonist considers himself a true man and is shocked when he fails, realizing by the end that the old-timer was correct. The man's final words are an admission of wisdom gained too late. Discuss the didactic nature of literature; why is it better to learn a lesson from the experiences of a fictional character rather than through one's own experience?

5. The dog, on the other hand, has evolved to survive in this climate. The man considers the dog an inferior being; yet, when the man realizes his own lack of warmth and endurance, he begins to envy the dog. The dog, whose ancestors lived in this region, has evolved a natural covering that protects it in the cold. However, it has more than fur to protect it; as a "brother" to the wild wolf, it has the instinct of self-preservation, a biological heritage of knowing when not to be outside: "It knew that it was no time for traveling. Its instinct told it a truer tale than was told to the man by the man's judgment." Although it lacks the man's knowledge of thermometers, its brute instinct enables the dog to survive the cold and the man's murderous desperation. Students should find examples in the text that show what the dog does to obey "the mysterious prompting that arose from the deep crypts of its being." Also, discuss how and why the dog chooses instinct over social training. When does it obey the man and when does it disobey? Discuss London's message that instinct and fur covered skin are superior in this environment to human reason and human-made tools like matches and clothing.

RESOURCES

Biography

Carolyn Johnston, *Jack London—An American Radical?* (Westport, Conn.: Greenwood Press, 1984).
A study of the development of London's politics, particularly his socialism. Johnston argues London should be considered a rebel rather than a radical and that his political views were complicated by his sympathetic but disdainful attitude toward the lower working class.

Alex Kershaw, *Jack London: A Life* (New York: St. Martin's Press, 1998).
A passionate, insightful biography of London, written in a breezy style.

Criticism

Jonathan Auerbach, *Male Call: Becoming Jack London* (Durham, N.C.: Duke University Press, 1996).
An important critical study of London's early life and writing career, particularly his contributions to literary Naturalism.

Leonard Cassuto and Jeanne C. Reesman, eds., *Rereading Jack London* (Stanford, Cal.: Stanford University Press, 1996).
A collection of essays by noted scholars, who examine London's Naturalism from a variety of theoretical approaches that include psychoanalytical, poststructuralist, Marxist, feminist, and New Historical.

James I. McClintock, *White Logic: Jack London's Short Stories* (Grand Rapids, Mich.: Wolf House Books, 1975); republished as *Jack London's Strong Truths* (East Lansing: Michigan State University Press, 1997).
McClintock's book analyzes, among other things, the Darwinian ideas explored in London's stories of adventure and death in a hostile Arctic environment.

Nancy A. Walker, ed., *Jack London* (New York: Twayne, 1994).
A collection of essays that includes "The Literary Frontiersman," by Earle Labor and Jeanne Campbell Reesman, which analyzes London's imagery and symbolism in "To Build a Fire." Labor and Reesman argue that the Naturalistic setting—the bitter winter in the Yukon—is a character in the story, mythical and antagonistic.

Charles Child Walcutt, *Jack London* (Minneapolis: University of Minnesota Press, 1966.
A pamphlet that provides an overview of London's writing. Walcutt pays particular attention to the influence of Darwin, Nietzsche, and Marx.

—*Matthew Teorey*

Edwin Arlington Robinson, *Collected Poems*
(New York: Macmillan, 1937)

Although his work fell into critical neglect almost immediately after his death, Robinson ranked among the most prominent American poets early in the century. In 1922 he was awarded the first-ever Pulitzer Prize for poetry. Born in Head Tide, Maine, on 22 December 1869, Robinson was raised in nearby Gardiner. His parents, Edward and Mary, descended from solid, though not distinguished, New England stock; Mary claimed the early Puritan poet Anne Bradstreet as a distant relative. By the time the youngest of his three sons was born, Edward had amassed a comfortable fortune of $80,000 through lumber speculation. The family's move to Gardiner in 1870 was prompted by his retirement at the age of fifty-one.

Robinson began writing as early as eleven or twelve without much encouragement. Near the end of his high school years he joined a group of amateur poetry enthusiasts called the Gardiner Poetry Club, headed by Alanson Tucker Shumann, who prescribed technical exercises that instilled in Robinson the necessary discipline of craft. Beginning in 1888, however, a series of family disasters threatened to derail his ambition to write full-time. Robinson worked on his poetry throughout this period and privately published his first collection of poems, *The Torrent and the Night Before* (1896), just ten days after his mother's death. The collection demonstrated his mastery of various verse forms such as the sonnet and his lifelong preference for rhymed and blank verse as opposed to the more formless free verse popularized by Whitman. Despite the collection's small print run (some three hundred copies) and the fact that Robinson personally mailed editors copies of the collection, *The Torrent and the Night Before* received a surprising amount of press, with notices appearing in prominent outlets such as *Bookman*. In part because Robinson eschewed the elevated language of poets such as James Whitcomb Riley, Thomas Bailey Aldrich, and Richard Henry Stoddard, his outlook was misinterpreted as stark and pessimistic. As he complained to a friend, "Because I don't dance on [an] illuminated hilltop and sing about the boblinks and bumble-bees, they tell me that my world is a 'prison house, etc.'"

In 1897 Robinson expanded *The Torrent and the Night Before* with forty-three additional poems in his first commercially distributed collection, *The Children of the Night*. Among the new inclusions was "Richard Cory," a portrait of gilded gentility reputedly based on the suicide of a prominent Gardiner resident. Narrated from the perspective of "we people on the pavement," the poem explores the deceptiveness of public appearances. Despite Cory's enviable wealth and social poise ("In fine, we thought that he was everything / To make us wish that we were in his place"), this epitome of gentlemanly grace commits a desperate act that those admiring him from a distance cannot begin to fathom:

> So on we worked, and waited for the light,
>   And went without the meat, and cursed the bread;
> And Richard Cory, one calm summer night,
>   Went home and put a bullet through his head.

In his later years Robinson expressed disgruntlement that anthologists selected "Richard Cory" to represent his entire career. His ambivalence toward the poem may reflect its muted autobiographical origins. At the time of its composition, the author was living in the family home in Gardiner with an increasingly embittered and volatile brother. Robinson did enjoy the support of a coterie of artistic friends in Gardiner, including the city's most famous author, Julia Ward Howe's daughter Laura E. Richards (1850–1943).

Yet, family tensions proved too stifling for Robinson to remain at home. His middle brother, Herman, had wooed away the love of Edwin's life, Emma Shepard, creating an irreparable fracture between the brothers. After one particularly explosive confrontation, Robinson agreed to leave Gardiner, even though he and not Herman had maintained the house over the course of their parents' decline. Despite his exile, Robinson's feelings for Emma never faded. He would ask her to marry him on the heels of Herman's death in 1909 and again in 1918 and 1927. Not surprisingly, romantic triangles are a recurrent motif in Robinson's poetry. "Eros Turannos" (1913), in particular, is an empathetic exploration of Emma's dependency on Herman. The poem at once condemns the traditions that lock a woman in an unhappy marriage while respecting its protagonist's dread of being alone: "But what she meets and what she fears / Are less than are the downward years, / Drawn slowly to the foamless weirs / Of age, were she to lose him."

After leaving Gardiner, Robinson briefly affiliated with a group of bohemian writers in New York. Among them was Alfred H. Louis, a colorful tale-teller who inspired the title poem of Robinson's third book, *Captain Craig* (1902). At two thousand lines, *Captain Craig* is the poet's first foray into the long-form verse that dominated his later career. The poem is also Robinson's most overt statement of philosophy, rejecting pessimism and despair in favor of an Emersonian optimism tempered by the wizened awareness of life's ultimate defeats. "There is no servitude so fraudulent / As of a sun-shut mind," the Captain preaches. "For 't is the mind / That makes you craven or invincible, / Diseased or puissant." Robinson found this roseate outlook difficult to sustain during a nearly two-year effort to find a publisher for the piece. Houghton Mifflin finally agreed to issue it—but only if Robinson's chief supporters, Laura E. Richards and John Hays Gardiner (a Harvard professor), agreed to subsidize printing costs. The poem's tortured journey may explain its author's wavering opinion of its merits over the years; ultimately, the poem is more intriguing as a character sketch than compelling as a credo. Of more interest is one of the half-dozen shorter poems Robinson also included in *Captain Craig*. "Isaac and Archibald," a meditation on aging, accomplishes the technical feat of creating a dual point of view in which the narrating "I" speaks as both a child and an adult, not unlike James Joyce's story "Araby":

> The old men smoked while I sat watching them
> And wondered with all comfort what might come
> To me, and what might never come to me;
> And when the time came for the long walk home
> With Isaac in the twilight, I could see
> The forest and the sunset and the sky-line,
> No matter where it was that I was looking:
> The flame beyond the boundary, the music,
> The foam and the white ships, and two old men
> Were things that would not leave me. . . .

With poetry proving unremunerative, Robinson was forced to seek employment for the first time in his life. In 1898 he worked briefly for Harvard president Charles W. Eliot before returning to New York. President Theodore Roosevelt read *The Children of the Night* and, impressed, secured for him a position at the New York customhouse. Roosevelt's patronage also paid a literary dividend: thanks to a glowing review of *The Children of the Night* that Roosevelt published in *Outlook,* Scribners released a new edition of the book.

Robinson produced little poetry during his four years at the customhouse, preferring to dabble in playwriting. One poem he did complete in this otherwise uninspiring period was "Miniver Cheevy," a light satire about a man obsessed with the "mediaeval grace" of the past:

> Miniver Cheevy, born too late,
>   Scratched his head and kept on thinking;
> Miniver coughed, and called it fate,
>   And kept on drinking.

For many biographers, the poem represents Robinson's mocking of his own susceptibility to nostalgia and his disinterest in material possessions. The character's name even captures his estimation of his career as he neared forty: he was a poet of "minimum achievement."

Robinson's sinecure ended when Roosevelt left the presidency in 1909. He repaired to Maine to assist his sister-in-law in raising his nieces and to prepare *The Town Down the River* (1910), a collection of verse portraits that, not surprisingly, features a prominent tribute to Roosevelt. The volume is notable for the variety of forms it attempts: in addition to the light verse of "Miniver Cheevy," there are sonnets, dramatic monologues, and elegies. Despite its maturity, the book received only modest reviews.

For the next several years, Robinson again focused on drama, eventually publishing two plays of middling quality, *Van Zorn* (1914) and *The Porcupine* (1915). Their completion was enabled by summer residencies at MacDowell Colony in Peterborough, New Hampshire. Although Robinson was initially leery of the colony, he flourished in its supportive atmosphere and found the rustic environment helped him control his drinking. Beginning in 1911, he returned annually for the rest of his life.

Robinson's career finally took off in 1916 with the publication of *The Man against the Sky*, a rapturously reviewed collection that includes some of the poet's most accomplished work. Several poems, including "Eros Turannos," "Gift of God," and "The Poor Relation," offer stirring insight into the romantic disappointments of women, reflecting his continued compassion for Emma. "Ben Jonson Entertains a Man from Stratford" is a long dramatic monologue exploring the rivalry between Shakespeare and his titular contemporary, while "The Man against the Sky" itself plumbs the global mood of anxiety and despair brought on by the Great War. The collection's reception inspired a dozen supporters to contribute to a $1,200-per-year stipend to ease Robinson's financial pressures. Equally important, the book's critical success vaulted him to the forefront of American poetry. Robinson died of pancreatic cancer on 6 April 1935.

TOPICS FOR DISCUSSION AND RESEARCH

1. Because Robinson was opposed to verbal abstraction and preferred to write within traditional forms and meters, his verse can appear deceptively old-fashioned, despite the fact that his simplified diction and avoidance of archaic language were quite novel for its time. Compare Robinson's innovations to the insistent experimentation of contemporaries such as T. S. Eliot, Ezra Pound, William Carlos Williams, Wallace Stevens, and even Robert Frost, with whom Robinson maintained a testy rivalry. As the modernist canon came to define the development of post–World War I poetry, Robinson's prodigious output—twenty volumes, the bulk of it after 1916—declined in both popularity and stature. What was the basis for the critical support from enthusiasts such as James Dickey, Donald Hall, and W. S. Merwin, who continued to advocate for a renaissance of interest? Robinson is remembered by many for a single

poem, "Richard Cory" (1897), which the folk-pop duo Paul Simon and Art Garfunkel adapted to song in 1965. Consider the effect of the transformation of Robinson's poem to music.

2. *The Torrent and the Night Before* introduced Robinson's fictional "Tilbury Town" poems, proto-*Winesburg, Ohio* character sketches that glimpse into the despair beneath the placid surfaces of small-town life. In efforts such as the oft-anthologized "Luke Havergal" as well as "John Evereldown," "The Dead Village," "The Clerks," and "The House on the Hill," Robinson fused deceptively simple language with a tonal Realism that demonstrated how even within the formal rigor of a meter and rhyme scheme poetry could speak disconcertingly directly in expression. Discuss the effect of Robinson's character sketches. Is his simple, direct language and formal meter and rhyme effective?

3. The apparent simplicity of Robinson's style has worked against his reputation, with the directness of his expression seeming to leave little room for interpretation. Nevertheless, his Realism and diction mark important breaks from the contrived, self-consciously poetic language of the preceding generation, and his empathy for the Miniver Cheevys and Mr. Floods—the beautiful losers of the world—offers a compassionate alternative to the satire with which modernists treated their Mauberlys, Prufrocks, and Sweeneys. Is poetry less effective or less interesting if it fails to invite interpretation?

RESOURCES

Biography

Scott Donaldson, *Edwin Arlington Robinson: A Poet's Life* (New York: Columbia University Press, 2007).

The definitive biography, drawing from recently unsealed correspondence and providing and fresh insight on a poet previously considered too placid and reserved for biographical analysis.

E. A. Robinson, *Untriangulated Stars: Letters of Edwin Arlington Robinson to Harry de Forest Smith, 1890–1905,* edited by Denham Sutcliffe (Cambridge, Mass.: Harvard University Press, 1947).

Often cited in Robinson's biographies and criticism, a selection of correspondence between Robinson and his close friend that allows one to witness the poet formulating his aesthetics in his early years.

Chard Powers Smith, *Where the Light Falls: A Portrait of Edwin Arlington Robinson* (New York: Macmillan, 1965).

Until Donaldson's biography, the most in-depth view of the poet available. The work is particularly important for its treatment of Robinson's feelings for Emma Shepherd and is marred only by Smith's insistent commentary on the poetry.

—*Kirk Curnutt*

Upton Sinclair, *The Jungle*
(New York: Doubleday, Page, 1906)

Upton Sinclair (1878–1968) was the author of ninety books and the recipient of a Pulitzer Prize in 1943 for *Dragon's Teeth* (1942). Best known for his socialist politics, Sinclair developed an early interest in social justice as a result of his own troubled upbringing. Born in Baltimore, Sinclair's childhood was marked by poverty and hunger as his alcoholic father struggled to provide for his family. Having to rely on his mother's more well-to-do family for assistance, Sinclair saw firsthand the disparity of wealth in America. His family eventually moved to New York, where he was educated at both City College of New York and Columbia University. To finance his studies Sinclair began a career as a hack writer, composing stories about life at West Point. In 1906 he founded Helicon Home Colony, a short-lived utopian community in New Jersey. He also ran for Congress on the Socialist Party ticket and later for the California governorship. Throughout his life Sinclair corresponded and enjoyed relationships with such public figures as Arthur Conan Doyle, William Dean Howells, Sinclair Lewis, Jack London, Margaret Sanger, George Bernard Shaw, Theodore Roosevelt, Winston Churchill, Mohandas K. Gandhi, and Albert Einstein. Despite such an extensive literary career, Sinclair is best remembered for his sixth book, *The Jungle* (1906).

Dedicated to "the workingmen of America," *The Jungle* is an exposé of the brutality and injustice suffered by the working class in Chicago's meat-processing industry. Set in Packingtown, the hub of the city's stockyards, *The Jungle* opens amid the frenzied celebration of a wedding feast in honor of the narrative's protagonist, Jurgis Rudkus, and his young bride, Ona Lukoszaite. Recent immigrants from Lithuania, this couple and various relatives have come to the stockyards hoping to improve their way of life. Despite their early optimism, Jurgis and his family soon learn that their attempts to secure their portion of the American Dream are futile. Where they once believed America to be a place where "rich or poor, a man was free," they soon find themselves bound to the drudgery and horror of the "killing beds" and the other industries connected to the packing plants that have made them pawns to America greed—cogs in a machine whose only aim is increased production. Despite their best efforts to get ahead, the family suffers one tragedy after another. Soon Jurgis finds himself alone and penniless, having lost nearly all that is dear to him. His wanderings as a hobo, time in jail, and participation in Chicago's corrupt political scene finally give way to his conversion to socialism at the end of the text, underscoring Sinclair's solution to the wrongs meted out upon the nation's working poor.

Dubbed by London "the *Uncle Tom's Cabin* of wage slavery," *The Jungle* has also been called America's first proletarian novel. Its origins can be traced to this nascent tradition along with a number of key events. In 1904 thousands of laborers in Chicago's stockyards protested in vain against their low wages and poor working conditions. Sinclair's recent embrace of socialism and interest in the *Appeal to Reason*, a weekly socialist newspaper, persuaded him to write a manifesto in support of the strikers' plight for publication in the paper. The editor promised Sinclair $500 for serialization rights. Thus, in 1904 Sinclair moved to Chicago, where he lived for seven weeks in a settlement house among those he called the "wage slaves of the Beef Trust."

Although the characters and setting for *The Jungle* emerge from his time interacting with the laborers and examining the filthy and oppressive working conditions, the book was just as much a reflection of Sinclair's personal life. In his autobiography he explains that "externally, the story had to do with a family of stockyard workers, but internally it was the story of my own family." The suffering he, his wife, and infant son endured while living in a small, rustic cabin in New Jersey during the harsh winter while he was writing *The Jungle* and the periods of want and hunger he suffered as a child clearly inform this text. After having been rejected by five different publishers because of the story's graphic and controversial nature, *The Jungle* was finally published in hard covers by Doubleday, Page in February 1906.

The impact of *The Jungle* was monumental. While Sinclair's objective was to convey the plight of the American worker to a national audience, the novel exposed the horrendous conditions characterizing the country's meat supply. As Sinclair observed, "I aimed at the public's heart, and by accident I hit it in the stomach." Americans called for immediate inspections of the nation's meat industry, while the owners of the packing plants rejected Sinclair's claims by providing their own testimonials as to the safety and sanitation of their facilities. Thus a press battle ensued between Sinclair and companies such as Armour with articles representing both sides of the charges appearing in *The Saturday Evening Post* and *Everybody's Magazine*.

The claims in *The Jungle* also captured the attention of government officials, and Theodore Roosevelt requested Sinclair's presence at the White House to discuss the matter. The impact of *The Jungle* also had international repercussions. A journalist and member of Parliament at the time, Winston Churchill wrote two articles in an English newspaper praising Sinclair's work. Such high-profile responses to *The Jungle* brought instant fame to Sinclair, but, more important, facilitated significant changes to the meatpacking industry. Coupled with the "embalmed beef" scandal during the Spanish-American War, when thousands of soldiers died from eating tainted meat, Sinclair's work demanded immediate change. In the same year that *The Jungle* was published, the Pure Food and Drug Act and Meat Inspection Act were signed into law.

The Jungle continues to be read as both a significant historical document and an important novel that speaks to the political, social, and economic conditions of the early twentieth century. Since its 1906 publication, the novel has been translated into many languages and adapted to both the stage and film.

TOPICS FOR DISCUSSION AND RESEARCH

1. Consider the relationship of *The Jungle* to two of the primary literary trends at the turn of the century: Naturalism and Realism. What evidence do you find that aligns *The Jungle* with these movements? Various critics have considered Sinclair a lesser naturalist writer than his contemporaries Theodore Dreiser, Frank Norris, and Stephen Crane. What reasons can you find in the text to support this claim? In your response, consider Sinclair's depictions of Jurgis

throughout the text and particularly in the final chapters. How do various conclusions of *The Jungle* noted above affect a Naturalist reading?

2. Along with the works of French Naturalist writers Honoré de Balzac and Émile Zola, Sinclair was influenced by the father of American Realism, William Dean Howells. Despite Sinclair's concern for the "truth" to be revealed in his portrayal of the plight of America's laboring classes, how authentic is this work to their experiences in light of the depictions of Jurgis throughout the text? How would you argue for or against a Realist reading based on the representation of the American immigrant experience Sinclair portrays?

3. Many readers have commented on the conclusion of *The Jungle* as a bizarre shift from the rest of the narrative. What do you make of the final chapters? In your response compare the traditional conclusion to *The Jungle*, which ends with a speaker urging a crowd to believe that "CHICAGO WILL BE OURS!" with the original ending, that appeared in *One Hoss Philosophy*, which is available in *The Jungle: The Uncensored Original Edition*. How does their difference influence how you interpret the text? How does Sinclair justify the differences?

4. In the final chapter of *The Jungle* Nicholas Schliemann addresses a particular view of marriage and its effects on women. A few pages later, Sinclair references the work of Charlotte Perkins Gilman, whose *Women and Economics* is most certainly the work from which Schliemann derives his ideas. What do Schliemann's and Gilman's commentaries regarding marriage and women say about gender in turn-of-the-century America? Do such positions justify the fate of Ona and other women throughout *The Jungle*?

5. How would you describe Sinclair's portrayal of Chicago's minority groups? Are there differences in the amount of sympathy by which they are depicted? How would explain such discrepancies, if any?

6. Following the death of Antanas, Jurgis flees Chicago to take up as a tramp riding the rails through the Midwest looking for work. This flight from the city to the country represents a powerful theme in Western literature that pits idyllic rural settings against the ill effects of industrialization. How does Jurgis's experience compare? Does Sinclair reproduce this common theme or does he complicate it?

RESOURCES

Primary Works

The Jungle: An Authoritative Text, Contexts and Backgrounds, Criticism, edited by
    Clare Virginia Eby (New York: Norton, 2003).
Includes the 1906 Doubleday, Page version along with the conclusion that appeared in the *Appeal to Reason*. The book contains useful excerpts by the author about his literary program as well as commentary from Sinclair's day on the meatpacking industry and the life of the immigrant laborer. A range of criticism about *The Jungle* concludes this text.

The Jungle: The Uncensored Original Edition (Tucson, Ariz.: Sea Sharp Press,
    2003).
One-third longer than the commercial version.

Biography

Kevin Mattson, *Upton Sinclair and the Other American Century* (Hoboken, N.J.:
    Wiley, 2006).
Examines Sinclair's contributions to the sociopolitical landscape of the twentieth
century, emphasizing his political, rather than literary, career. Mattson provides
useful information about Sinclair's early years and his ongoing commitment to
exposing the negative side of America's rise to economic might.

Upton Sinclair, *The Autobiography of Upton Sinclair* (New York: Harcourt, Brace
    & World, 1962).
Provides valuable insight into Sinclair's literary career and the particular circumstances that motivated and shaped *The Jungle*. The work begins with his earlier
childhood and comments on many of his works and career as a socialist.

Sinclair, *My Lifetime in Letters* (Columbia: University of Missouri Press, 1960).
Includes letters Sinclair received from some of the most celebrated intellectuals
of the first half of the twentieth century.

Criticism

Michael Brewster Folsom, "Upton Sinclair's Escape from *The Jungle:* The Nar-
    rative Strategy and Suppressed Conclusion of America's First Proletarian
    Novel," *Prospects*, 2 (1979): 237–266.
Examines the structural and thematic challenges Sinclair encountered writing
The Jungle and charts the effects of his publishers on the conclusions drawn
in the text.

Orm Øverland, "*The Jungle:* From Lithuanian Peasant to American Socialist,"
    American Literary Realism, 37 (Fall 2004): 1–23.
Considers *The Jungle* as both historical and literary text, examining the veracity
of Sinclair's observations in the stockyards and his complicated relationship with
Naturalism.

—Paul Formisano

Frank R. Stockton, "The Lady, or the Tiger?"

Century, 25 (November 1882): 83–86; collected in *The Lady, or the Tiger? and
Other Stories* (New York: Scribners, 1884)

Though relatively unknown today, the stories of Frank R. Stockton (1834–1902)
once challenged the popularity of writers such as Mark Twain and William
Dean Howells. Stockton wrote prolifically and in many genres, from science
fiction and adventure to fantasy. In the 1960s Maurice Sendak illustrated two of
Stockton's children's stories—"The Bee-Man of Orn" (1883) and "The Griffin
and the Minor Canon" (1885). Recently critics have acknowledged Stockton's
contributions to the fairy-tale genre. Stockton's interest in fairy tales can be

seen in "The Lady, or the Tiger?" (1882), his most anthologized short story. It remains compelling because of its timeless themes: the notion of free will, the cruel arbitrariness of fate, and the twin emotions love and jealousy. The open-ended conclusion forces readers to think carefully about specific details and the characters' underlying motivations. In doing so, it offers an excellent introduction to literary analysis.

Stockton wrote "The Lady, or the Tiger?" after some friends requested that he create an amusing story for some guests at a dinner party. He was already well known as an editor and contributor to *St. Nicholas,* a magazine for children, and he had published many books for adults and children. At the party, Stockton failed to narrate what would become his most famous story because he was reluctant to tell a story that lacked a clear resolution. Throughout his literary career, Stockton celebrated family and domesticity; yet, here was a story that did not present itself that way. Before publication, he attempted no fewer than five different conclusions. None satisfied him. Eventually he gave up and submitted the "unfinished" work to the *Century* shortly before setting sail on a long vacation to Europe. Stockton was abroad when the literary pandemonium began that would change his life.

Following the fairy-tale paradigm, the story occurs at an indeterminate time and place. A "semi-barbaric" king learns of his daughter's affair with a man he finds unsuitable. The king has devised what he feels is the ideal justice system, one that rests on its utter impartiality and reliance on fate as ultimate judge. The accused must choose between two doors—one hides a beautiful maiden (not the princess) ready to marry him, and the other hides a hungry tiger and a dreadful end. The princess, who is there to witness the judgment, has divined the secret behind the doors. To complicate matters, she knows and resents the maiden because in the past she had seen what she assumed to be flirting between her lover and the maiden. When her lover enters the arena, the princess covertly signals the door to the right. Without hesitation, he moves to open that door. At this very moment—the climax of the story—it ends. For an additional page, the narrator speaks directly to the audience about what might have happened next, but the last line leaves the question for readers to decide: "Which came out of the opened door,—the lady, or the tiger?"

Immediately after publication, the *Century* was inundated with mail demanding that the author explain what had really happened. The deluge was relentless and lasted for years. More than a decade later Stockton's wife claimed that every few years there was a renewed interest in the story followed by more correspondence and suggested outcomes. Until Stockton's death twenty years later, his readers tried to corner him about what "really" happened when the door opened. Exasperated, Stockton answered his critics with the story "His Wife's Deceased Sister" (1884). In this story a writer decides to withhold rather than publish a potentially famous story. The title "The Lady, or the Tiger?" (fortunately changed from Stockton's original "In the King's Arena") became so well known that popular culture referenced it well into the twentieth century.

As Stockton anticipated, the literary world has largely forgotten him. There are, however, a handful of critical overviews that students will find valuable. Sarah

Madsen Hardy's explication of "The Lady, or the Tiger?" in *Short Stories for Students,* volume 3 (1998) connects the story's subversive nature with Stockton's manipulation of the fairy-tale genre. Jack Zipes argues in his book *When Dreams Came True: Classical Fairy Tales and Their Tradition,* second edition (2007), that Stockton's fairy tales are important because his mature themes influenced L. Frank Baum (1856-1919), who wrote the *Wizard of Oz* books. Tanya Gardiner-Scott, in an essay also included in *Short Stories for Students,* expands on some of the religious themes in the story that Henry Golemba noted in his critical biography *Frank R. Stockton* (1981). Golemba does not spend a great deal of time on "The Lady, or the Tiger?" but focuses on Stockton's other works in an effort to revive Stockton's reputation as a writer generally.

TOPICS FOR DISCUSSION AND RESEARCH

1. The gender issues raised in the story account for a large part of its appeal. According to the fan mail Stockton received, women tended to believe the tiger would emerge from behind the door, whereas men thought it would be the maiden. What explains this difference? A quick survey of males and females in a modern classroom would likely renew many of the enthusiastic gender debates this story triggered more than a century ago.
2. Students' understanding of the story and the gender issues it raises will be enhanced by recognizing the fairy-tale paradigm that Stockton subverted when he wrote it. As Madsen Hardy has noted, the story contains many of the elements common to fairy tales: it takes place in an indeterminate time and place; its main characters include a king and a princess; and the male lead in the story, a man too far "beneath" the princess to be considered suitable, might well be compared with the kiss-seeking frog, Beauty's Beast, or even Cinderella, all characters who found similar obstacles to their ambitions. Fairy tales of this type operate as literary comedies: young lovers, mixed identities, and happy marriages are the raw materials here. Readers of fairy tales have come to expect that obstacles will be overcome and true love must be vindicated by a "happy ever after" conclusion. Stockton denies such expectations. Instead, he places the essential ingredients of the fairy-tale comedy inside the king's arena, the classic domain of tragedy. Given the story's parameters, neither of the two choices Stockton offers his readers allows the princess and her lover to become united. It is worth noting that many of Stockton's fans, desperate for a happy ending, suggested elaborate and contrived ways that the lovers might have outmaneuvered the king, but the text supports none of these possibilities. Support your conjectures with specific passages.
3. Stockton does an excellent job manipulating reader response and using dramatic irony to create tension. Opinions naturally split on which of the two possible outcomes seems most likely. Students should look closely at how much text Stockton devotes to describing each outcome, particularly in the last section, where the narrator speaks directly to the audience. Based strictly on this single measure, the princess's lover appears headed for trouble. Stock-

ton ratchets up the tension even further by describing the princess's jealousy of the maiden who, she suspects, has flirted with her lover in the past. Finally, students may overlook the simple fact that the princess actually debates whether or not she should send her lover to a gruesome death—in effect, she considers a kind of premeditated murder. Thus, while the fairy-tale genre has conditioned the audience to seek a happy resolution, Stockton emphasizes details that suggest (but certainly do not guarantee) a tragic outcome. It is worthwhile to explore the dynamic schism between these expectations.

4. Like her father, the princess is described as barbaric, although exactly what Stockton implies by this word is unclear. Barbarism in this story relates to power, specifically the power to determine the lover's fate. The princess uses "gold, and the power of a woman's will" to divine what no one has been able to learn: the secret of what lies behind the doors. Connections between different kinds of power, barbarism, and "the feminine" suggest themselves throughout the story and should be explored.

5. Knowing the depths of the princess's power, her lover comes to the arena fully confident that she will know the secret behind the doors. That he immediately follows her instruction to open the door on the right signifies his blind trust not only in her power but also in the purity of her love and good will toward him. Readers, however, know better. Although he correctly understands her power, he appears oblivious to the vacillations caused by her jealous heart. If Stockton intended these nameless, "everyman" characters to be interpreted symbolically, what is he implying about the underlying truth of love?

6. This question becomes more complex if students consider the arena and its two doors metaphorically. Stockton would not be the first author to suggest that we are but pawns in a chaotic world ruled by chance. In Stockton's other works marriage serves as a bulwark against life's absurdities. With a good partner, Stockton seems to say, a person can overcome and even laugh at life's obstacles. But in "The Lady, or the Tiger?" Stockton undermines this thesis with the terrifying possibility that in fact—and unknown to us—we stand in life's arena alone. What makes the story so compelling is that this idea ultimately remains only a possibility, not a certainty. Without a clear ending, readers must decide for themselves whether the story is a comedy or a tragedy. As Stockton rightly explained when he was asked, the way in which a reader interprets the ending may say more about that reader and how that reader views the world than anything else. Consider what their interpretation of the ending says about them.

RESOURCES

Criticism

Henry L. Golemba, *Frank R. Stockton* (Boston: Twayne, 1981).

Claims that Stockton deserves to be read again and includes a solid biography in the first third of the book followed by literary analysis of the novels and stories. To highlight Stockton's other achievements, Golemba delays analyzing "The Lady, or the Tiger?" until the end. The book includes an excellent annotated bibliography of primary and secondary works.

"The Lady, or the Tiger?" in *Short Stories for Students,* volume 3, edited by Kathleen Wilson (Detroit: Gale, 1998), pp. 177–193.
Excellent overview of the story and its themes that includes two interpretive essays on "The Lady, or the Tiger?" by Tanya Gardiner-Scott and Sarah Madsen Hardy. The entry also includes commentary by William Dean Howells.

Jill P. May, "Frank R. Stockton," in *Dictionary of Literary Biography,* volume 42: *American Writers for Children Before 1900,* edited by Glen Estes (Detroit: Bruccoli Clark Layman/Gale, 1985), pp. 332–338.
Good summary of Stockton's life and works. May interprets the suspense in "The Lady, or the Tiger?" as stemming from "the idea that love can destroy as well as redeem."

Frank R. Stockton, "How I Wrote 'The Lady, or the Tiger?' and What Came of the Writing of It," *Ladies' Home Journal,* 10 (November 1893): 1–2.
Discusses the many creative endings to the story people had sent the author in the decade after publication.

Jack Zipes, "Frank Stockton, American Pioneer of Fairy Tales," *When Dreams Came True: Classic Fairy Tales and Their Tradition,* second edition (New York: Rutledge, 2007), pp. 187–194.
Analysis of Stockton's important contributions to the American fairy-tale genre.

—*Michael Smedshammer*

Mark Twain, *The Adventures of Tom Sawyer*
(Hartford, Conn.: American Publishing, 1876)

Samuel Langhorne Clemens (1835–1910), better known by his pseudonym, Mark Twain, is a major figure in American and world literature. Born in Hannibal in the slave state of Missouri, Clemens grew up hearing a rich mixture of dialects: African American, Missourian (several), Southern (numerous), as well as Northern dialects of those traveling up and down the river. He developed a keen ear for the multifarious sounds of the human voice in conversation. He developed, too, a keen sense of irony, drawn partly from the inherent contradictions of living in a country that prided itself on freedom and independence even while keeping slaves in bondage. As a boy he was confronted by this stark contradiction early and often, as his family kept slaves. When Clemens was six years old, his father sold a slave for ten barrels of tar.

Like Benjamin Franklin, Clemens began his literary career early by working for his older brother's newspaper. In the 1850s he wrote many humorous pieces drawing on the variety of types once experienced in a village on the Mississippi River. Throughout his career, his life in Hannibal contributed to his literature. Nowhere is that contribution so profound as in *The Adventures of Tom Sawyer*.

Twain's young hero is a brash, self-confident raconteur who quickly wearies of humdrum routines and longs incessantly for excitement and escape. Along with his friend Joe Harper, he often skips school to fish. With Huckleberry Finn, the outcast son of the town drunk, Tom and Joe play Robin Hood on Cardiff Hill, pretend to be pirates on Jackson's Island, and explore McDougal's cave. Tom is cared for by his Aunt Polly and Cousin Mary. His cousin Sid, the perfect child, provides a foil for Tom's mischievous antics.

Clemens based the character Tom and the book itself on several models. One such work was *The Story of a Bad Boy* (1869), by his friend Thomas Bailey Aldrich. Readers will find it illuminating to read some of Clemens's earlier works such as "The Story of the Bad Little Boy That Bore a Charmed Life" (1865) and "The Story of the Good Little Boy Who Did Not Prosper" (1870). In such works Clemens burlesqued the genre known as "Sunday School books," moralizing tales that were intended to model proper behavior for children. In lampooning this genre, Clemens often rewarded bad behavior and punished good behavior, as evidenced by the perverse titles he chose.

One sees the influence of these early burlesques on *The Adventures of Tom Sawyer.* Structurally, the book is interesting because of its inherently episodic nature, typical of childhood, in which one event follows another, interrupted only by the occasional obligations of church and school. Beyond this natural structure, however, one sees as well the importance of Sunday School books to the story. Such books told of good little children who always did right and who were rewarded, often on earth, but if they died, certainly in heaven. Twain inverts this by telling stories of good little boys and girls who came to grief and of bad little boys and girls who made good. One sees this element in the character Tom Sawyer, who always emerges victorious, regardless of how bad he has been. This is most obvious in the famous whitewashing episode in chapter 2. Found to have played hooky, Tom is punished by having to spend Saturday whitewashing Aunt Polly's fence. Tom turns the punishment to his advantage by conning other boys to do the work for him—and to pay him for the privilege. In so doing he amasses a small fortune: a one-eyed kitten, a broken piece of blue glass, and a dead rat on a string, among other treasures.

One of Twain's great achievements was the use of first-person narration in *The Adventures of Huckleberry Finn* (1884). For this reason, Ernest Hemingway said in *The Green Hills of Africa* (1935) that "All modern American literature comes from one book by Mark Twain called *Huckleberry Finn.*" After completing *The Adventures of Tom Sawyer*, Twain felt that perhaps he had made a mistake in using a third-person, omniscient narrator. But just as it is now impossible to imagine Huck's story told in the third person, it is difficult to imagine Tom's story told in the first person. Much of the charm of *The Adventures of Tom Sawyer* stems from the adult narrator's restrained but mordant commentary on the story. The disjuncture between Tom's sensibility and the ironic awareness of the adult narrator helps to develop several important themes, particularly those involving religion and slavery. Clemens wrote other works featuring Tom as a character, including *Tom Sawyer Abroad* (1894) and *Tom Sawyer, Detective* (1896). Tom also features prominently in the unfinished works "Huck Finn and

Tom Sawyer among the Indians" (written circa 1885), "Tom Sawyer's Conspiracy" (written between 1897 and 1900), and "Tom Sawyer's Gang Plans a Naval Battle" (written circa 1900). Indeed, so compelling is the character Tom Sawyer that Mark Twain could never entirely forget him; neither have critics or readers.

TOPICS FOR DISCUSSION AND RESEARCH

1. "Church ain't shucks to a circus," as Tom Sawyer phrases it, sums up the attitude toward divine services in the book. As a form of entertainment, church has little to recommend it—except when untoward events happen. One of these is when Tom's pinch bug gets loose and pinches a dog on the nose during the sermon. The dog becomes a "wooly comet" that adds a bit of diversion to the usual Sunday fare. Twain's depictions of church services in the book stem from a letter he wrote his wife, Olivia, in 1871 in which he recounts attending a small country church that transports him back to his childhood. His description of the pastor, the unruly choir, the bored children, and others directly contributed to his writing of such scenes in *The Adventures of Tom Sawyer*. Discuss Twain's attitude toward religion in the novel. Is he critical or simply using the solemnity of the service as a means of characterizing Tom?

2. Serious thematic concerns about religion include the hypocrisy of religious people who seem much more devoted to the "letter that killeth" than they are to "the spirit that giveth life." The book's chapter 4 is a perfect example. Oblivious to the beauty of the natural world that has its own "benediction," Aunt Polly delivers a "grim sermon" that seems Mosaic in its legalism. Despite such depictions, Twain's book is not antireligion per se. Indeed, the author lavishes such attention to the details of organized religion that one must say the tone is affectionately ironic. Does Twain feel that the devout characters in his book are better than their religion?

3. Twain wrote his masterpiece, *The Adventures of Huckleberry Finn* (1884), as a sequel of sorts to *The Adventures of Tom Sawyer* but chose to foreground issues of slavery and racial justice in the later work. By comparison, *The Adventures of Tom Sawyer* has suffered from the assumption that it has little to say about race. The books do differ, of course, but the earlier book has its own ways of bringing up issues of race. In some instances the African American characters are used primarily for their "comic darky" aspect common to literature of the time. The figure of the slave Jim, for example, rises above caricature in some instances in the later work, but in *The Adventures of Tom Sawyer* he remains ever the gullible, superstitious slave, incapable of even reflecting on his involuntary servitude. Does Twain's attitude toward race differ in the two novels?

4. Despite the fact that Tom and Huck are close friends, in chapter 27 the narrator informs readers that Tom does not like to be seen with Huck in public. In the very next chapter Huck, though at the very bottom of white society, is seen to have his prejudices as well. Despite the fact that a slave named

Uncle Jake generously provides him food and shelter, Huck is anxious not to have that fact widely known, for "A body's got to do things when he's awful hungry he wouldn't want to do as a steady thing." Discuss the divisions of class and race that exist even among Petersburg's most honest citizens, and pay particular attention to the children.

5. Mark Twain is one of the most written about American writers. Books and articles on the writer and his work abound. The most important book-length treatments of *The Adventures of Tom Sawyer* are Charles A. Norton's *Writing Tom Sawyer* (1983), which includes chapters on the composition history of the work, Clemens's involvement in adaptations of the book for the stage, and early reviews of the work. Walter Blair's *Mark Twain's Hannibal, Huck, and Tom* (1969) is important for bringing together many of the working notes and related material. Research the composition of the novel. How did Twain's method of composition affect his novel?

RESOURCES

Biography

Samuel L. Clemens, *The Autobiography of Mark Twain,* edited by Charles Neider (New York: Harper Perennial, 1990).

Reflects on his childhood in Missouri and provides invaluable commentary on his own life and work.

Justin Kaplan, *Mr. Clemens and Mark Twain* (New York: Simon & Schuster, 1966).

The classic biography of Mark Twain, more critical in its judgments than Paine's important work.

Albert Bigelow Paine, *Mark Twain: A Biography* (New York: Harper, 1912).

The official biography. Paine had unparalleled access to the author and his records. At the same time, his judgments are frequently hampered by that intimacy. This work remains an indispensable resource but should be supplemented by other biographies.

Dixon Wecter, *Sam Clemens of Hannibal* (Boston: Houghton Mifflin, 1952).

A meticulously researched volume that is an invaluable scholarly tool and eminently readable story of the author's early years. The work includes many obscure facts about Twain's family and background that other biographers have overlooked.

Criticism

Walter Blair, *Mark Twain and Huck Finn* (Berkeley: University of California Press, 1960).

A critical and analytical work that is important for understanding the relationship between *The Adventures of Tom Sawyer* and *The Adventures of Huckleberry Finn.*

Blair, ed., *Mark Twain's Hannibal, Huck and Tom* (Berkeley: University of California Press, 1969).

An important compendium of many of Clemens's working notes for his various projects involving Tom Sawyer.

Richard Chase, *The American Novel and Its Tradition* (Garden City, N.Y.: Doubleday, 1957).

Helps situate Twain between the aesthetic practices of Romance and Realism. Chase also discusses the character Tom in relation to the "good boy" and "bad boy" in American literature.

Joe B. Fulton, *The Reverend Mark Twain: Theological Burlesque, Form, and Content* (Columbus: Ohio State University Press, 2006).

Discusses the structure of *The Adventures of Tom Sawyer*, paying close attention to the generic contributions such as the Sunday School book.

Charles A. Norton, *Writing Tom Sawyer: The Adventures of a Classic* (Jefferson, N.C.: McFarland, 1983).

Provides a valuable discussion of the book's genesis and development as well as a discussion of Twain's other projects involving the character Tom Sawyer.

—*Joe B. Fulton*

Mark Twain, *The Adventures of Huckleberry Finn*

(London: Chatto & Windus, 1884); republished as *Adventures of Huckleberry Finn* (New York: Charles L. Webster and Co., 1885)

Mark Twain was a prominent figure in the American Realist movement. Samuel Langhorne Clemens (1835–1910) adopted the pen name Mark Twain while a reporter for the *Virginia Territorial Enterprise* in 1863 and used the literary persona to explore an array of issues—social, political, aesthetic—that arose during the post–Civil War period. He began his career as a writer while still a typesetter for his brother Orion's newspaper in Hannibal, Missouri, by composing short sketches and, later, as a correspondent during his travels east and west. His experiences as an itinerant typesetter and steamboat pilot, wildcat miner, reporter, and lecturer shaped his narrative voice and his practice of realistic writing. He left newspaper work after his first book, *The Innocents Abroad* (1869), became a national success (it was his best-selling book throughout his life). He devoted the rest of his life to writing across genres, from novels to travel writing, from short fiction to essays, from lectures to political and social polemic. During his most prolific years (1870–1897), along with short fiction and essays, he published eighteen books including *Roughing It* (1872), *The Gilded Age* (with Charles Dudley Warner, 1873), *The Adventures of Tom Sawyer* (1876), *A Tramp Abroad* (1880), *The Prince and the Pauper* (1881), *Life on the Mississippi* (1883), *A Connecticut Yankee* in *King Arthur's Court* (1889), *The Tragedy of Pudd'nhead Wilson* (1894), *Personal Recollections of Joan of Arc by the Sieur Louis de Conte* (1896), and *Following the Equator* (1897). From 1900 until his death in 1910 Twain shifted his attention primarily to nonfiction with a series of anti-imperialism essays, a diverse collection of aborted manuscripts, and his autobiography.

The Adventures of Huckleberry Finn was written from the late summer of 1876 through late 1884. The novel was begun as the sequel to *The Adventures of Tom Sawyer,* and the opening chapters return to the picaresque design of the earlier novel as Huck and Tom engage in various kinds of play, most of which is dictated by Tom's love of the romance. The immediate difference is the point of view from which the story is told. Instead of the omniscient narrator of *The Adventures of Tom Sawyer,* the new tale is told by Huck himself in a first-person tour de force that allows readers to see the world through the eyes of a disenfranchised and much-abused adolescent. Twain was clear about the value of Huck's voice when he wrote to William Dean Howells that he had begun "Huck Finn's autobiography" and that he had struck the right note when he decided to use Huck as the narrator. The decision grounds the novel within Huck's experience, and his no-frills, vernacular language offers a deadpan description of his life.

That decision to have Huck tell his own story inspired Twain, and he quickly composed roughly the first eighteen chapters of the novel. He halted only after Huck and the runaway slave Jim, together on a raft, are run over by a steamboat and Huck finds himself among the Grangerford clan. In chapter eighteen, Huck asks Buck Grangerford, "What's a feud?" and it is at this point that Twain put the manuscript away, a practice that he described as writing until the well ran dry and then setting work aside until the creative well filled up again. While Twain waited for the well to fill, he turned to other projects: during 1877 he wrote the first twelve chapters of *The Prince and the Pauper* and during 1878–1879 he traveled in Europe and wrote *A Tramp Abroad.* The continual writing helped Twain work through the issues underlying *The Adventures of Huckleberry Finn.* In fact, he saw the relationship between *The Adventures of Huckleberry Finn* and the story line and childhood experiences of Tom Canty and Edward Tudor in *The Prince and the Pauper* as so allied that his initial plan was to publish the two novels as a set, though the story of the prince and the pauper was published alone in 1881.

A visit to the Mississippi and its shoreline communities during 1882 (his first extended trip to the South since the Civil War) prompted Twain to write *Life on the Mississippi* and, more important, to complete the final chapters of *The Adventures of Huckleberry Finn,* including a drastic change to the end of the Sherburn episode: at first Twain was willing to have Sherburn spirited away by friends as the lynch mob approaches. In what seems a fit of frustration, Twain penciled in directions to let the mob hang the man, but instead he ended the episode with Sherburn's direct and sustained rant against mobs and mob mentality. Both the Wilkes episode and the final evasion chapters were written in a burst during the summer of 1883. The book was published in England in 1884 to preserve Twain's copyright; it was published in the United States in 1885.

The novel is essentially the tale of a runaway, Huck, who teams with a runaway slave, Jim, on an improvised and ultimately failed attempt to find freedom. As the story begins, Huck is constrained by the social order and false piety of St. Petersburg and the Widow Douglas and her sister Miss Watson. When his father reappears (in chapter five) to claim Huck's part of the treasure found at the end of *The Adventures of Tom Sawyer*, he abducts Huck and brings him back to a life outside society. Because of his father's abusive ways, Huck decides to run away, which he does by designing his own murder (chapter 7). Huck's journey changes radically when he finds the runaway slave Jim on Jackson's island (chapter 8), and the two quickly become dependent upon one another as they make their way down the river. Jim's hope to escape to freedom and to rescue his wife and children from slavery form an underlying tension in the novel as Huck is forced to face the reality that he is helping a slave escape a system that is not and has not been a threat to him. As they are swept along by the river's current, soon the two have journeyed past the free state of Ohio and have been drawn deeper into the South. Along the way, Huck and Jim face their own demons as well as a series of external threats from a corrupt and parsimonious society, including the Grangerford and Shepherdson feud, the arrival of the con men the Duke and the King and their several scams, the Sherburn episode, and (with the aid of Tom Sawyer) an attempt to free Jim from bondage after he is imprisoned at the Phelps farm. Finally, after a harrowing and absurd escape plot, Tom Sawyer delivers the news that Jim has already been manumitted and Huck once again faces the possibility of social constraints from Aunt Sally Phelps, who wants to adopt him. He announces his intention to flee into the West, but it not clear in the novel about whether this is a real possibility.

TOPICS FOR DISCUSSION AND RESEARCH

1. *The Adventures of Huckleberry Finn* has had a long and complex critical history. American readers and critics have adjusted their interpretations of the novel because they have been influenced by the times in which they have lived and in a profound way by the reactions of prior readers of the text. The novel, however, does not change. Readers and critics and their interaction with the novel change based on their own needs and interests during the decades since publication. For example, the novel was immediately banned after its publication in 1885; however, the reason was not tied to race or the conflicts over racial image and language. The book was banned because Huck was not a proper role model for young readers: he lied, stole, and used bad language. Times and readers change. Our sensitivity to race has been a focal point to the popular and academic discussions of this novel, especially since the mid 1950s and the arc of the modern Civil Rights Movement. Today the novel's pointed descriptions of alcoholism and abuse seem disturbing. It is the Realism of Huck's point of view, his language, his interests, and his conflicts that allow different generations of readers to approach the novel with fresh eyes. That shift in perspective allows the novel to continue to live as a touchstone

for our understanding of social and domestic relations, which is a primary focus of Mark Twain's storytelling. Students are advised to consider how their own cultural experiences shape their response to the novel.

2. *The Adventures of Huckleberry Finn* can be viewed from a variety of perspectives. Students can enter the critical discussion by asking questions that focus on aesthetics, with special attention to whether the final "evasion" chapters of the novel adversely affect the novel's structural integrity, as well as how Twain's use of dialect affects our understanding of his characters. Because the tale is set in the 1840s antebellum South, it cannot be defined as an antislavery novel; however, students should ask how nineteenth- and twentieth-century political and social concerns affect and determine interpretation as well as how the concerns with identity and the impact of race, issues prominent during the 1870s and 1880s when Twain is writing, affect their reading of the novel. Do those concerns affect the actions of the characters as they interact during their journey on and along the river? How do Huck and Jim struggle with how they are defined by the society that holds them in thrall? How do they define each other as they work to come to terms with who they are as individuals within a hostile social system? Does Huck grow to an understanding of Jim as a person? Does contact with characters and communities along the river affect Huck's awareness of Jim's humanity? And, if so, how? As the novel introduces a series of episodes during which Huck must either turn Jim in or take an active role in abetting his escape, how does the tension in these scenes affect Huck's self-awareness and his reliance on social and even theological beliefs? Does that tension make an argument in favor of freedom? Of course, the issue of freedom is complex, and Twain's realistic treatment of race and class may at times undermine the possibilities for full-throated freedom for either character.

3. The novel's concern with race has become more prominent during the past fifty years as American society has addressed questions of racial identity and racial prejudice. The novel is often still indicted for its use of racist language—the fact that the word "nigger" appears over two hundred times in the novel presents a challenge to those who would interpret the text as an argument for racial transcendence. The issue is also made more complex by the image of Jim in the final chapters and the interpretation of that image as embedded within nineteenth-century minstrelsy. Students should consider how Twain's use of racial language and images affects Jim's place in the novel both as a character supporting racial stereotypes and as a character that challenges those stereotypes. How can readers remain open to and come to terms with the novel's range of contrasting interpretations of race?

4. Finally, it is also possible to use the novel to explore issues of class and the impact of physical and mental abuse within a destructive domestic environment; for example, how does Pap Finn's treatment of Huck influence the novel's challenge to social order? How does the novel introduce the experience of the disenfranchised and does its description of the reality of child and domestic abuse prompt questions about the effects of abuse on the emotional and spiritual well-being of adults and especially children? Huck's sense of self is affected

by his status within and the outside the various communities portrayed as well as by his experience within his own family. How does Huck's sense of self affect his interaction with Jim and how does his reliance on and craving for friendship influence our reading of major episodes of the novel? Huck's relationship with Pap affects his understanding of race and family, but does it also affect his potential for and search for compassion as he makes his way through experiences with the Widow Douglas, the Duke and the King, Mary Jane Wilkes, Sally Phelps, Tom Sawyer, and, perhaps most importantly, Jim?

RESOURCES

Primary Work

Adventures of Huckleberry Finn, edited by Victor Fischer and Lin Salamo with Walter Blair (Berkeley: University of California Press, 2003).
The definitive text of the novel, edited at the Mark Twain Project. The text includes material restored from the manuscript and the original illustrations. Most useful is the introduction by the editors, which offers a full discussion of the background for the text and the history of composition.

Biography

Fred Kaplan, *The Singular Mark Twain: A Biography* (New York: Doubleday, 2003).
Runs counter to the long-established idea in Twain biography, growing out of Justin Kaplan's *Mr. Clemens and Mark Twain* (New York: Simon & Schuster, 1966), that there is a split between Samuel L. Clemens and his literary persona, Mark Twain. Here the focus is on the way that the two personae come together in one integrated personality. A refreshing analysis, it allows readers to ponder the strength of a single creative power.

Albert Bigelow Paine, *Mark Twain: A Biography*, 3 volumes (New York: Harper, 1912).
The first authorized biography of Mark Twain and still a standard reference work. While later biographies have superseded Paine because of the wider availability of material and a less-biased point of view, this edition is still the starting point for learning about the life of Samuel L. Clemens.

Ron Powers, *Mark Twain: A Life* (New York: Free Press, 2005).
In the tradition of the Clemens/Twain dichotomy. The study updates the image of Mark Twain and devotes considerable space to his background and the impact on the development of the literary voice.

Criticism

Victor A. Doyno, *Writing Huck Finn: Mark Twain's Creative Process* (Philadelphia: University of Pennsylvania Press, 1991).
Genetic study of the second half of the manuscript for *The Adventures of Huckleberry Finn*, tracing both the composition history of the novel and Mark Twain's

careful editing process. This study is the primary examination of Twain's precise creation of dialect in the novel and offers insights into the creative mind.

James S. Leonard, Thomas A. Tenney, and Thadious M. Davis, eds., *Satire or Evasion? Black Perspectives on Huckleberry Finn* (Durham, N.C.: Duke University Press, 1992).

Sixteen essays demonstrating a variety of perspectives and interpretations from African American scholars. The collection explodes the idea of a monolithic approach to the novel and introduces readers to a range of nuanced readings of the novel in relation to issues of race.

Robert Sattelmeyer and J. Donald Crowley, eds., *One Hundred Years of Huckleberry Finn: The Boy, His Book, and American Culture* (Columbia: University of Missouri Press, 1985).

Twenty-four essays giving a coherent summary of the state of criticism and the approaches to the novel marking its centennial. The contributors examine the novel in terms of the creative imagination, craft, contexts, contemporary concerns, and cultural legacy.

—*Michael J. Kiskis*

Walt Whitman, *Drum-Taps*
(New York, 1865)

Born on Long Island, New York, the second of nine children to parents of modest means and Quaker leanings, Walt Whitman (1819–1892) seemed an unlikely candidate to become the great American poet that he is known as today. Indeed, Walt Whitman (as he was known since boyhood) had very little formal education, worked at a number of odd jobs—from office boy to typesetter to teacher to journalist to editor—none for very long, and published a variety of articles, short stories, and a temperance novel, *Franklin Evans* (1842), before publishing the first edition of *Leaves of Grass* (1855).

While Whitman did publish prose pieces during his lifetime—*Democratic Vistas* (1870), *Specimen Days* (1882), and *November Boughs* (1888) are all lengthy prose projects—he was known then and is known now as the poet of democracy and the father of free verse. He published his poems in the ever-expanding editions of *Leaves of Grass* that came out every few years between 1855 and his death. Nine editions were published during Whitman's life. With each edition Whitman altered the poems from the previous one (sometimes even omitting some entirely), shifting their order and layout, and incorporating new poems. Although Whitman had published three editions by the time the Civil War broke out in 1861, the war brought with it what was, momentarily, a new project: a stand-alone book of fifty-three poems about the war that he titled *Drum-Taps* and that he published in 1865.

Some of the poems in *Drum-Taps* had been drafted before Whitman had any direct contact with the war ("Beat! Beat! Drums!" and "First O Songs for Prelude" in particular), but the poems at the heart of this book describe and were inspired by the war he saw firsthand. Unlike two of his brothers, who enlisted in the Union army, Whitman did not go to war. His contact with the war came through the wounded soldiers whom he met first during his visits to New York hospitals and later during his work as a volunteer nurse in Washington, D.C. He had made his way to Washington in search of his brother George, whom he feared had been wounded, but upon seeing the makeshift hospital and the injured soldiers from all over the nation, he stayed to help. Many of the poems in *Drum-Taps* grew out of the interactions Whitman had with these soldiers and were informed by the stories they told him and the deep attachment he felt to them.

After Abraham Lincoln was assassinated in 1865, Whitman wrote eighteen more poems, many of which were tributes to the late president ("When Lilacs Last in the Dooryard Bloom'd" and "O Captain! My Captain!" are the most famous of these), but because *Drum-Taps* had already gone to press, he incorporated them into the next edition, which he published under the title *Sequel to Drum-Taps* (1865–1866). Whitman absorbed these poems into the next edition of *Leaves of Grass* (1867) with their original order rearranged. When people refer to "Drum-Taps" today, they are usually referring to the forty-three poems that make up the section by that title in the final three editions of *Leaves of Grass*.

TOPICS FOR DISCUSSION AND RESEARCH

1. "Drum-Taps" is often read as a sequence in which the poems move from one outlook, perspective, or interest in the war to another. Some of these moves can be characterized as a shift from a hopeful call to arms to an awareness of the deaths that the call produces, or, put another way, from an interest in the more abstract issues to those of individual existence and suffering. Reading "Drum-Taps" as a sequence whose movements can be mapped in these ways not only allows students to identify the themes and issues that recur, but exposes them to Whitman's use of a wide variety of formal and stylistic strategies. In other words, while all of these poems are in some way about the Civil War, each one approaches the problem of representing the war differently. What are some of the different narratives about the war that are embedded in this sequence? What poems rupture those narratives? Michael Warner's essay discusses the narrative strategy of "Drum-Taps."

2. When dealing with the poems individually, there is a group of five at the center that look closely at the lives and deaths of the soldiers. These are particularly accessible poems because in them Whitman renders his own attachment to these men in deeply emotional ways. Looking closely at these poems—"Come Up from the Fields Father," "Vigil Strange I Kept on the Field One Night," "A March in the Ranks Hard-Prest, and the Road Unknown," "A Sight in Camp in the Daybreak Gray and Dim," and "As Toilsome I Wander'd Virginia's

Woods"—allows you to identify and characterize both the different ways that Whitman tells these men's stories and the similarity of sentiment that runs through all of them. You might, for instance, identify what the relationship is between the poem's level of remove from the battlefield and the kind of story it tells. Even more specifically, how does the setting of each poem affect the syntax Whitman uses? With every poem Whitman attempts a new way to see these soldiers, and if students can characterize the various relationships that he establishes in these poems, they can come to understand the complex strategies he uses for making the soldiers' deaths real. In other words, how does Whitman balance his desire to represent the horrors of mass death and retain the humanity and individuality of the dead soldiers? He tells the story of a letter arriving to a soldier's home, describes in lush language the fields that his parents work in, and renders, in jagged syntax, the worry they register on receiving a letter that is not in their son's handwriting. The poem navigates knowledge of the soldier's state carefully, as the omniscient poet-speaker is the only one who knows of his death, yet the mother has intuitive knowledge of this fact. In "Vigil Strange I Kept on the Field One Night" the people in the poem are no longer at one remove from the war, but are the soldiers themselves. The setting now is in a field, and the speaker is a soldier holding a vigil in the night for one of his fallen comrades. This is a scene of both death and romance. Michael Moon will be a useful resource as you begin to consider the physicality of Whitman's poetry.

3. In "A March in the Ranks Hard-Prest, and the Road Unknown" the soldier-speaker comes upon a makeshift hospital during a night march. He lingers on the sight of such a place that contains so much suffering, a place described as "a sight beyond all the pictures and poems ever made." In "A Sight in Camp in the Daybreak Gray and Dim" the seeing takes place in the morning, but the wounded are still present and he views three bodies—those of an old man, a child, and a young man. It is as if with every poem Whitman attempts a new way to see these people, and it is in this poem that he turns the anonymous dead into a deeply meaningful figure: "Young man I think I know you—I think this face is the face of the Christ himself, / Dead and divine and brother of all, and here again he lies." "As Toilsome I Wander'd Virginia's Woods" is the last in this set of poems and here readers are not faced with the dying or the dead, but instead with the sign that a solder has died in this spot: "a tablet scrawl'd and nail'd on the tree by the grave." The words written in haste on that tablet are haunting in what they say and cannot say: *"Bold, cautious, true, and my loving comrade."* After consulting Davis's book, which analyzes the effect of Whitman's experiences as a nurse during the war, consider whether the different perspectives in these poems are related to experience or narrative strategy.

4. Whereas all of these poems are narrated by the poet, who brings himself as close as possible to these different situations and then describes them in all their complexity, some of the more challenging poems employ different voices. "Song of the Banner at Daybreak," "The Centenarian's Song," and

"The Wound-Dresser," for instance, are at least more than one level removed from the lives of the young boys on the battlefield. What is the effect of having so many different kinds of poems about the war in this sequence? Erkkila may help clarify your approach to this topic.

5. Although it is not the last poem in the section, "Reconciliation"—a six-line poem that can easily be memorized and recited—reads like a finale. A perfect combination of the best of Whitman's sounds and rhythms, and of his long and short lines, this poem magnifies the emotions expressed in the individual poems as its speaker looks at his dead enemy and slowly and deliberately narrates his move of reconciliation. What does Whitman mean by "reconciliation" and how does he imagine the country might get there?

RESOURCES

Biography

David S. Reynolds, *Walt Whitman's America: A Cultural Biography* (New York: Knopf, 1995).

Presents the details of Whitman's biography in relation to the shifts in the social and political climates of nineteenth-century America, telling the stories of the man and the nation simultaneously.

Criticism

Robert Leigh Davis, *Whitman and the Romance of Medicine* (Berkeley: University of California Press, 1997).

Analyzes the influence of Whitman's experience as a nurse during the Civil War on his writing, arguing that it is in those poems that he develops his fullest sense of the democratic experience.

Betsy Erkkila, *Whitman the Political Poet* (New York: Oxford University Press, 1989).

Explores a number of nineteenth-century political struggles (including the Civil War), Whitman's own political ideology, and the effect of both on Whitman's ongoing poetic project.

Ted Genoways, "Civil War Poems in 'Drum-Taps' and 'Memories of President Lincoln,'" in *A Companion to Walt Whitman,* edited by Donald D. Kummings (Malden, Mass.: Blackwell, 2006), pp. 522–538.

Offers one way through the sequence by characterizing the poems in each stage by the following terms: "Recruiting Poems," "Journalistic Poems," "Soldier Poems," "Hospital Poems," and "Memories of President Lincoln."

Michael Moon, *Disseminating Whitman: Revision and Corporeality in* Leaves of Grass (Cambridge, Mass.: Harvard University Press, 1991).

Analyzes the first four editions of *Leaves of Grass* in relation to issues of the body, desire, and homosexuality that Moon argues guides Whitman's "revisions."

M. Wynn Thomas, *The Lunar Light of Whitman's Poetry* (Cambridge, Mass.: Harvard University Press, 1987).
Analyzes the social and political contexts within which Whitman was working—capitalism and the Civil War, in particular—and argues that his poems were directly affected by them.

Michael Warner, "Civil War Religion and Whitman's *Drum-Taps,*" in *Walt Whitman: Where the Future Becomes the Present,* edited by David Haven Blake and Michael Robertson (Iowa City: University of Iowa Press, 2008), pp. 81–90.
Suggests that "Drum-Taps" does not tell the narrative of this particular war but instead is preoccupied with larger issues of history, time, and mortality and often casts those issues in religious language and tone.

—Alexandra Socarides

Edith Wharton, *Ethan Frome*
(New York: Scribners, 1911)

Born into a well-to-do New York family, Edith Wharton (1862–1937) was an astute observer of old New York society. She came of age accustomed to travels throughout Europe; in fact, she often appeared far more at ease in Europe than in America. In Europe she could escape the role of debutante that plagued her in her native New York. From early on a shy, imaginative, and intellectual child, Wharton found both Europe and literature havens from the encroachment of such a social and invasive lifestyle that was New York at the time. While many of her novels (for example, *The House of Mirth,* 1905; *The Custom of the Country,* 1913; and *The Age of Innocence,* 1920) focus upon the countless nuances and limitless strata of class distinctions and rules, there is a novella that emerges like a diamond in the rough amid these other novels: *Ethan Frome.* To use Wharton's own imagery, *Ethan Frome* and its characters are like "granite outcroppings," rarely noticed and often inarticulate but present and enduring nonetheless. Wharton wrote a book a year in the twenty-six years of her life after *Ethan Frome.* She died of a heart attack on 11 August 1937 at her eighteenth-century house in Saint-Brice-sous-Forêt and is buried in the American cemetery in Versailles, France.

Ethan Frome was first published serially in *Scribner's Magazine* in the summer of 1911. It was published in book form in September of that year, and its relative lack of success was one reason Wharton ended her partnership with the house of Scribner. With the recent revival of interest in her writings, however, *Ethan Frome* has attracted renewed attention. There was a 1993 film based on the novella. Although set in the fictional village of Starkfield, Massachusetts, the novella was written while Wharton resided in Paris, and the first draft was crafted in French as an exercise in improving her language proficiency. It was later translated into English by Wharton as her marriage was dissolving and during her affair with Morton Fullerton. Torn between a life of literary, cultural, and sexual freedom and life with her often ill, mentally troubled, and extremely nervous husband, Wharton created one of her most haunting characters, Ethan Frome.

Told within a frame narrative, *Ethan Frome* is the tale of a disturbingly stark love triangle: Ethan Frome; his wife, Zenobia (Zeena); and Zeena's young cousin, Mattie Silver. Ethan married Zeena after she cared for his mother until her death. Alone on the stark Massachusetts farm, Ethan turned to Zeena for companionship, but he soon discovered that she was not nearly as stoic and strong as he thought. She is frequently sick and helpless, testing every new medical treatment and offering little comfort to Ethan. To help out, Mattie has come to live with the Fromes and she does what she can to earn her keep. Soft and spirited, Mattie is the antithesis of Zeena, and Ethan falls deeply in love with her. Upon discerning the truth of the situation, Zeena sends Mattie away and hires a girl to replace her. Ethan is trapped in this situation. On the way to the train station, Ethan and Mattie decide to commit suicide by sledding down the mountain and smashing into a large elm. The sledding scene, perhaps the most famous in all of Wharton's fiction, turns grotesquely wrong. Ethan is left disfigured and limping, and Mattie is left paralyzed; both are left at the mercy of Zeena, who ironically becomes their caregiver. All three are trapped in the bleak house with their squandered hopes and dreams.

TOPICS FOR DISCUSSION AND RESEARCH

1. One of the most structurally adept features of the novella is Wharton's use of a frame tale. The opening and closing of the novella is narrated by an unnamed outsider in Starkfield on business. Frequently seeing Ethan, with his limp and his austere and silenced countenance, he cannot help but wonder about Ethan and his story. One evening Ethan offers to lodge the narrator at his home for the night. The opening frame ends with the narrator's remark: "It was that night that I found the clue to Ethan Frome, and began to put together this vision of his story." The reader is swept along by the tale that the narrator constructs, often forgetting that it is a "vision" only. The truth of Ethan's life is never revealed. In her introduction, Wharton notes that each of her "chroniclers contributes to the narrative just so much as he or she is capable of understanding of what, to them, is a complicated and mysterious case; and only the narrator of the tale has scope enough to see it all, to resolve it back into simplicity, and to put it in its rightful place among his larger categories." By the close of the novella, the narrator has gleaned some scattered facts, but the questions remain: Is the story constructed by the narrator accurate and true, and if so, does it matter?
2. In addition to her masterful use of the frame device, Wharton also achieves an extremely powerful counterpoint to her own life experiences. Both Ethan and Wharton are caught in marriages that they desperately wish to escape. Wharton,

who eventually divorced her mentally ill husband, struggled to earn a place in a New York society that prized women as wives and mothers, not as artists and thinkers. Ethan too had dreams before he married Zeena. With an interest in engineering, Ethan had hoped to move to Florida and follow his passion. Marriage to Zeena forced him to change his plans. As the narrator imagines, "She chose to look down on Starkfield, but she could not have lived in a place which looked down on her. Even Bettsbridge or Shadd's Falls would not have been sufficiently aware of her, and in the greater cities which attracted Ethan she would have suffered a complete loss of identity." In addition, both Ethan and Wharton were trapped caring for mates who suffered countless debilitating illnesses. The sole difference between them is that Wharton escapes and Ethan does not.

3. This novella also prefigures the modernist juxtaposition of the individual and the group. Faced with sending Mattie away because of the plotting of a jealous Zeena, Ethan considers leaving Zeena and running away with Mattie to the West, fulfilling his own desires and needs. He even goes so far as to write Zeena a goodbye letter. Ethan's conscience, however, will not allow him to go through with the plan. Because Zeena would be left on a farm she could not work or sell, Ethan realizes his fate will be to live out the rest of his days with her. Not until Mattie suggests suicide by sledding into the tree can Ethan conceive of a plausible escape from his fate.

4. Finally, one of the most significant features of the novella is Wharton's description of a hostile environment as setting. *Ethan Frome* is packed with connections between nature and the fates of the characters. A freak sickness of the town horses first introduces the narrator to Ethan. A terrible snowstorm provides an opportunity to discover Ethan and his home life at first hand. The cold snows of Starkfield blanket the town, creating an eerie silence that is mimicked and rivaled only by the starkness and silence of the Frome household. Even the cucumber vines outside the Frome home are withered and dying, much like Zeena and eventually Mattie and Ethan. As Wharton herself notes, "I had had an uneasy sense that the New England of fiction bore little—except a vague botanical and dialectical—resemblance to the harsh and beautiful land as I had seen it." She feared that "the outcropping granite" had "been overlooked." The characters in *Ethan Frome* are like the "granite outcroppings," inarticulate and easily ignored, but worthy of attention.

5. Wharton offers a realistic representation of rural New England life in the novella, which she was at pains to distinguish from the more sentimental treatments of the region by Sarah Orne Jewett and Mary E. Wilkins Freeman. She attains a perspective on her characters missing in her previous work. In addition, she provides a glimpse into her own life.

RESOURCES

Biography

Hermione Lee, *Edith Wharton* (New York: Knopf, 2007).
The first British biography of Wharton, demonstrating both her modernism and her ties to Europe.

Cynthia Griffin Wolff, *A Feast of Words: The Triumph of Edith Wharton* (New York: Oxford University Press, 1977; revised edition, Reading, Mass.: Addison-Wesley, 1985).
A psychobiography that traces Wharton's development as a writer.

Criticism

Elizabeth Ammons, *Edith Wharton's Argument with America* (Athens: University of Georgia Press, 1980).
Discusses Wharton's fiction in the context of feminism or "the Woman Question."

Ammons, "The Myth of Imperiled Whiteness and *Ethan Frome*," *New England Quarterly,* 81 (March 2008): 5–33.
An analysis of the "largely hidden" racist and anti-immigrant subtext of the novella.

Kenneth Bernard, "Imagery and Symbolism in *Ethan Frome*," *College English,* 23 (December 1961): 178–184.
Argues that, given her cast of inarticulate characters, Wharton solved the problem of portraying them "in a masterful way by her use of imagery and symbolism."

Denise D. Knight, ed., Ethan Frome *and* Summer: *Complete Texts with Introduction, Historical Contexts, Critical Essays* (Boston: Houghton Mifflin, 2004).
Authoritative texts of the short novels as well as a rich selection of contextual material and critical essays.

Melissa McFarland Pennell, *Student Companion to Edith Wharton* (Westport, Conn.: Greenwood Press, 2003).
An introduction to Wharton's career with a chapter devoted specifically to *Ethan Frome.*

Orlene Murad, "Edith Wharton and Ethan Frome," *Modern Language Studies,* 13 (Summer 1983): 90–103.
An analysis of the narrative technique in the novella.

Cynthia Griffin Wolff, "Cold Ethan and 'Hot Ethan,'" *College Literature,* 14 (Fall 1987): 230–245.
An autobiographical reading of the novella in light of Wharton's relationships with Morton Fullerton and her husband.

—Rachel Harmon

Edith Wharton, "Roman Fever"

Liberty (10 November 1934): 10–14; collected in *The World Over* (New York & London: Appleton-Century, 1936)

Edith Wharton (1862–1937) is best known for her intimately detailed portraits of class conflict, and in particular of the so-called leisure class, traditional and hypocritical social mores and practices, and relationships between and among men and women that are psychological, at times compromised, and always complicated. Born into a wealthy family in New York City, Wharton lived on inherited wealth as an adult, which allowed her frequent and lengthy travels in Europe. Her early stories began to appear at the end of the Victorian era; early reviewers praised her craftsmanship, but, Helen Killoran explains, "they held two culturally ingrained prejudices against her"—first, she was a female writer, one of Nathaniel Hawthorne's "scribbling women," and second, she belonged to old money of Manhattan. "Charges abounded," Killoran notes, "that her upper-class characters, based on the privileged 'four hundred,' constituted too narrow a subject matter." During Wharton's life "critics grudgingly admired her craftsmanship, but backhandedly referred to it as too clever and too artificial. Then, as if in an attempt to explain the mystery of such artificially clever fiction, they created a myth that imagined her seated at the feet of the man who became known as the 'The Master,' Henry James." Yet, *The House of Mirth* (1905), *The Age of Innocence* (1920), for which she won the Pulitzer Prize, several collections of short fiction, letters, poems, and an autobiography, *A Backward Glance* (1934), published three years before her death, cemented her place in the pantheon of American literature. Critics, however, would not elevate her into such rarefied air until the release of her private papers in 1968 and R. W. B. Lewis's Pulitzer Prize–winning biography of Wharton in 1975.

Among her short stories, "Roman Fever" is one of the best known. It encapsulates not only the travels of wealthy Americans tourists in Europe, a theme that Wharton returns to again and again, but also the incisive and barbed world of women of this social set in the early decades of the twentieth century. These are women who knew their best exercise of power came among, and often at the expense of, each other. Millicent Bell suggests that Wharton "distinguished herself from those fashionable women whom she satirized years later in 'Roman Fever' by turning the pleasure of Italy into a fact of knowledge and enlightened creative labor."

The product of a trip to Rome, "Roman Fever" is set on a terrace restaurant overlooking the ruins of Rome and at first seems to be little more than a sketch of reminiscences between two women, described by the narrator as "two American ladies of ripe but well-cared-for middle age," who have both traveled to Rome with their now-adult daughters. Two matriarchs of respected families, Mrs. Alida Slade and Mrs. Grace Ansley have been lifelong friends, due to their common social class, rather than any true liking of each other. What is clear are their feelings, not quite of contempt for each other, but of a distrusting wariness based on some historical moment in their relationship that is revealed at the end of the story.

That Wharton has set this story in Rome—outside of the United States—illustrates the tension she felt in American society. "She inevitably found," Katherine Joslin and Alan Price suggest, that her significant time abroad and "her developing sensibility put her out of step with the native rhythms of the United States." As an adult, she, like so many other women writers such as Jane Addams,

Charlotte Perkins Gilman, and Alice James, underwent neurologist S. Weir Mitchell's "rest cure," as a way, Joslin and Price note, "to curb the intellectual and artistic tendencies of women, whose duties supposedly belonged to the prosaic world of upper-middle-class domesticity." Still, it was to this world she returned, setting her characters within the Europe that she knew so well, but bringing with them the baggage of being an American of a certain social and cultural class.

The seemingly calm demeanor of "Roman Fever," however—two middle-aged women sitting on a terrace engaged in conversation and knitting—contains a more biting indictment than perhaps either Mrs. Slade or Mrs. Ansley realize. Their two daughters, who have left their mothers that afternoon to realize more exciting possibilities in Rome, say of their mothers: "'let's leave the young things to their knitting'; and a voice as fresh laughed back: 'Oh, look here, Babs, not actually *knitting*—'Well, I mean figuratively,' rejoined the first. 'After all, we haven't left our poor parents much else to do.'" Alice Hall Petry suggests that the daughter's appraisal of their mothers as "young things" is "mocking," and the "implication is clearly that the ladies are physically, emotionally, and intellectually capable of nothing more than the traditionally passive, repetitive, and undemanding task of knitting. By having the daughters patronize their mothers in this fashion, Wharton is predisposing the reader to perceive the ladies as stereotypical matrons; and the rest of the story is devoted to obliterating this stereotype, to exposing the intense passions that have been seething in both women for more than twenty-five years."

As "Roman Fever" unfolds, the reader learns that Slade and Ansley first met as young women visiting Rome with their families, and have lived most of their adult lives across the street from each other in New York, eyeing each other's comings and goings with both a noticeable commonality—both have been widowed—and unexpressed competitiveness. Now, they have returned to Rome decades later with their daughters: Jenny Slade is dull and sensible, and Barbara Ansley is vivid and dramatic, apparently unlike either of her parents. Mrs. Slade even says of her own daughter: "Oh, my girl's perfect; if I were a chronic invalid I'd—well, I think I'd rather be in Jenny's hands. There must be times . . . but there! I always wanted a brilliant daughter . . . and never quite understood why I got an angel instead."

The climactic moment in the story comes at the end, when the women's conversations escalate the obvious tension of some personal travesty unstated, but known by both of the women. The narrator reveals, through the women's dialogue, the long-simmering crisis, pinpointed to a time in their blossoming youth when both were in Rome and being courted. Alida Slade is finally angry enough to confront Grace Ansley for having gone to meet her fiancé illicitly in the shadows of the Colosseum. "'Well,'" she says, "'you went to meet the man I was engaged to—and I can repeat every word of the letter that took you there.'" Mrs. Ansley's "unsteady" rise to her feet, and her knitting bag and gloves sliding to the ground in a "panic-stricken heap" is all the confirmation the reader needs to know that the accusation is true, a seething, simmering secret harbored for years finally publicly acknowledged.

But there are three last damaging admissions. Mrs. Slade admits to writing the letter and signing her fiancé's name. Cognizant of the concerns about contracting "Roman fever" (malaria is the less romanticized name of the disease) from the cold dampness that settled among the ruins at night and which provided attractive cover for trysts between lovers, the young Alida deliberately lured the young Grace to the same ruins in the hope that Grace would contract the illness. Recounted family history of the "dreadfully wicked" great-aunt Harriet, who sent her young sister out to the Forum after sunset purportedly to gather flowers, but, according to speculation, because she and her sister were in love with the same man, sets the scene for the revelation between Alida and Grace to follow. That the great-aunt's story ends in tragedy—her younger sister did, in fact, die of the fever—establishes the awful stakes such women engaged in as they sought to protect their futures as married women. ("Roman fever" also is used by Henry James in his novella *Daisy Miller* [1878] to punish the flirty young American woman of the title, who contracts the fever after visiting the Colosseum at night.)

Yet, as damning as Alida's forged love letter is to Grace, it is Grace who has the last two most powerful plays. Once Alida announces her trickery, the narrator notes that "The flame of her wrath had already sunk, and she wondered why she had ever thought there would be any satisfaction in inflicting so purposeless a wound on her friend." Seeking to justify her actions, Alida admits to Grace the fear she had of losing Delphin, her fiancé. "So in a blind fury I wrote that letter." What she fails to realize, however, was that the tryst between Grace and Delphin did occur that evening years ago because Grace had answered the letter: "I told him I'd be there. So he came."

And what results is the most damning twist of all in "Roman Fever" and the lives of its two middle-aged matriarchs. Alida Slade, after having finally confessed to the forgery and the jealousy she felt so many years ago, capitulating but proud that "Yes, I was beaten there. But I oughtn't to begrudge it to you, I suppose. At the end of all these years. After all, I had everything; I had him for twenty-five years. And you had nothing but that one letter that he didn't write." Grace Ansley, hurriedly married to another man two months after the rendezvous on the Forum with Delphin, simply replies: "I had Barbara."

TOPICS FOR DISCUSSION AND RESEARCH

1. What had seemed at the outset to be a story of middle-aged American tourists resting for an afternoon on a restaurant terrace in Rome concludes with incidences of sexual promiscuity and infidelity, pregnancy outside of marriage, innuendo and lies, savage cruelty, and a now-chaotic microcosmic family structure and macrocosmic social structure. Susan Elizabeth Sweeney argues even more pointedly that the title of "Roman Fever" alludes to the differences that Rome represents to each generation of women in this story: "'sentimental dangers,' filial disobedience, love-sickness, sexual jealousy, illegitimate pregnancy, and the longing for new or foreign experiences

that Wharton elsewhere calls 'travel-fever.' These different things have one common characteristic: all are experiences prohibited to women." And these women's experiences are worth exploring in "Roman Fever" and other works by Wharton. How, for example, do Ansley and Slade live typical women's lives according to their class? How do their daughters, the next generation, compare to them? Why are men absent in the story, particularly when compared to other Wharton stories and novels where men play more prominent roles? Sweeney also notes how Henry James had used the trope of illness, or "Roman fever," in *Daisy Miller*. Does Wharton in effect respond to James in her story?

2. As Cynthia Griffin Wolff argues, the satire Wharton employs in the short story places an enormous amount of responsibility on the reader. "The stakes are not clear (as they might be in a business transaction), nor is the eventual outcome. Who was the winner of this convoluted game? . . . Can an astute reader make a more accurate assessment?" For the story to end with the declaration by Grace Ansley that the one-night tryst resulted in a child requires that the reader, as Wolff avers, determine if there ever can be "a winner in a competition that has been defined in the way this one has." And this is, perhaps, the striking subtlety of "Roman Fever," a slowly building story of longtime competitors who find that their real power lies in their womanhood, and learn that such power is fleetingly compromised and readily stolen, at best. As critics at the start of Wharton's career and those over the past century have noted, she possessed a keen and sharp sense of human nature and women's sensibilities and an exquisite pen that allowed language to flourish and incisively cut through the social complications of early-twentieth-century America.

RESOURCES

Biography

Cynthia Griffin Wolff, *A Feast of Words: The Triumph of Edith Wharton* (New York: Oxford University Press, 1977).

A biographical account of Wharton's development as an important novelist, accompanied by detailed readings of her major novels and of her unpublished fictions and autobiographical recollections.

Criticism

Millicent Bell, ed., *The Cambridge Companion to Edith Wharton* (Cambridge, England & New York: Cambridge University Press, 1995).

A collection of essays by distinguished scholars that covers Wharton's most important novels, as well as some of her shorter fiction. The introduction supplies a valuable review of the history of Wharton criticism; a detailed chronology of her life and publications and a useful bibliography of important books for further reading are also provided.

Katherine Joslin and Alan Price, *Wretched Exotic: Essays on Edith Wharton in Europe* (New York: Peter Lang, 1993).
Considers Wharton as a cross-cultural writer, a self-described "wretched exotic"—an American by birth but a European by inclination.

Helen Killoran, *The Critical Reception of Edith Wharton* (Rochester, N.Y.: Camden House, 2001).
Traces and analyzes the development of Whartonian literary criticism in its historical and political contexts; also considers Wharton's own criticism.

Alice Hall Petry, "A Twist of Crimson Silk: Edith Wharton's 'Roman Fever,'" *Studies in Short Fiction,* 24 (Spring 1987): 163–166.
Considers the motif of knitting in the tale as a "complex personal emblem."

Susan Elizabeth Sweeney, "Edith Wharton's Case of Roman Fever," in *Wretched Exotic: Essays on Edith Wharton in Europe,* edited by Katherine Joslin and Alan Price (New York: Peter Lang, 1993), pp. 335–354.
Focuses on the story's setting within the historical context of Rome and the fear of Roman fever, as well as the technical, medical phenomenon of malaria. The article also considers Wharton's use of the trope of illness in relationship to Henry James's use of Roman fever in *Daisy Miller.*

Cynthia Griffin Wolff, "Introduction," in Wharton's *Roman Fever and Other Stories* (New York: Collier, 1987), pp. ix–xx.
Notes that Wharton shows her skill "in dissecting the elements of emotional subtleties, moral ambiguities, and the implications of social restrictions." Specifically, Wolff suggests Wharton takes particular aim at women's lives within marriage, and the sociopolitical restrictions in which their lives operate.

—Laura Behling

Part IV
Annotated
Bibliography

Lars Åhnebrink, *The Beginnings of Naturalism in American Fiction* (Cambridge, Mass.: Harvard University Press, 1950).
Locates certain American writers in terms of an emerging Naturalism but also discusses European influences, particularly French, Russian, and Scandanavian, most notably the work of Émile Zola, Ivan Turgenev, and Henrik Ibsen. Henry James, William Dean Howells, Stephen Crane, Frank Norris, and Hamlin Garland are principal subjects.

American Literary Realism (1968–present). Published since 1999 by the University of Illinois Press.
The premier scholarly journal in the field of late-nineteenth- and early-twentieth-century American fiction.

George Becker, ed., *Documents of Modern Literary Realism* (Princeton: Princeton University Press, 1963).
A comprehensive collection of documents from mostly European writers on the principles and theory of Realism, including Zola's *Le Roman expérimental* (1880). Together, the documents show that Realists were reacting against Romanticism and at the same time developing literary means that were unified in this opposition but sometimes in conflict with one another. The collection of statements has been translated into English, and the editor supplies a comprehensive introduction and useful headnotes. A basic book for anyone seeking to understand foreign influences on American Realism.

Michael Davitt Bell, *The Problem of American Realism: Studies in the Cultural History of a Literary Idea* (Chicago: University of Chicago Press, 1993).
Contends that "Realism" and "Naturalism" were, in effect, ideological rather than literary terms that promoted a version of reality that was gender and class inflected. For many of the male writers of the period, including Howells, Norris, Crane, and Theodore Dreiser, the claim to be a Realist or Naturalist was a way to fend off suspicions of femininity.

Bert Bender, *Evolution and "The Sex Problem": American Narratives during the Eclipse of Darwinism* (Kent, Ohio: Kent State University Press, 2004).
A wide-ranging book that explores the "sex problem" as it was inherited from Darwinism in Norris, Crane, Jack London, Dreiser, Gertrude Stein, Willa Cather, and many others. A theory of sexual selection was important to how one might understand contemporary life, though such theories were difficult to treat in the Victorian era. Bender argues for a continuity between Darwinism and Freudianism and that Freud extended evolutionary contexts for understanding. Particularly strong on London and Norris.

Warner Berthoff, *The Ferment of Realism: American Literature 1884–1919* (New York: Free Press, 1965).
A readable critical history of thirty-five years of American culture addressed not so much to the general reader as to those who already have a broad acquaintance with the era. The first chapter describes the emergence of Realism in response to a cultural ferment; the second treats specific writers (including James, William Dean

Howells, and Mark Twain) or genres (including Regionalism); the third chapter deals with what Berthoff calls the "literature of argument"—sociology, philosophy, criticism, history; and the fourth takes up Naturalism as well as the "new poetry."

Daniel H. Borus, *Writing Realism: Howells, James, and Norris in the Mass Market* (Chapel Hill: University of North Carolina Press, 1989).
Selects Howells, James, and Norris as principal authors because each justified writing as a "profession" through published commentary that was meant to describe a "systematic theory of Realism and its practice." The book is also valuable in detailing the differences between the antebellum and postbellum literary marketplace, differences that include publicity and publishing practices, readers' and editors' expectations, and so forth.

Richard H. Brodhead, *Cultures of Letters: Scenes of Reading and Writing in Nineteenth-Century America* (Chicago: University of Chicago Press, 1993).
Argues that high-culture literature did not render ordinary life so much as create it for a status-conscious reading public. One of the ironies of Regionalist writing, according to Brodhead, is that it reassured the upper middle class that America remained homogenous, despite considerable evidence to the contrary, and that they could feel superior to that same class. Sarah Orne Jewett and Charles Chesnutt became victimized by this arrangement because they were restricted by editors in their treatment of subject matter they knew well and wished to write about.

Edwin H. Cady, *The Light of Common Day: Realism in American Fiction* (Bloomington: Indiana University Press, 1971).
A series of interconnected essays on Realist writers that is more personable than polemical in its approach to the subject. The volume begins with a sweeping but reader-friendly attempt at a definition of Realism. Cady argues that Realism cultivates a certain "common vision" in readers and has certain characteristics, including a critical view of the past, a greater interest in character than in plot, and a democratic focus. The successful Realist work dramatizes the relation between ordinary experience and art.

Donna M. Campbell, *Resisting Regionalism: Gender and Naturalism in American Fiction, 1885–1915* (Athens: Ohio University Press, 1997).
Argues that the popularity and critical approval women Regionalists acquired in the 1870s and 1880s derived from the cultural functions it performed—a certain nostalgic ease, a cultural continuity in community, and a regard for time-tested values. For some male writers, including Norris, Crane, and Dreiser, it appeared that literature had become feminized, and Naturalism, with its emphasis on the extreme and grotesque over the common and ordinary, sought to displace this effeminacy with a more-manly fiction.

John J. Conder, *Naturalism in American Fiction: The Classic Phase* (Lexington: University Press of Kentucky, 1984).
A thesis-driven book that seeks to mediate between the positions of Donald Pizer and Charles Walcutt—namely, to argue that Naturalism is deterministic but that freedom can exist within a determinist frame. Conder discusses several nineteenth- and twentieth-century writers in this context, from Crane, Norris, and

Dreiser to John Dos Passos, William Faulkner, and John Steinbeck. For Conder, Naturalists wrestled with the opposition between freedom and determinism and eventually came up with a logically consistent answer to the dilemma with the help of Henri Bergson and other philosophers.

Stanley Corkin, *Realism and the Birth of the Modern United States: Cinema, Literature, and Culture* (Athens: University of Georgia Press, 1996).
An interdisciplinary study of literary texts and films from 1885 to 1925 shaped by the financial, political, and social history of the period. Corkin treats Howells's major novels in connection with Thomas Edison's pioneering cinema, Dreiser's *Sister Carrie* and the films of Edwin S. Porter, and Ernest Hemingway's *In Our Time* in conjunction with D. W. Griffith's *The Birth of a Nation.*

Malcolm Cowley, "Not Men: A Natural History of American Naturalism," *Kenyon Review,* 9 (Summer 1947): 414–435; collected in Becker, *Documents of Modern Literary Realism* (Princeton: Princeton University Press, 1963) pp. 429–451.
A straightforward chronicle of the rise and fall of literary Naturalism from Norris and London through Steinbeck with a useful list of its characteristics (for example, "The effect of Naturalism as a doctrine is to subtract from literature the whole notion of human responsibility"). Cowley acknowledges that, their pose of dispassionate objectivity notwithstanding, the Naturalists "could not remain merely observers."

Donald A. Dike, "Notes on Local Color and Its Relation to Realism," *College English,* 14 (November 1952): 81–88.
A pioneering attempt to define local-color writing, which, according to Dike, has no necessary connection to Realism. Local-color writing, Dike concludes, "is writing that insists upon the special context of the events and characters with which it deals, that insists upon the primary importance of that special context to its meaning." He lists specific components of local-color writing; for example, it "fosters Americanism by documenting American history"; it exhibits "a semi-anthropological interest in local customs"; and/or it presumes to protect "regional interests—an economic system or a class structure."

John Dudley, *A Man's Game: Masculinity and the Anti-Aesthetics of American Literary Naturalism* (Tuscaloosa: University of Alabama Press, 2004).
Focusing on works by Norris, Crane, London, Edith Wharton, Charles Chesnutt, Paul Laurence Dunbar, and James Weldon Johnson, surveys the association of literary Naturalism with hypermasculinity and parallel developments in turn-of-the-century American culture: the rise of such spectator sports as boxing and football and the emergence of a pop-Darwinism that valorized male sexual conquest. Dudley underscores the Naturalists' disdain for the foppish aestheticism of Oscar Wilde. He also explains the ambivalent adoption of Naturalism by African American writers who resisted its hypermasculine values.

Jennifer L. Fleissner, *Women, Compulsion, Modernity: The Moment of American Naturalism* (Chicago: University of Chicago Press, 2004).
Challenges the conventional notion that literary Naturalism is necessarily a masculine form of fiction, given its frequent focus on the lives of young women.

Fleissner also proposes to replace the equation of Naturalism and pessimistic determinism with the notion of compulsion. The typical plot of a Naturalistic novel "is marked by neither the steep arc of decline nor that of triumph, but rather by an ongoing, nonlinear, repetitive motion . . . that has the distinctive effect of seeming also like a stuckness in place." Her examples include Dreiser's Carrie Meeber, Norris's Trina McTeague, Wharton's Lily Bart, and Charlotte Perkins Gilman's Jane in "The Yellow Wallpaper." Such fiction is "as much (if not more) about domesticity, details, and women's inner lives" as they are about men.

Alfred Habegger, *Gender, Fantasy, and Realism in American Literature* (New York: Columbia University Press, 1982).
A lively book with a surprising argument—that American Realism did not descend from European examples but from a group of popular American women novelists who challenged male writers to respond. Two "sissies," he says, effected the transition from these popular women novelists to the masculine narratives of the Naturalists: Henry James and Howells. Habegger argues that one cannot understand Realism without also understanding gender and its influence on Realist narratives.

Hamlin Hill, "There Ought to Be Clowns: American Humor and Literary Naturalism," *Prospects*, 5 (1980): 413–422.
Argues that humor functions as defense mechanism and/or supplies comic relief in some works of Naturalism, specifically in some of the humor writings of Ambrose Bierce, Eugene Field, Harry Graham, and William Cowper Brann.

Barbara Hochman, *Getting at the Author: Reimagining Books and Reading in the Age of American Realism* (Amherst: University of Massachusetts Press, 2001).
A reassessment of late-nineteenth-century reading practices. Hochman demonstrates the ambivalence of the Realists toward their own purported objectivity and how their ambivalence shaped standards of literary merit for the modernists.

Richard Hofstadter, *Social Darwinism in American Thought* (Boston: Beacon, 1955).
An excellent intellectual history of the period. Particularly valuable is the chapter "The Vogue of Spencer."

June Howard, *Form and History in American Literary Naturalism* (Chapel Hill: University of North Carolina Press, 1985).
A highly theoretical treatment of Naturalism as a genre. For Howard, literary history may be studied in terms of forms that represent the cultural assumptions of the period. Thus, for example, the representation of proletariat characters, whatever their creators may have thought, in fact are ideological constructs derived from the prevailing dominant culture. Howard analyzes selected texts of Norris, London, and Dreiser, with briefer treatments of Crane and Upton Sinclair.

William Dean Howells, *Criticism and Fiction* (New York: Harper, 1891).
A literary and aesthetic credo by the leading American theorist of Realism and prominent realistic novelist. Howells based the book on his editorial columns in *Harper's Monthly,* in which he repeatedly argued that "fidelity to experience and probability of motive are essential conditions of a great imaginative literature." When Realists begin to "map" life rather than "picture" it, "Realism will perish" just as literary romance became passé. The Realist "finds nothing insignificant; all tells for destiny and character; nothing that God has made is contemptible."

Gene Andrew Jarrett, *Deans and Truants: Race and Realism in African American Literature* (Philadelphia: University of Pennsylvania Press, 2007).
Interrogates the idea of "racial Realism" and the category of African American literature, standards that have "shackled the creative decisions and objectives of many black authors." These standards have been promulgated by critics, "de facto deans," as different as Howells, Alain Locke, Richard Wright, and Amiri Baraka. Jarrett calls for a definition of African American literature and an expansion of the African American literary canon to include writings by black authors, such as Paul Laurence Dunbar, George S. Schuyler, and Frank Yerby, who did not always write about race.

Amy Kaplan, *The Social Construction of American Realism* (Chicago: University of Chicago Press, 1988).
Undertakes to redefine Realism in terms of what Realist novels do and how they function culturally. The work of Howells, Wharton, and Dreiser reflects a sense of "unreality" in middle-class American life, brought about alternatively by disruptive class conflict and a homogenizing mass culture, at the same time that it combats these forces through social constructions of reality.

Harold H. Kolb Jr., *Illusion of Life: American Realism as a Literary Form* (Charlottesville: University Press of Virginia, 1969).
A relatively brief book that emphasizes Realism as a literary manner, though Kolb also gives a lengthy and insightful definition of Realism that is not at all limited to this element. He sees the rejection of omniscient narration in favor of a restricted narrative consciousness in Henry James, Twain, and Howells as a common quality that unites these three important Realists.

Robert Paul Lamb and G. R. Thompson, eds., *A Companion to American Fiction, 1865–1914* (Malden, Mass.: Blackwell, 2005).
Important essays include Winfried Fluck's "Morality, Modernity, and 'Malarial Restlessness': American Realism in its Anglo-European Contexts" (pp. 77–95), a thorough review of the influence of European Realists on American fiction in the late nineteenth century; and Bert Bender's "Darwin, Science, and Narrative" (pp. 377–394), a précis of Bender's books on the impact of Darwin's theories on such American Realists/Naturalists as Howells, James, Kate Chopin, Garland, Crane, and London.

Mary Lawlor, *Recalling the Wild: Naturalism and the Closing of the American West* (New Brunswick, N.J.: Rutgers University Press, 2000).
Proposes to "get at the shifting meanings of the West as an imaginative geography and as the national concept at the moment when official recognition of the frontier" ended at the turn of the twentieth century. Lawlor traces the making of Western American myth in the writing of James Fenimore Cooper and how the Romantic myth changed under the influence of Darwinism and French Naturalism. American literary Naturalists such as Crane, Norris, and London constructed the West in material terms, as a geography or landscape of forces limiting individual volition and endeavor.

Richard Lehan, "American Literary Naturalism: The French Connection," *Nineteenth Century Fiction*, 38 (March 1984): 529–557.
Details the significance of Zola for the "hundreds of novels" by Americans "which did for America after the Civil War what Zola did for the Second Empire. . . . The cumulative effect of these novels is more impressive than the individual achievement of most of these authors, almost all of whom have fallen out of the canon." According to Lehan, every Naturalistic novelist, "particularly in America," was "directly or indirectly in his debt."

Lehan, *Realism and Naturalism: The Novel in an Age of Transition* (Madison: University of Wisconsin Press, 2005).
A provocative intellectual, cultural, and literary history that considers the narrative mode of American, British, French, and Russian Realism/Naturalism not as an evolutionary cul-de-sac but as a hinge between romance and modernism. Sailing against the tide of the New Historicism, Lehan insists on treating scientific laws and historical events not as intellectual constructs or discursive practices but as contexts for the novels. Such an approach invites intertextual study of such novels as E. W. Howe's *The Story of a Country Town* (1884) and Sherwood Anderson's *Winesburg, Ohio* (1919); Norris's *McTeague* (1899) and Dreiser's *Sister Carrie* (1900); and Chopin's *The Awakening* (1899) and Wharton's *The House of Mirth* (1905).

Eric Carl Link, *The Vast and Terrible Drama: American Literary Naturalism in the Late Nineteenth Century* (Tuscaloosa: University of Alabama Press, 2004).
Emphasizes "literary Naturalism as an aesthetic movement—an art form, a way of writing" rather than a constellation of intellectual doctrines. Link challenges the notion that American Naturalists were deeply influenced by Zola's theory and practice, given the differences between what Zola wrote and what Norris, Dreiser, and others wrote. Link contends, like Norris, that American literary Naturalism was a form of literary romance—an inner circle of romance—rather than a development of Realism.

Sämi Ludwig, *Pragmatic Realism: The Cognitive Paradigm in American Realist Texts* (Madison: University of Wisconsin Press, 2002).
Traces the influence of William James and pragmatism on literary Realism. Such an approach reaffirms Henry James's position in the Realist canon beside

Howells and Twain. Ludwig also asserts the importance of Chesnutt's conjure tales in his chapter "The 'Pragmatist Deconstruction' of Racism."

Jay Martin, *Harvests of Change: American Literature 1865–1914* (Englewood Cliffs, N.J.: Prentice-Hall, 1967).
Surveys the monumental changes that occurred during this fifty-year period—in education, immigration, science and technology, book publishing, and other arenas—and analyzes a vast array of literary works as the harvest of those changes. Martin is less interested in advancing some definition of Realism or Naturalism than giving a panoramic view of the period. The author comments on Regionalist writers, utopian writers, humorists, and others; he reserves separate chapters for Twain and Henry James.

Ronald E. Martin, *American Literature and the Universe of Force* (Durham, N.C.: Duke University Press, 1981).
Explores the determinism of Herbert Spencer as a source for Naturalism. Philosophers and scientists agreed that a concept of force was inherent in the universe, and Spencer offered what he called a synthetic philosophy of force, as it was expressed in evolutionary terms, in virtually every aspect of life. Martin points out that Spencerism was not really a science at all, but that writers such as Dreiser and Norris responded positively to this vision and dramatized it in their fiction.

Walter Benn Michaels, *The Gold Standard and the Logic of Naturalism* (Berkeley: University of California Press, 1987).
A New Historicist interpretation of American Naturalism that argues that the movement can best be understood in terms of the economic conditions of the time. The author does not limit himself to texts that explicitly deal with economic themes; instead, he contends economic realities, especially the debate over the gold or silver standard for currency, enter into every aspect of life and often in unexpected ways. He reads the work of Norris, Wharton, and Dreiser in this light.

Lee Clark Mitchell, *Determined Fictions: American Literary Naturalism* (New York: Columbia University Press, 1989).
Claims that Naturalist writers challenge the premises of Realism, particularly with regard to moral agency and the existence of an independent autonomous self. In separate chapters, Mitchell analyzes the style of Naturalism in London's "To Build a Fire," Norris's *Vandover and the Brute,* Dreiser's *An American Tragedy,* and Crane's *The Red Badge of Courage.*

Brenda Murphy, *American Realism and American Drama, 1880–1940* (Cambridge, England & New York: Cambridge University Press, 1987).
A pioneering study of the dramatic literature of Howells, James, Twain, and Bret Harte—the four wrote a total of about sixty plays, many never produced and most utterly neglected—as well as the plays of more-minor figures, such as Hamlin Garland, Susan Glaspell, and Clyde Fitch. Murphy describes the theory of drama the American Realists proposed in their criticism; examines how this

theory informs their own dramatic literature and how the plays changed over time; and explains how the work of the Realists anticipated the early plays of Eugene O'Neill.

Thomas Peyser, *Utopia and Cosmopolis: Globalization in the Era of American Literary Realism* (Durham, N.C.: Duke University Press, 1998).

Evaluates utopian and realistic fiction by Edward Bellamy, Charlotte Perkins Gilman, Howells, and Henry James in the light of contemporary notions of globalization, or "what it might mean to be a citizen of the world." That is, Peyser recontextualizes fiction of the period in regard to the emergence of consumer culture, debates over immigration and imperialism, and the rivalry of socialism and capitalism.

Donald Pizer, *The Cambridge Companion to American Realism and Naturalism: Howells to London* (Cambridge, England & New York: Cambridge University Press, 1995).

To a degree, conceived in response to poststructuralist assessments of Realism and Naturalism as they were expressed in Eric Sundquist's *American Realism: New Essays*. In his introduction Pizer analyzes the problem of defining Realism and Naturalism. The remaining essays are divided into three categories: "Historical Contexts" (the American and European background); "Contemporary Critical Issues" (recent critical approaches and the expansion of the canon of Realism); and "Case Studies" (seven essays on individual works). This book is a useful volume for the student of the period.

Pizer, "Late Nineteenth-Century American Literary Naturalism: A Re-Introduction," *American Literary Realism*, 38 (Spring 2006): 189–202.

A corrective to the more theoretical approaches to literary Naturalism. Pizer emphasizes that Naturalism was a form of "radical expression" designed to evoke strong responses in contemporary readers. "Naturalism in its own day was often viewed as a threat to the established order because it boldly and vividly depicted the inadequacies of the industrial system that was the foundation of that order."

Pizer, "*Maggie* and the Naturalistic Aesthetic of Length," *American Literary Realism*, 28 (Fall 1995): 58–65.

Given the consensus view that a Naturalistic text must be substantial in length and detail, addresses two questions: why is the typical Naturalistic novel so long, and how does Crane "achieve a Naturalistic effect without a reliance on length?" The answer centers on "Crane's art of compression" or "Naturalistic aesthetic of brevity."

Pizer, "Nineteenth-Century American Naturalism: An Essay in Definition," *Bucknell Review*, 13 (December 1965): 1–18.

Contends that the melodrama, sensationalism, and moral confusion some critics attack in Naturalistic novels of the period are "essential constituents" of such works as Norris's *McTeague*, Dreiser's *Sister Carrie*, and Crane's *The Red Badge of Courage*. That is, Pizer argues for a coherence or internal consistency to American Naturalism other critics deny.

Pizer, *Realism and Naturalism in Nineteenth-Century American Literature* (Carbondale: Southern Illinois University Press, 1966).

Attempts to answer two questions: how can one describe Realism and Naturalism in fiction (a question of definition), and how do Realism and Naturalism relate to the criticism of the age (a cultural and historical matter)? For Pizer, Realism is ethically idealistic, even though there was increasing awareness of the limitations, both biological and social, placed upon the individual. Naturalism, while both deterministic and pessimistic, nevertheless posits an ethical affirmation by asserting the value of all life no matter how low or compromised.

Pizer, ed., *Documents of American Realism and Naturalism* (Carbondale: Southern Illinois University Press, 1998).

Conceived as supplementary to George Becker's *Modern Literary Realism,* concentrates on American statements and reactions. This collection is composed of three sections—The Critical Debate, 1874–1950; The Early Modern Period, 1915–1950; and Modern Academic Criticism, 1951–1995. It contains a healthy selection of critical statements by the practitioners of Realism, including Howells and Garland, as well as more-recent essays and excerpts of critical commentary. Pizer's general introduction and his introductions to the three sections are instructive.

Tom Quirk and Gary Scharnhorst, eds., *American Realism and the Canon* (Newark: University of Delaware Press, 1994).

A collection of twelve essays illustrating the flexibility of Realism as a literary mode. Contributions include essays on women's poetry and women's humor, representations of Chinese Americans, eastern European Jewish immigrants, and Native Americans in Realist fiction, and the evolution of canonization and anthologizing of writers during this period. Among the writers discussed are Charles Chesnutt, Abraham Cahan, Anzia Yezierska, Sui Sin Far, and Emma Lazarus, as well as Henry James, Twain, and Harte.

Philip Rahv, "Notes on the Decline of Naturalism," in his *Image and Idea* (New York: New Directions, 1949), pp. 128–138.

An analysis of the inherent contradictions of literary Naturalism rooted in its "scientific bias." Rahv attributes the exhaustion of the strategy to the modern scientific challenges to the notion of *reality,* particularly from the psychological sciences.

David E. Shi, *Facing Facts: Realism in American Thought and Culture, 1850–1920* (New York: Oxford University Press, 1995).

A rich "synthetic" account of the presence of Realism in American culture. Shi shows in a highly readable way the desire among many philosophers, artists, writers, and architects to "face the facts" of modern life. The book includes ample testimony on the part of individuals to participate in this cultural movement. Divided into five sections, it explores the social and intellectual underpinnings of Realism, the achievement in the arts of Realists in various art forms, the Naturalistic response to more extreme realities, and the rise of modernism, in which a new Realism emerged.

Studies in American Naturalism (2005–present). Published by the University of Nebraska Press.

Includes scholarship on American literary Naturalism across all genres from its origins in the writings of Norris, Crane, and London to its contemporary manifestations in the writing of Don DeLillo and Joyce Carol Oates.

Eric Sundquist, ed., *American Realism: New Essays* (Baltimore: Johns Hopkins University Press, 1982).

A collection of fourteen essays that do not cohere as a unified statement about Realism. To the contrary, as the editor maintains, they propose "no specific ideological or theoretical program on behalf of Realism." Instead, they identify in diverse ways the complexity of responses writers had to their own time, and this very complexity defines the period.

Brook Thomas, *American Literary Realism and the Failed Promise of Contract* (Berkeley: University of California Press, 1997).

A study of the relation between law and literature that argues that Realism assumes that negotiation and agreement between equal parties is possible and just but that corporate capitalism, segregation, gender bias, and other infringements on social justice thwarted this ideal. Thomas provides extended analyses of a substantial number of novels of the period, many unfamiliar to most readers.

Charles C. Walcutt, *American Literary Naturalism: A Divided Stream* (Minneapolis: University of Minnesota Press, 1956).

Walcutt maintains that Naturalism is the "offspring" of the Transcendentalism of an earlier era, but that that movement divided into idealism, on the one hand, and a mechanistic determinism, on the other hand. Most Naturalist writers were caught between these two expressions of Transcendentalism and could not resolve the tension. Norris and London, for example, permitted moral judgments to enter into otherwise deterministic stories. Crane and Dreiser were more successful in integrating the polar oppositions in their fictions.

Kenneth W. Warren, *Black and White Strangers: Race and American Literary Realism* (Chicago: University of Chicago Press, 1993).

Argues that late-nineteenth-century literary Realism was shaped by and in turn helped to shape post–Civil War racial politics. Warren demonstrates the centrality of race in late-nineteenth-century American Realism and puts writers not usually associated with one another in critical conversation. He shows that even works not directly concerned with race assisted after Reconstruction in a return to a racially segregated society.

Christopher P. Wilson, "American Naturalism and the Problem of Sincerity," *American Literature*, 54 (December 1982): 511–527.

Traces the devotion of working-class authors to a democratic (yet commercial) literature. The Naturalists sought to synthesize romance and Realism in order to achieve a brand of sincerity. Significantly, many of the authors of early-twentieth-century business manuals were magazine editors "for whom the Naturalists often worked and wrote." That is, the American literary marketplace at the turn of the twentieth century spawned its own aesthetic, which celebrated "the language of business." Wilson challenges the simplistic notion of Naturalism as "pessimistic determinism" given its valorization of positive thinking or "triumph of the will."

Molly Winter, *American Narratives: Multiethnic Writing in the Age of Realism* (Baton Rouge: Louisiana State University Press, 2007).
Recovers the work of four marginalized writers from the period 1890 to 1915: Mary Antin, a Jewish immigrant and author of *The Promised Land* (1912); the Sioux author Zitkala-Ša; Sutton Griggs, the African American author of *Imperium in Imperio* (1899); and Sui Sin Far, the Chinese American and author of *Mrs. Spring Fragrance* (1912). Winter contends that the emphases of these writers on ideas of ethnicity and national identity place their work squarely within the Realist camp.

Nicolas Witschi, *Traces of Gold: California's Natural Resources and the Claim to Realism in Western American Literature* (Tuscaloosa: University of Alabama Press, 2002).
An ecocritical study of the writings of late-nineteenth-century Western American Realists, among them Harte, John Muir, and Mary Austin, who existed at the intersection of cultural and material or industrial production. "Western narratives of nature prove, upon closer examination, to be narratives of natural resources, the result of an ideology of Realism inextricably tied to the material unconscious of western American culture."

Henry B. Wonham, *Playing the Races: Ethnic Caricature and American Literary Realism* (New York: Oxford University Press, 2004).
Demonstrates that ethnic caricature, far from antithetical to realistic fiction, was integral to it. In this study of the novels of Howells, Twain, James, Wharton, and Chesnutt and their illustrations, Wonham suggests that caricature restores the narrator's sense of "racial privilege even as it calls attention to the dubious legitimacy of that privilege" and that the "same images work to destabilize the very categories they are meant to police." Ironically, the age of Realism was also the age of caricature, and Wonham explains how the two forms of representation were complementary. The difference between text and image, as in Twain's *The Adventures of Huckleberry Finn* and E. M. Kemble's controversial illustrations for the novel, is thus not as dramatic as critics have often alleged.

Larzer Ziff, *The American 1890s: Life and Times of a Lost Generation* (New York: Viking, 1966).
Contends that this generation of writers was "lost" owing to social disturbances and a loss of old certainties. Nostalgia and romance were present among some, but another group of social Realists were the precursors of twentieth-century art and culture. Ziff analyzes the works of individual writers (James, Howells, Twain, Dreiser, and others) and also groups of writers (journalists, women writers, and poets). These writers contributed to the formulation of a "new nationalism" that emerged in the early years of the new century.

Part V
Glossary

Aestheticism   A late-nineteenth-century literary movement that valued artistic values over moral or political ones; it is sometimes referred to as the "art for art's sake" movement. Aesthetes were often criticized as "decadent," though they embraced the term. Oscar Wilde is probably the most accomplished and notorious of the decadents.

Agrarianism   A social philosophy that asserts that a rural or semirural way of life, with the farmer in control of the means of production, is more sustainable and contented.

Anarchism   A political philosophy that holds that government itself is evil and urges free associations of groups opposed to private property. In the 1880s anarchists unsuccessfully tried to infiltrate the American labor movement.

Burlesque   A comic technique that ridicules, through exaggeration, the style or tone of a certain kind of literary work. Unlike parody, which ridicules particular writers or texts, burlesque typically satirizes literary forms.

Censorship   During this period, censorship was actively practiced by United States Postal Inspector Anthony Comstock, who influenced the passage of the so-called Comstock Law of 1873, prohibiting the transportation or delivery of any lewd or lascivious material in the United States. Comstock was, in his mind, upholding a certain Victorian propriety, and his censorship even extended to prohibition of some anatomy textbooks or any information about birth control.

Chinese Exclusion Act   The first act to exclude Chinese immigration, passed by Congress in 1882. In part, the act was in opposition to so-called coolie wages paid to the immigrants, but the Chinese were also demonized as a threatening "yellow peril."

Color line   A phrase given currency by the publication of W. E. B. Du Bois's *The Souls of Black Folk* (1903), in which he defined the problem of the twentieth century as that line that divides lighter and darker races, which gives rise to discrimination, undermines democracy, and fosters conflict. Later in his life, Du Bois recognized that prejudicial boundaries exist in the world on the basis of cultural differences that were not exclusively marked by color.

Conspicuous consumption   A phrase coined by economist Thorstein Veblen in *The Theory of the Leisure Class* (1899) to describe the behavior of the nouveau riche whose lavish display of wealth was an effort to establish their status in society.

Didacticism   An attempt to teach or preach.

Dime novels   Pulp novels popular in the mid to late nineteenth century for juvenile readers; they often cost no more than ten cents.

Direct address   A literary device wherein the narrator speaks directly to the reader. It is sometimes considered a form of narrative intrusion because the author is telling the reader what to think or how to feel about certain imaginative events. In works by writers such as Walt Whitman, the device is more artistic than moralistic, and it is sometimes forgotten that the whole of *The Adventures of Huckleberry Finn* is addressed to the reader.

Doppelgänger   Literary double.

Dramatic monologue   A passage, usually of verse but sometimes prose, in which the speaker reveals his or her inner self. Unlike a soliloquy, an internal monologue presumes a hearer or audience.

Expatriate   One who resides permanently or temporarily in a country other than his or her birthplace. Among nineteenth- and early-twentieth-century American expatriates are Bret Harte, Harold Frederic, Ambrose Bierce, Henry James, and Edith Wharton.

Feminism and suffrage   The activist pursuit of equal rights for women, including their right to vote. The chief aim of nineteenth-century American feminism was women's suffrage, or the extension of the vote to include women. In 1869 the National Woman Suffrage Association and the American Woman Suffrage Association were founded. Through marches, petitions, and other forms of protest, feminists made some strides in acquiring the vote, particularly in Western states and territories, but it was not until the ratification of the Nineteenth Amendment to the Constitution in 1920 that universal women's suffrage was achieved.

Fin de siècle   Literally, end of century; usually associated with decadence at the close of the nineteenth century.

Frame tale   Sometimes referred to as the "box tale," a form of comic sketch featuring a genteel narrator who introduces the narrative and comes in contact with a rustic vernacular narrator who tells a story in his own idiom. Ordinarily, the genteel narrator returns at the end of the sketch to round things off. The form was later adapted to serious purposes. Mark Twain did so in "A True Story"; Henry James's *The Turn of the Screw,* Edith Wharton's *Ethan Frome,* and Sarah Orne Jewett's *The Country of the Pointed Firs* may be considered variations of this literary mode.

Free verse or vers libre   A poetic form that self-consciously refuses to observe strict rhyme schemes but is recognizable as poetry by other patterns or conventions. Walt Whitman is the most famous nineteenth-century American poet to adopt this poetic manner.

Frontier or borderland   Literally, the area beyond some boundary. The American frontier was constantly receding due to what was understood to be a civilizing process of the West. Historian Frederick Jackson Turner, however, maintained that what was best in the American character evolved out of the tension between settlements and the rugged individualism just beyond it. When the U.S. Census Bureau declared the frontier officially closed in 1890, some believed a new era had begun in the development of the country.

Genteel tradition   A literary tradition that emphasized sexual propriety, refinement, and complacent optimism. After World War I, writers were in active revolt against this tradition.

Higher criticism   Literary analysis of the Bible. It concentrates on chronology, sources, and historical analysis to understand Scripture instead of naive faith and sometimes disputes the authenticity or authorship of some parts of the Bible. Many Christians are highly critical of the practice, believing that Scripture itself is the best guide to understanding.

Impressionism   A literary manner derived from the example of the French impressionist painters. It attempted to paint with words, to disclose individual impressions under given circumstances uncorrected by mental or moral adjustments. The best of American impressionists is Stephen Crane; Hamlin Garland and Henry James also engaged in this form of writing.

Initiation story or bildungsroman   A story of development (German *Bildung*), usually about a young male protagonist who undergoes rites of passage from innocence to experience or from ignorance to knowledge.

Internal monologue   A conversation with oneself, or thinking in words, as in stream-of-consciousness writing.

International novel   Unlike novels that emphasized American individualism and mobility, usually to the West, a novel that dramatized the experience of the American point of view as it confronted the old world of Europe. Henry James is the most notable practitioner of this form, and some of his works in this vein include *Daisy Miller, The American, Portrait of a Lady,* and *The Ambassadors.*

Irony   A broad term referring to the recognition by characters or the reader that expected consequences or meanings are far from reality. Irony may occur as verbal phrasing, in dramatic situations, or even in cosmic terms. Stephen Crane's "The Blue Hotel" is a good example of a story employing all of these forms. Irony may be used for comic purposes; often, however, it is serious, even tragic.

Leisure class   In the stratified class structure of the Gilded Age, the wealthy class that enjoyed privileges unavailable to the working or underclass. The economist Thorstein Veblen coined the phrase in his book *The Theory of the Leisure Class* (1899).

Local color   Writing that attempted to render the peculiarities or distinct qualities of a given region—its customs, dialects, attitudes, and natural setting.

Melodrama   Originally associated with drama and operetta, its features include stock characters (unmistakable heroes, heroines, and villains), high drama, and sensationalism. Naturalist novels are sometimes described as melodramatic, though lacking the self-conscious effort at sentimental drama of justice and reform.

Muckraking   Journalistic writing designed to expose corruption in business and politics. Lincoln Steffens's *The Shame of the Cities* (1904) and Ida Tarbell's *The History of the Standard Oil Company* (1904) are the most famous examples of this form.

Narrative point of view   The perspective of the teller of a world of fiction. As Harold Kolb observed, Realist writing tends to be "antiomniscient" in the sense that reality is essentially social and individuals have a common but still partial understanding of the world. For that reason, first-person narratives were common because they dramatized an individual sense of experience (*The Adventures of Huckleberry Finn* is the most famous example of that sort of narrative). Another form of first-person narration presents an unreliable narrator who, due to a variety of reasons including self-delusion, madness, or conniving, presents a story that the reader is expected to be skeptical of;

Henry James's *The Turn of the Screw* is an example. James, Edith Wharton, and others offer a limited omniscient perspective wherein the point-of-view character offered a center of consciousness that was restricted but still allowed for authorial commentary and clarification. Naturalist writers, on the other hand, tended to favor third-person, omniscient narrators who understood the significance of events according to biological or economic and social forces that were quite beyond the grasp of their characters. For that reason, authorial intrusion, wherein the author comments directly to the reader on the significance of narrated events, was more common with Naturalists.

Naturalism   Although writers such as Jack London, Frank Norris, and Theodore Dreiser called themselves Realists, their assumption about truth and their literary manner differed markedly from Realists in the Howellsean vein. The historian David Shi has described these writers as "savage Realists." The Naturalist writer tends to take a scientific point of view toward his or her subject; his or her characters are motivated by forces (biological and/or economic) beyond their understanding or control. Often those baser instincts are best displayed in extreme circumstances; London favored the extreme cold of the Alaskan tundra, and Norris concludes his novel *McTeague* in Death Valley. In other words, Naturalists embraced sensationalist and melodramatic elements that Realists tried to avoid. Vernon Parrington identified these characteristics of Naturalism: attempted objectivity, frankness, an amoral attitude toward the subject, a philosophy of determinism, pessimism, and a projection of strong characters of a marked animal or neurotic nature.

Nouveau riche   French for "newly wealthy": a class that has accumulated wealth and influence but has neither the education nor refinement to know how to behave according to more traditional and genteel standards. The so-called Robber Barons were seen in this light, and in fiction Henry James's Christopher Newman or William Dean Howells's Silas Lapham are somewhat sympathetic portraits of this type.

Parlor magazine   A magazine, such as the *Atlantic Monthly* or *Harper's Monthly*, designed for a middle-class to genteel readership.

Parody   The technique of satirizing a writer or work by lowering the significance or manner of treatment of the subject.

Persona   A literary "mask" often used by humorists as a comic device. Among the masks were the Dandy, the "Muggins" (someone self-assured but lacking judgment), the Tenderfoot, and the Sentimentalist.

Picaresque narrative   A highly episodic narrative, typically involving travel and comic adventures, in which the main character is a "picaro" (Spanish for rogue or rascal). *The Adventures of Huckleberry Finn* is sometimes characterized in this way, though Huck Finn is hardly a rogue.

Populism   The political movement that seemed to advocate the interests of the common man. The People's Party was organized in 1892 to protect the interests of farmers, including falling prices and foreclosures. It joined the Democratic Party in support of William Jennings Bryan for president in 1896; when Bryan lost, the Populists lost their national influence and eventually dissolved.

Pragmatism   William James published a volume by that name in 1907 and said it was a new name for a very old philosophical method. Pragmatism is not merely a practical attitude toward life; it was a "meliorative" way of negotiating or settling intellectual disputes. To oversimplify, according to James, if the answer to a given question would not make a practical difference in one's daily life, the question is really not worth asking.

Progressivism   The movement that promoted the transition of American society to an industrial base. From 1901, with the election of Theodore Roosevelt, until 1917, the political establishment attempted to institute reforms to correct the grosser abuses of corporations and to regulate and to combat monopolies. Constitutional amendments also ensured a more direct form of democratic representation.

Proletarian novel   A novel that exposes the exploitation of the workers under a capitalist system. Upton Sinclair's *The Jungle* is a notable example.

Psychological Realism   A form of Realism most often associated with Henry James. He emphasized the drama of consciousness in his characters and the moment-by-moment apprehension of experience, which is often bewildering and very nuanced.

Realism   Broadly speaking, a literary movement in France, England, and America devoted to representing life as it is lived and experienced; thus, the subject matter is often common or ordinary, and the literary manner is representational (the subject is rendered in a certain way). Realist writers were generally opposed to idealistic or sentimental fiction and often dramatized the ill effects brought about by such sentimentality. Mark Twain is sometimes described as a vernacular Realist, William Dean Howells as a doctrinal Realist, and Henry James as a psychological Realist. In a response to a questionnaire given to Americanists at a Modern Literature Association meeting, the following were identified as characteristics of Realism: "fidelity to actuality, objectivity (or neutrality—the absence of authorial judgment), democratic focus (particularized, ordinary characters), social awareness (and critical appraisal), reportorial detail, and colloquial expression."

Reconstruction   From 1865 until 1877 the U.S. government sought to repair the devastated economy of the South and, in an orderly fashion, to readmit those states that had seceded from the Union, though a great deal of bitterness on both sides remained. In 1877 federal troops were removed from the South.

Revolt from the village   A phrase coined by Carl Van Doren in 1920 to designate those writers who challenged the Romantic idea that the village was characterized by goodwill, virtue, and hospitality. He had in mind twentieth-century works such as Sherwood Anderson's *Winesburg, Ohio* (1919); however, Edgar Watson Howe's *The Story of a Country Town* (1883), Twain's *The Man that Corrupted Hadleyburg* (1899), and Edgar Lee Masters's *Spoon River Anthology* (1915) are earlier examples of the same impulse to expose the fraudulence, venality, and corruption of village life.

Satire   Both a genre and a literary manner in which the deficiencies of certain attitudes or practices are pointed out through humor and wit. An author may be satiric without writing a full-fledged satire. (Twain is a good case in point.) The satirist may be gentle or biting in his or her treatment of the subject matter but in either case should aim to correct rather than demean; in that sense satire can be understood as a moral form of literary expression.

Sentimentality   A literary device that cultivates in the reader responses excessive of the circumstances that occasion them. The death of Little Nell in Charles Dickens's *The Old Curiosity Shop* is an epitome of sentimentalism, but many writers recognized certain forms of affection, ideas about love and marriage, or patriotism as other forms of sentimentality.

Social Darwinism   An application of evolutionary principles to social behavior. Among other things, Social Darwinism, derived from the work of Herbert Spencer, justified or at least extenuated the existence of powerful millionaires because they were specimens of the survival of the fittest.

Social gospel   An intellectual movement of the late nineteenth and early twentieth centuries, composed of liberal Protestants who were intent on applying Christian ethics to social and political problems and were part of the liberal element in the Progressive movement.

Veritism   Hamlin Garland's term for Realism.

Vernacular   The language native to a particular nation or locale, often considered nonstandard and colloquial. Dialect is a form of speech marked by vocabulary, pronunciation, grammar, and sometimes accent. Dialect writing was particularly popular among local-color writers and was sometimes, though not always, used for comic effect.

Wild West   A popular perception of the American West fostered by William F. ("Buffalo Bill") Cody, who staged a type of Western show, often imitated, that featured shooting contests, frontier warfare, and such celebrities as Annie Oakley, Sitting Bull, and James Butler "Wild Bill" Hickok. Cody's Wild West Show spent nine of its thirty-three years in Europe, and an estimated fifty million people saw Cody in person, more than any other figure in history to that time, and at his death in 1917 he was arguably the most famous person in the world.

Yellowback   Cheap fiction novels with brightly colored covers, often reprints of cloth editions. They were advertised as entertainment reading and created in part as a response to increased rail travel. Routledge Publishing called their series of such books their "Railway Library."

Yellow journalism   A type of cheap or sensational journalism usually associated with the Hearst newspapers (for example, the *New York American,* the *San Francisco Examiner,* the *Boston American*) in the late nineteenth and early twentieth centuries. Named perhaps for featuring the cartoon character "The Yellow Kid," or perhaps for the high sulphur content of the newsprint, which turned yellow within a day or two of publication.

Index

burlesque, 211
Butler, Jim (character), 131

C

"Caballero's Way, The," 140
Cabbages and Kings, 139
Cable, George Washington, 57, 61, 113
Caesar's Column, 53
Cahan, Abraham, 38, 41
Calamity Jane, 67
California, 56, 74, 166
    Oakland, 158
    San Francisco, 79, 123, 158
    San Joaquin, 52
California Fish Patrol, 158
Call of the Wild, The, 46, 154, 158
Call of the Wild: A Naturalistic Romance, The, 155
"Call of the Wild: Parental Metaphor, The," 155
Calvinism, 47
Cambridge Companion to Nineteenth-Century American Women's Writing, The, 75
Cambridge History of American Literature, The, 39
camera
    box, 12
Canada
    Montreal, 123
Cane, Aleta Feinsod, 75
Canty, Tom (character), 178
capitalism, 50, 52
Captain Craig, 163
Cardiff Hill (fictional location), 174
Carleton, Will, 44
Carlyle, Thomas, 13–14
Carnegie, Andrew, 11, 16, 51
Carter, Lieutenant-Colonel (character), 62
Carter, Nick, 32
Carteret, Major (character), 85
Carteret, Olivia (character), 85
Cather, Willa, 46, 49, 69, 75–76, 88, 150
Catholics, 10, 59
Cats, 117
Cawelti, John G., 32, 34
censorship, 88, 211
Census Bureau, 212
Century, The, 17, 63, 74, 88, 95, 158, 169, 170

Chaney, John Griffith (See London, Jack), 158
Chaney, William, 153
"Chapters from My Autobiography," 28
Charles (character), 154
Chase, Richard, 22
Château de Chillon, 147
Cherbuliez, Victor, 14
Chesnutt, Charles Waddell, 4, 9, 29, 38, 58, 83
Chesterton, G. K., 34
Children of the Night, The, 162–163
Children of the Poor, The, 56
Children of the Tenements, 56
China
    Shanghai, 123
Chinese Americans, 10, 39, 123
Chinese Exclusion Act, 211
Chin Yuen (character), 124
Chopin, Kate, 4, 13–14, 73–75, 87, 92, 113
Chopin, Oscar, 88
Christianity, 56
    Orthodox, 212
Churchill, Winston, 166–167
"Church Mouse, A," 125
Circular Staircase, The, 36
Cisco Kid (character), 140
City College of New York, 166
Civil War, 3, 8, 11–12, 28, 57, 61–63, 65, 67, 73, 79, 150, 182
Clarel, 66
Clark, Charles Heber (See Adeler, Max), 43
Clemens, Orion, 177
Clemens, Samuel Langhorne (See Twain, Mark), 43, 173
Cleveland, Grover, 9
Cocktail Party, The, 117
Cody, William F. (Buffalo Bill), 68, 216
Colburne, Edward (character), 62
Coleridge, Samuel Taylor, 13
Collected Poems of Edwin Arlington Robinson, 161
Collected Works (Bierce), 79
Collier, P. F., 53
Collier's, 53
Collier's Once a Week, 53
Colonel's Dream, The, 83
Colored American Magazine, 74, 76

color line, 211
Colosseum, 147, 191
Columbia University, 29, 166
Commodore (ship), 100
Complete Poems of Emily Dickinson, The, 104
Comstock, Anthony, 211
Comstock Law, 211
Comte, Auguste, 46, 50
Confederacy, 80
Confederate army, 61, 63, 65
*Conflicting Stories: American Women
    Writers at the Turn into the Twentieth
    Century,* 75
Congregationalism, 126
Conjure Woman, The, 83
Conklin, Jim (character), 96
*Connecticut Yankee in King Arthur's
    Court, A,* 9, 14, 178
Connolly, C. P., 53
conspicuous consumption, 11, 16, 211
Constitution, 212
Cooke, Rose Terry, 73–74
Cooper, James Fenimore, 5, 67, 72
copyright laws, 147
Corbett, Elizabeth Burgoyne, 53
Cornell University, 112
Cornhill, 146
Cosmopolitan, 17, 79
Costello, Aunt (character), 147
Council, Stephen (character), 131
Country Doctor, A, 150
Country of the Pointed Firs, The, 17, 73,
    212
Cowley, Malcolm, 5
Crane, Stephen, 3–5, 7, 10, 13–14, 16–17,
    21, 46, 49, 59, 63, 69, 80, 95, 99, 140,
    213
Crane Log, The, 101
Cranston (character), 63
Crédit Mobilier scandal, 11
Creole culture, 88, 113
crime fiction, 32–36
criminology, 33
Crisis, The, 41
criticism, 22
    Aristocratic, 20
    higher, 212
    idealistic, 19
    sentimental, 19

Criticism and Fiction, 3
Cruise of the Dazzler, The, 158
Cruise of the Snark, The, 158
Crumbling Idols: Twelve Essays on Art,
    130
Cuba, 12, 56, 95, 100
Cumberland Mountains, 61
Curie, Marie, 23
Current-Garcia, Eugene, 140
Custer, George Armstrong, 67
Custom of the Country, The, 186

D

daguerreotypists, 8
"Daisy Miller," 4, 14, 17, 146
Daisy Miller, 192, 213
Daisy Miller: A Study, 146
Damnation of Theron Ware, The, 61
Dandy, The (character), 214
Daniel Deronda, 14
Danish Americans, 39
Darwin, Charles, 3, 5–6, 14–15, 21, 46,
    75, 131
Daudet, Alphonse, 13
Daughter of the Middle Border, A, 130
Davis, Rebecca Harding, 9, 73, 76
Dayton Herald, 108
Dayton Tattler, 108
Dead Letter, The, 33
Deadwood Dick, The Prince of the Road,
    67
Deadwood Dick series, 33, 67, 72
"Deal of Wheat, A," 56
"Death of the Hired Man, The," 7
Death Valley, 21, 214
Debs, Eugene, 158
decadence, 21
"Defence of Detective Stories," 34
De Forest, John W., 3, 17, 19, 62, 64–65
Deland, Margaret, 127
Delmonico's (restaurant), 11
Democratic Party, 214
Democratic Vistas, 182
Denmark, 56
Depression of 1873, 9
Derrida, Jacques, 23
Descent of Man, The, 15, 75
"Desirée's Baby," 5, 92
detective fiction, 32

Finn, Huckleberry (character), 58, 174, 178, 214
Fireside Poets, 7
First National Bank, 139
"First O Songs for Prelude," 183
First Principles, 16
Fiske, John, 12
Flaubert, Gustave, 13–14
Fleming, Henry (character), 7, 64, 95
Flink, Andrew, 155
Florida
    Jacksonville, 100
Fluck, Winfried, 13
Following the Equator, 28, 178
Ford, Paul Leicester, 27
Ford, Worthington Chauncey, 27
"Foreign Influence on American Fiction," 13
For the Major, 74
Foss, Sam Walter, 44
Founding Fathers, 27
Four Million, The, 10, 139
Four Quartets, 117
frame tale, 212
France
    Paris, 117, 146, 186
    Versailles, 186
Franklin, Benjamin, 27, 173
Franklin, Ralph, 104
Franklin Evans, 182
Frank R. Stockton, 171
Frederic, Harold, 61, 212
Freeman, Mary E. Wilkins, 3, 7, 16–17, 33, 58, 73–75, 125
free verse, 212
French Americans, 39
French Revolution: A History, 14
Freud, Sigmund, 16, 23
From Canal Boy to President, or, The Boyhood and Manhood of James A. Garfield, 27
Frome, Ethan (character), 187
Frome, Zenobia (character), 187
From Farm Boy to Senator, Being the Boyhood and Manhood of Daniel Webster, 27–28
frontier thesis, 67
Frost, Robert, 7
Fullerton, Morton, 187

"Furnished Room, The," 140
Fusion Party, 85

G

gambling, 11
Gardiner, John Hays, 163
Gardiner-Scott, Tanya, 171
Gardiner Poetry Club, 161
Garland, Hamlin, 3–4, 9, 16, 20–22, 46, 57, 95, 130, 213, 216
Gass, William H., 23
Gates, John W., 11
Gates Ajar, The, 56
Gautier, Armand, 13
Gearson, George (character), 144
genteel tradition, 212
Gentle Grafter, The, 139
George, Henry, 16
George's Mother, 95
George V, 146
Georgia, 57, 63
Georgia Scenes, 18
German Americans, 39
Germany, 56
Ghost Dog (character), 155
"Gift of God," 164
Gilded Age, 28, 53, 213
"Gilded Age, The," 8
Gilded Age, The, 177
Gilman, Charlotte Perkins, 4, 53, 75, 134, 137, 141, 191
Giovanelli, Mr. (character), 147
Glasgow, Ellen, 46, 64–65
Godey, Louis A., 74
Godey's Lady's Book, 73
Goethe, Johann Wolfgang von, 27
Golden Bowl, The, 22
Golding, William, 80
Gold Standard and the Logic of Naturalism, The, 23
Golemba, Henry, 171
Goncourt, Edmond, 13
Goncourt, Jules, 13
"Good Fellow's Wife, A," 131
"Goodness of St. Rocque, The," 58
Goodness of St. Rocque and Other Stories, The, 112–113
"Gospel of Wealth, The," 11
Gould, Philip, 75

humor, 79
humorists
    frontier, 18
humor writing, 43
Hungry Hearts, 38

I

Ibsen, Henrik, 13
idealism, 58
Illinois
    Chicago, 43, 53, 68, 109, 166
Imagism, 21–22
immigration, 4
Immigration Restriction League, 10
imperialism, 12, 74
Imported Bridegroom and Other Stories of the New York Ghetto, The, 38
Impressionism, 7, 22, 57, 213
impressionism, literary, 21
"Impressions of an Indian Childhood," 29, 74
Incidents in the Life of a Slave Girl, 38
Indiana
    Baldwinsville, 45
Indianapolis Journal, 109
"Indian Teacher among Indians, An," 29
industrialization, 9
Industrial School for Colored Girls (Delaware), 112
initiation story, 213
Innocents Abroad, The, 28, 177
Interstate Commerce Act, 11
In the Tennessee Mountains, 74
Iowa, 130–131
Iron Heel, The, 53, 158
irony, 213
Irving, Washington, 140
"Isaac and Archibald," 163
Italian Americans, 10, 39
Italy
    Rome, 147, 190

J

Jackson, Helen Hunt, 68, 74
Jacksons Island (fictional location), 174
Jacobs, Harriet, 38
Jamaica, 123

James, Henry, 3–4, 7, 11, 13–14, 16–17, 19, 22, 28, 59, 83, 146, 151, 190, 192, 212–215
James, Alice, 191
James, William, 22, 146
Jewett, Sarah Orne, 3, 7, 16–17, 57, 73–74, 76, 150, 155, 212
Jewish Americans, 39, 47
Jewish Daily Forward, 41
Jews, 10, 29, 38
Jim (character), 179
Jim Crow, 9
Joe (character), 174
Johanningsmeier, Charles, 96
John (character), 83
Johns Hopkins University, 65
Johnson, James Weldon, 10, 38, 41
Johnson, Thomas H., 104
Joshua (father of Paul Lawrence Dunbar), 108
Josiah Allen's Wife (See Holley, Marietta), 43
Joslin, Katherine, 190
journalism, 18, 99
    muckraking, 11, 31, 53, 56
    yellow, 216
"Journalization of American Literature, The," 140
Joyce, James, 22, 163
Judson, Edward Z. C. (See Buntline, Ned), 68, 72
Jungle, The, 4–6, 9, 14, 53, 166, 215
Jury of Her Peers: American Women Writers from Anne Bradstreet to Annie Proulx, A, 75

K

Kai Tzu (character), 123
Kansas, 131
Kant, Immanuel, 13
Kaplan, Amy, 23
Kate Chopin: A Critical Biography, 88
Kelso, Perley (character), 52
Kennedy, Craig (character), 33
Kentucky, 57
Kilburn, Annie (character), 52
Kilcup, Karen, 75
Killoran, Helen, 190
Klondike, 6